MW00809485

The Contemporary History Play

Methuen Drama Engage offers original reflections about key practitioners, movements and genres in the fields of modern theatre and performance. Each volume in the series seeks to challenge mainstream critical thought through original and interdisciplinary perspectives on the body of work under examination. By questioning existing critical paradigms, it is hoped that each volume will open up fresh approaches and suggest avenues for further exploration.

Series Editors
Mark Taylor-Batty
University of Leeds, UK
Enoch Brater
University of Michigan, USA

Titles in the series include:
Contemporary Drag Practices and Performers:
Drag in a Changing Scene Volume 1
Edited by Mark Edward and Stephen Farrier
ISBN 978-1-3500-8294-6

Performing the Unstageable: Success, Imagination, Failure
Karen Quigley
ISBN 978-1-3500-5545-2

Drama and Digital Arts Cultures
David Cameron, Michael Anderson and Rebecca Wotzko
ISBN 978-1-472-59219-4

Social and Political Theatre in 21st-Century Britain: Staging Crisis
Vicky Angelaki
ISBN 978-1-474-21316-5

The Contemporary History Play

Staging English and American Pasts

Benjamin Poore

methuen | drama

LONDON • NEW YORK • OXFORD • NEW DELHI • SYDNEY

METHUEN DRAMA
Bloomsbury Publishing Plc
50 Bedford Square, London, WC1B 3DP, UK
1385 Broadway, New York, NY 10018, USA
29 Earlsfort Terrace, Dublin 2, Ireland

BLOOMSBURY, METHUEN DRAMA and the Methuen Drama logo are
trademarks of Bloomsbury Publishing Plc

First published in Great Britain 2024

ISBN: HB: 978-1-3501-6963-0
        ePDF: 978-1-3501-6965-4
        eBook: 978-1-3501-6964-7

Series: Methuen Drama Engage

Typeset by Integra Software Services Pvt. Ltd.

To find out more about our authors and books visit www.bloomsbury.com
and sign up for our newsletters.

For Varsha, in all the timelines.

Contents

Acknowledgements

This book has been six years in the making, and I couldn't have got here without the support and encouragement of friends, family and colleagues.

I first tried out some of the ideas in *The Contemporary History Play* at Sheffield University's School of English Research Seminar in 2017; thanks to Michael Kindellan and Frances Babbage for inviting me. Since then, I've presented on this topic at numerous conferences, most frequently at the International Federation for Theatre Research World Congress as part of the Political Performances Working Group. Thank you to the group's convenors, Julia Boll, Cristina Delgado-García and Trish Reid for the welcoming, invigorating and generous space that they have curated.

At Methuen Drama, warm thanks are due to Anna Brewer, to Aanchal Vij and to the Engage series editors Enoch Brater and Mark Taylor-Batty for their very helpful review comments and suggestions.

My thanks also go to the colleagues who have been so supportive in giving feedback on individual book chapters: Chris Megson, David Barnett, Rebecca Benzie, Bridget Foreman, Liz Tomlin and members of the Cultures, Histories and Legacies Research Cluster at York who gave early feedback on the Introduction. David Barnett has also been my research mentor for this whole period, and has always offered support, reassurance and sound advice. Rebecca Benzie warrants further thanks and gratitude for the research conversations that we have shared since 2019, and the teaching, thinking and writing that has developed from them. I couldn't wish for a better collaborator on history plays. I'm grateful to the creative insights of Poppy Corbett, May Sumbwanyambe, Steve Waters and Selma Dimitrijevic, whose ideas and practice in playwriting and dramaturgy have informed and enriched this book.

Very special thanks go to Varsha, who is a vital source of intellectual energy, inspiration and awesomeness. I'm so thankful that we've had the chance to get to know each other again. Thank you to my parents and step-parents, who have supported and believed in me through the changes of the last few years. And thanks to my children Lydia and Harry, for the water fights, the songs, the PowerPoints, the colours and the numbers — for bringing me back into the present.

Introduction

A woman leaves her farm in the 1880s and walks through time. She reappears at a series of turning points for the global oil industry over the next two centuries. A company of actors try to put on a play about a genocide in Africa, but ultimately collapse into desperate, anxious, embarrassed laughter. A teenager in Bootle takes a series of smartphone photos inspired by Caravaggio, who steps through time to see them. A playwright defiantly introduces a banned performance of a documentary drama, purporting to reveal the truth about a young couple's mysterious disappearance.

These scenarios are not what is usually understood by the term, 'history play'.[1] History plays are either strongly associated with the works of Shakespeare, particularly those that dramatize the Wars of the Roses, or else they are assumed by default to be modern plays staged in a realist style and based faithfully on historical facts. By contrast, in this book, any play that states or indicates that it is set in the past, whatever its genre or mode, is a history play. If we broaden our definition this way, we immediately see that history is everywhere on our stages, but few scholars and critics are talking about it. Ignoring this key element of contemporary playwriting means that we only see these plays as 'new writing', rather than texts which respond to a varied history of representing the past through theatre. Instead of viewing the plays in this book as only contemporary dramas or only history plays, *The Contemporary History Play* considers them as both.

---

[1]   The plays alluded to in the opening paragraph are *Oil* by Ella Hickson, *We Are Proud to Present … * by Jackie Sibblies Drury, *The Seven Acts of Mercy* by Anders Lustgarten and *Rapture* by Lucy Kirkwood.

Every new play stands on the cultural ground of what came before: a nation's own history, theatre history, the patterns, tropes and structures that are regularly used to represent the past on stage – and the wider influences of television, film, museums, galleries, games, books and heritage attractions that process, package and circulate the past as history. In a country such as England, saturated with historical awareness and interpretation through its media, education, its leisure activities and its politics, a history play is both an expression of, and an intervention into, that historicized and historicizing society. In my first book, *Heritage, Nostalgia and Modern British Theatre: Staging the Victorians* (2012), I investigated the changing structures of feeling about the Victorians from the 1960s to the 2000s, as expressed and negotiated through theatre.[2] By contrast, this book is founded on the premise that we can better understand the stage representation of any specific historical period by first looking at how contemporary history plays operate as a category, whatever their period setting (or settings). To illustrate this common ground, I identify a range of approaches that have been used by contemporary playwrights since the opening decade of the twenty-first century. I also show how styles of history play that began to be produced in the last century have evolved and mutated to reflect changing theatrical and political circumstances.

Why This Book?

Something is happening with the contemporary history play for which, currently, there are few analytical or comparative tools. Faced with new writing such as *Oil* by Ella Hickson (2016), *Love and Other Acts of Violence* by Cordelia Lynn (2021) or *Marys Seacole* [*sic*] by Jackie

---

[2] The phrase 'structure of feeling' is derived from the critic Raymond Williams: 'The term is difficult, but "feeling" is chosen to emphasize a difference from more formal concepts of "world-view" or "ideology" … we are concerned with meanings and values as they are actively lived and felt' (Raymond Williams, *Marxism and Literature* (Oxford: Oxford University Press, 1977), 132).

Sibblies Drury (2022), critics are sometimes bemused, patronizing or even hostile, trying to fit these works into conventional categories of drama.[3] It is my contention in this book that many contemporary history plays are becoming more complex and layered in their aesthetic approaches, as playwrights work through the experience of being surrounded by numerous and varied forms of historical representation in the twenty-first century. The categories of history play that this book proposes will help us to name and critically analyse what is happening. For theatre scholars, *The Contemporary History Play* offers a means of interpreting how new writing relies on the past and notions of historicity to generate meaning and resonance in the present. For playwrights and students of playwriting, the book is a guide to the history play's recent past, and to the state of the art: what techniques and formulas have been popular, the tropes that are widely used, and how artists have found ways of renewing or overturning established conventions.

Since Richard H. Palmer's *The Contemporary British History Play* in 1998, this aspect of contemporary new writing has only been fitfully addressed in theatre scholarship. In that time – the first quarter of the twenty-first century – some decisive shifts have been taking place in the way that history is both consumed as entertainment and deployed in politics. Historical drama is now available on-demand via streaming services, in a variety of flavours of nostalgia, realism, documentary drama, revisionism and fantasy, from *Call the Midwife* (2012–) to Shane Meadows's *This Is England* film and TV series (2006–15), via *Bridgerton* (2020–) and *The Crown* (2016–23). Perhaps in response to the abundance of historical stories available elsewhere, theatre's representation of the past has moved away from historical realism, and towards the fracturing and splitting of narratives, characters and realities, towards encounters with possible pasts and their futures, towards history plays as enactments of 'time that won't quit', as Suzan-Lori

---

[3] See this book's discussion of the critical reception of *Marys Seacole* in Chapter 2, and of *Love and Other Acts of Violence* and *A Museum in Baghdad* by Hannah Khalil in Chapter 4. For reviewers' responses to *Oil*, see Benjamin Poore, "'You Can't Be Here": The Playwriting Dialectic in Ella Hickson's *Oil*', *Modern Drama* 63, no. 1 (2020): 21–38.

Parks puts it.[4] Most of the works analysed in this book are concerned with what theatre as an art form can bring to our understanding of the past, and its relationship with the present and future. They respond to theatre's specific properties and affordances, taking up the challenge in Parks's question: '*Why* does this thing I'm writing *have* to be a *play*?'[5]

At the same time as our cultural engagement with history has transformed, much in the surrounding political environment has changed since the late 1990s. In place of the 'long boom' of the late 1990s and early 2000s, the UK has undergone a series of political and economic shocks that have, according to the sociologist William Davies, led to the collapse of liberalism: 'one liberal convention after another was openly tossed aside ... basic assumptions and constraints that had governed public life and policy were discarded'.[6] Most of the history plays discussed in this book were first produced in England in the years between 2010 and 2022, a period dominated by Conservative Party rule in Westminster and bookended by two periods of imposed austerity by different Conservative governments. To distract from the dysfunction at the heart of government, right-wing politicians from

---

[4] Suzan-Lori Parks, *The America Play and Other Works* (London: Nick Hern, 1995), 15. In this respect, theatre in England has been slow to develop these more experimental dramaturgies compared to the theatre of continental Europe. See note 32 below.

[5] Parks, *The America Play*, 7. Various recent iterations of this idea are usefully collected by Maddy Costa in 'The Well-Made Play and the Play Made Well': '[Vinay Patel] wonders why so much theatre doesn't "think more theatrically. Why does this have to be a play? What is it about this as a thing to sit with in time and space?" Faced with a lot of issues-based drama, Featherstone asks another question: "What's the difference that turns something into a piece of theatre, that could be told better in a documentary or a really good news article?" Or, as Emily McLaughlin, then head of the New Work department at the National Theatre, puts it: "What can you detonate as a playwright, in a way that can only happen on a stage, in front of a live audience?"' (Maddy Costa, 'The Well-Made Play and the Play Made Well', *Write A Play* (blog), *The Bruntwood Prize for Playwriting*, 5 March 2019. Available online: www.writeaplay.co.uk/the-well-made-play-and-the-play-made-well-by-maddy-costa/(accessed 3 February 2023)).

[6] William Davies, *This Is Not Normal: The Collapse of Liberal Britain* (London: Verso, 2021), 1–2. Davies cites as examples such moments as Prime Minister Boris Johnson's proroguing of Parliament in 2019, which was declared unlawful by the Supreme Court; the *Daily Mail* newspaper labelling high court judges 'Enemies of the People' in 2016, and the government's denial of access to ministers and press briefings for those media organizations deemed to be critical of the Conservative Party (Davies, *Not Normal*, 2). Readers who observed the Trump presidency of 2017–21 in the United States will no doubt recognize such patterns of behaviour.

prime ministers and cabinet ministers to advisers and backbenchers became increasingly vocal on 'culture wars' issues, attempting to stoke the flames of regional and social division that had been ignited by the EU Referendum vote in 2016. New writing staged in English theatres in this period, therefore, is inevitably a response to a national environment that has been increasingly hostile to both the arts and to historical questioning. Populist and right-wing UK governments have sought to control what are reasonable or permissible views of their national past.

Far from recognizing the legacies of Empire, slavery and White supremacy in the modern British state, UK governments in the 2010s and early 2020s seemed intent on discrediting any uncomfortable information or critical views about its past. In this, they were abetted by aligned organizations and individuals in the press, in pressure groups, and on radio, television and social media.[7] These coalitions sought instead to reassert nationalist myths, whilst at the same time nurturing a sense of grievance against those who would critically examine those myths. As early as 2004, Paul Gilroy pointed to a mood of 'postcolonial melancholia' in the early twenty-first century, where the British had come to regard themselves as Empire's victims.[8] More recently, journalist Nesrine Malik picked up on this theme, describing it as the 'myth of a virtuous origin',[9] a myth that combines, as Gilroy has argued, a false memory of the British as imperial 'benevolent trustees' who brought 'civilization' to Indigenous peoples, which has been connected in retrospect with the notion of Britain 'sacrificing' its empire in resisting the Nazis.[10] Malik goes on to state that 'empire and [Second World] war mythology are not flaws in the machine of British politics, they are the machine, one that was not repurposed once its functions ceased'.[11]

---

[7] This process was facilitated by the close relationship between government and the right-wing press, and the elevation of journalists such as Boris Johnson and Michael Gove to political leadership positions. See Davies, *Not Normal*, 178–85.

[8] Paul Gilroy, *Postcolonial Melancholia* (New York: Columbia University Press, 2005), 93–4.

[9] Nesrine Malik, *We Need New Stories* (London: Weidenfeld and Nicolson, 2019), 171.

[10] See also Peter Mitchell, *Imperial Nostalgia* (Manchester: Manchester University Press, 2021), 197, 251.

[11] Malik, *New Stories*, 190.

Similarly, Robert Eaglestone has called Empire and the Second World War the 'two dominant forms of affect memory in the UK at the moment'; in moving from living memory into myth, '[w]hat once was the living sea has become sediment, petrified as sentiment, a thick, significant layer in the geology of British memory'.[12] For Katie Donington, these historical distortions are indicative of Svetlana Boym's 'restorative nostalgia'. Using a UKIP pamphlet,[13] *Restoring Britishness*, as a starting point, she observed in 2019: 'These acts of historical suppression chime with Boym's assertion that "The nostalgic desires to obliterate history and turn it into private or collective mythology." The plaintive cries of historical desecration emanating from the far-right conceal the ways in which it is engaged with a process of historical destruction through the closing down of critical debate.'[14] Historian David Andress noted this process in 2018, highlighting the distillation of right-wing history-as-myth into 'a disconnected series of images' that is 'the opposite of a coherent history'.[15] Malik also noted the development of this process in the US, where the 'imaginary place, a selective collage of past greatest hits' was used to mask the emptiness of the slogan 'Make America Great Again' during the Trump campaign and presidency.[16]

While political conservatism has long been grounded in nostalgia and tradition, what is new about these coalitions of politicians, pressure groups and media is that their appeal to the past is at the expense of the present and future. As Andress argues, 'Politicians of earlier generations did not try to turn the clock back to what had never been. Even Margaret Thatcher [had] a vision of new opportunities for new

---

[12] Robert Eaglestone, 'Cruel Nostalgia and the Memory of the Second World War', in *Brexit and Literature: Critical and Cultural Responses* (Abingdon, Oxon: Routledge, 2018), 97, 104.

[13] UKIP is the United Kingdom Independence Party, which was highly influential in the early 2010s, and especially during the 2016 Referendum campaign on membership of the European Union.

[14] Katie Donington, 'Relics of Empire? Colonialism and the Culture Wars', in *Embers of Empire in Brexit Britain*, ed. Stuart Ward and Astrid Rasch (London: Bloomsbury Academic, 2019), 125.

[15] David Andress, *Cultural Dementia* (London: Head of Zeus, 2018), 417.

[16] Malik, *New Stories*, 190.

economic sectors.'[17] Despite the tropes of 'Victorian values', imperial nostalgia and a fondness for quoting Kipling, Thatcherism dressed itself in traditional costume to disguise its ruthless modernizing programme of deindustrialization and financialization of the economy. Anthony Barnett expands on this point, recalling that Stuart Hall, who coined the term 'Thatcherism', described it as 'reactionary modernisation'; despite the 'collective fantasy' of her rhetoric, she was driven by market values oriented to the future.[18] Thatcherism was thus a 'Janus-faced combination of reaction and modernity'.[19] Under the New Labour governments of 1997–2010, as under Thatcher, the emphasis was on 'modernization', which usually meant the expansion of marketization into every aspect of political and cultural life. As Barnett records, Prime Minister Tony Blair even went so far as to dismiss the value of history in this neoliberal new world order; he told the US Congress in 2003: 'Never has there been a time … when, except in the most general sense, the study of history provides so little instruction for our present day.'[20]

The future is the element that has become increasingly etiolated in political language over the last two decades. Growing in strength after the financial crash of 2007–8, the austerity rhetoric of the UK Coalition government (2010–15) was established on the principle that the past 'sins' of public spending must be paid for in the present. As Owen Hatherley has examined in detail, this embrace of austerity involved a conscious repackaging of the past as 'austerity nostalgia' with the 'Keep Calm and Carry On' poster, and its derivative merchandise, as the era's central emblem.[21] In the United States, Donald Trump's political campaigns made repeated use of 'back' and 'again' in their promises and rhetoric, such that for a brief period in 2016, the interests of a Trump presidency and a post-EU United Kingdom in 'turning back the clock'

---

[17] Andress, *Cultural Dementia*, 430.
[18] Anthony Barnett, *The Lure of Greatness: England's Brexit and America's Trump* (Harmondsworth: Penguin, 2017), 203.
[19] Barnett, *Lure of Greatness*, 203.
[20] Ibid., 30.
[21] Owen Hatherley, *The Ministry of Nostalgia* (London: Verso, 2017), 14, 18.

appeared to be aligned.[22] These developments marked a new phase in what Franco Berardi has called 'the slow cancellation of the future', which he theorizes as having taken root in the 1970s and 1980s, meaning the loss of 'the cultural expectations that were fabricated during the long period of modern civilization, reaching a peak after the Second World War'.[23] As explored by Mark Fisher in his essays, and in the book *Capitalist Realism*, we are in a general cultural condition in which 'life continues, but time has somehow stopped … it doesn't feel as if the 21st century has started yet' and the present age is characterized by 'a crushing sense of finitude and exhaustion … The feeling of belatedness, of living after the gold rush'.[24] Barnett, too, sees the 'reflexive impotence' of younger generations as being due in part to 'the absence of any convincing left-wing vision of the future'; 'the market' is all there is.[25] For critic and journalist Fintan O'Toole, a further element of this structure of feeling is the mourning of the welfare state, particularly by older generations, some of whom were themselves instrumental in its dismantling; in retrospect, the pre-Thatcher period is viewed as a lost golden age, because '[a] welfare state is about the future'.[26] Hence, a recurring theme in the writers surveyed here is that the dominant political culture denies responsibility for, and seeks to suppress the expression of, this pervasive pessimism, while offering very little for the future ('we're all in this together'; 'global Britain'; 'levelling up'; 'the age of optimism') that does not already draw implicitly on Victorian, imperial or Second World War mythology. As Edoardo Campanella and Marta Dassù put it, counter-intuitively, 'Nostalgia offers relief from

[22] Edoardo Campanella and Marta Dassù, *Anglo Nostalgia: The Politics of Emotion in a Fractured West* (Oxford: Oxford University Press, 2020), 22, 153–4. As they note, however, there was a fundamental tension between Trump's 'America First' outlook and the 'world island' narrative put forward by advocates of Brexit (Campanella and Dassù, *Anglo Nostalgia*, 167).

[23] Franco 'Bifo' Berardi, *After the Future* (New York: AK Press, 2011), 18.

[24] Mark Fisher, 'The Slow Cancellation of the Future', in *Ghosts of My Life* (London: Zero, 2014), 6, 8.

[25] Barnett, *Lure of Greatness*, 105.

[26] Fintan O'Toole, *Heroic Failure* (London: Head of Zeus, 2018), 9.

socio-economic angst. Yesterday is associated with progress; tomorrow with stasis or regression.'[27]

In such a political climate – in which theatre and the arts have frequently been targets of authoritarian demands and populist mockery – there is, this book will argue, an emancipatory potential in historical counternarratives and challenges, in radical upendings of familiar treatments of the past.[28] Theatre's potential, in this case, lies in its provisionality as a constructed representation, one that frequently, consciously exposes the conditions of its own making in performance. As Clare Finburgh Delijani suggests, '[T]heatre, perhaps better than any other medium, bears within its mechanics the possibility to disrupt the parts of our consciousness and senses with which we apprehend the world around us, and to foster new ways of understanding the hegemony of meaning-making and attendant practices of perception and power.'[29] If plays that make use of history can look towards the present and the future,[30] they can create a valuable space for thinking and feeling at one remove from the relentless repetition of 'affirmative history', of 'knowledge that is already known'.[31]

I have limited the scope of the present study to works performed at venues in England over this period. Partly this is because other scholarship has focused on new writing and identity in the other nations of the United Kingdom in connection with national identity, and these

---

[27] Campanella and Dassù, *Anglo Nostalgia*, 1.

[28] For example, in 2020 the UK Culture Secretary Oliver Dowden said he was writing to Netflix to demand that *The Crown* be labelled as fiction by a 'health warning' before each episode (Ellise Shafer, 'UK Culture Secretary Asks Netflix to Label "The Crown" as Fiction', *Variety*, 29 November 2020. Available online: https://variety.com/2020/tv/news/the-crown-fiction-uk-culture-secretary-1234841736/ (accessed 1 November 2021)). The *Daily Mail*, among other sections of the right-wing media, regularly runs news stories and opinion pieces mocking what it sees as the 'woke' excesses of the theatre industry (Christopher Hart, 'Is the West End Going Broke Because It's Gone All Woke?', *Daily Mail*, 6 June 2022. Available online: www.dailymail.co.uk/tvshowbiz/article-10887577/Is-West-End-going-broke-gone-woke-Writes-CHRISTOPHER-HART.html).

[29] Claire Finburgh Delijani, *Watching War on The Twenty-First Century Stage: Spectacles of Conflict* (London: Methuen Drama 2017), 56.

[30] See Michael Y. Bennett, *Narrating the Past Through Theatre: Four Crucial Texts* (New York: Palgrave, 2013), 77.

[31] Martin L. Davies, *Historics* (London: Routledge, 2006), 6, 1.

works have each been to some degree concerned with representations of that nation's history.[32] Partly, too, this decision reflects where I live and work as a scholar. But the strongest imperative is that in the UK, England is where the crises of identity and political legitimacy have been at their most acute over the last quarter-century. It is the Westminster government that has pursued 'culture wars' talking points with such vigour, whilst also promising to 'level up' the impoverished and neglected regions of England that Conservative policies have helped create and sustain. It is in England where, as Fintan O'Toole and Anthony Barnett have pointed out, the UK's exit from the European Union has reopened urgent questions about the purpose of the Union between Scotland, Wales, Northern Ireland and England since the end of Empire, and about regional representation in the UK's most populous nation.[33] Hence, it is the particular question of what is at stake in performing these plays in England that informs the chapters that follow. In addition, the last few years have seen a further decline in the production of plays originating in mainland Europe on English stages,[34] but an increase in new writing by dramatists from the United States. The present volume includes English productions of American plays, therefore, because they have contributed to conversations about identity, race, nation and history in English theatre. Plays by writers such as Anne Washburn, Jackie Sibblies Drury and Katori Hall have gained significant critical attention in English theatres and in theatre scholarship. In a period when the government in Westminster has been quite consciously

---

[32] See, for instance, Tom Maguire, *Making Theatre in Northern Ireland: Through and Beyond the Troubles* (Exeter: Exeter University Press, 2006); Ian Brown, *History as Theatrical Metaphor: History, Myth and National Identities in Modern Scottish Drama* (Cham, Switzerland: Palgrave, 2016); and Kirsty Sedgman, *Locating the Audience: How People Found Value in National Theatre Wales* (Bristol: Intellect, 2016).

[33] O'Toole, *Heroic Failure*, 193–201; Barnett, *Lure of Greatness*, 326–9.

[34] See Natasha Tripney, 'Why Does Radical European Work Get Such a Bum Deal in the UK?,' *The Stage*, 30 November 2022. For more on UK theatre's antagonism towards experimental European plays, see David Barnett, '"I've been told … that the play is far too German": The Interplay of Institution and Dramaturgy in Shaping British Reactions to German Theatre', in *Cultural Impact in the German Context: Studies in Transmission, Reception, and Influence*, ed. Rebecca Braun and Lyn Marvin (Rochester NY: Camden House, 2010), 150–66.

seeking to import American-style culture war divisions, these theatre artists' creative manipulations and interrogations of history are all the more salient.[35] Moreover, the above playwrights, alongside the work of Suzan-Lori Parks and Robert O'Hara in particular, have shaped this book's ideas about the history play.

What Is a Contemporary History Play?

As the opening paragraphs have indicated, by 'the contemporary history play' I mean, principally, plays written in our present century that make a claim to be set, wholly or in part, in a version of the past. That past, as the chapters that follow will show, can be either a single setting or multiple pasts; the past as rendered familiar from historical narratives or made strange by dissonant, jarring or anachronistic elements. In terms of the range of periods covered, I incline to Richard H. Palmer's position, that 'no specific length of time must pass to qualify an event as historical'.[36] Indeed, the present is, by definition, historical; we can historicize the present in order to better understand it.[37] Hence, recent works like *Value Engineering: Scenes from the Grenfell Inquiry* by Richard Norton-Taylor, dealing with the Grenfell Tower fire of June 2017 and the Public Inquiry that took place in 2020 and 2021, are history plays that make a powerful claim for the recent past *not* to be consigned to

---

[35] See, for example, Tim Shipman, 'How the Tories Weaponised Woke: Ministers Are Wading into Debates Over Trans Rights, Taking the Knee and Cricketers' Tweets. It's All Part of a Vote-Winning Plot Masterminded by Dougie Smith, the Most Powerful Man in Politics You've Never Heard Of. Tim Shipman Reports', *The Sunday Times*, 13 June 2021. Available online: https://advance.lexis.com/api/document?collection=news&id=urn:co ntentItem:62X2-G5H1-DYTY-C05R-00000-00&context=1519360 (accessed 21 March 2023). See also Davies, *This Is Not Normal*, 40–1.

[36] Richard H. Palmer, *The Contemporary British History Play* (Westport, CT: Greenwood Press, 1998), 10.

[37] In Bertolt Brecht's theoretical writings, in an imagined conversation between an Actor and a Spectator, he has the Spectator say, 'That is the main thing: these contemporary plays in particular should be performed historically' (Bertolt Brecht, *Brecht on Theatre*, ed. Marc Silberman, Steve Giles and Tom Kuhn (London: Bloomsbury Academic, 2015), 226).

history.[38] By recounting such recent events from a range of perspectives the play inevitably historicizes, but does so with urgency for the present and with the stated aim of making an impact on the future.[39]

In defining a history play as any play that makes a claim to be set in the past, however recent, I am conscious of broadening the scope of the term even beyond the generous bounds of Palmer's declaration that '[r]ather than confining ourselves to an ill-defined genre, we will examine the dramatic uses of history in whatever guise.'[40] In this book I include alternate-history narratives and impossible and fantastic events, as long as they specify a dateline, or multiple datelines, in the past. In other words, I trust the play's own announcement of its historicity. Attempting to define history plays by some other measure seems to lead to added complexities and contradictions. For instance, Nilhoufer Harben contends that 'a history play is a play that evinces a serious concern for historical truth or historical issues', which only serves to underline the epistemological challenges of establishing the qualities of 'seriousness' and 'historical truth'.[41] Mark Berninger posits that 'a history play is a play that deals with history … [but] a history play need not be exclusively or even mainly concerned with history'.[42] This definition would seem, on the one hand, to include dramas with exclusively contemporary settings where characters simply discussed history, but to exclude, on the other hand, plays with historical settings that seemed, to the beholder, somewhat arbitrary or unconvincing.

---

[38] A second Grenfell tribunal play, *Grenfell: System Failure*, was also performed at the Playground, Tabernacle and Marylebone Theatres in London in spring 2023. An unrelated production, Gillian Slovo's *Grenfell: In the Words of Survivors*, opened at the National Theatre in London in July 2023.

[39] As the publicity for *Value Engineering* explains, 'The intention behind the play is to help the public get an overview of the Inquiry's work and to hold the people and systems responsible for the tragedy to account' ('About', *Value Engineering: Scenes from the Grenfell Inquiry*. Available online: https://part1.grenfellsystemfailure.com/about.html (accessed 29 April 2023)).

[40] Palmer, *Contemporary British History Play*, 9.

[41] Nilhoufer Harben, *Twentieth-Century English History Plays* (New York: Barnes and Noble, 1988), 18.

[42] Mark Berninger, 'Variations on a Genre: The British History Play in the Nineties', in *British Drama of the 1990s*, ed. Annelie Knapp, Erwin Otto, Gerd Stratmann and Merle Tönnies (Heidelberg: Universitätsverlag C. Winter, 2002), 37.

Lastly, Brean S. Hammond considers history plays to be those which '[confront] directly the events taking place in tracts of historical time', which 'retain the ambition to dramatize involvement in the process of English history, and to make relevant connections between the nation's present and its past',[43] and declares on this basis, 'In British theater, history is virtually unrepresented.'[44] Conversely, I propose that it is unnecessary for a play to have a theory of historical change to qualify as a history play; indeed, many of the plays discussed in this book undermine or mock attempts at a totalizing intellectual framework, or theatre's suitability for conveying any such thesis.

Having defined 'history play' and 'contemporary' for the purposes of the present study, I will add for clarity what I mean by 'history'. I make a distinction between the past, as any and all events that have taken place up to the present moment, and history, as the attempt to systematize and narrativize that past. In a widely cited explanation by the historian Keith Jenkins, 'history is a discourse about, but fundamentally different from the past ... The past has occurred. It can only be brought back again by historians in very different media, for example in books, articles, documentaries, etc., not as actual events. The past has gone and history is what historians make of it when they go to work.'[45] This chimes with Alex von Tunzelmann's observation that '[a]ny written history, even the blandest of documents, can only ever be a map, not the actual territory of history, which vanishes as soon as it has happened.'[46] The past is, in Jerome de Groot's words, 'a chaos that society attempts to frame as "history".'[47] The history plays that this book takes as its case studies often peel away these ideas of a settled history to examine the chaos of the past that lies behind it.

---

[43] Brean S. Hammond, "'Is everything history?'": Churchill, Barker and the Modern History Play', *Comparative Drama* 43, no. 1 (Spring 2007): 3. doi:10.1353/cdr.2007.0004.

[44] Hammond, "'Is everything history?'" 2.

[45] Keith Jenkins, *Re-thinking History* (London: Routledge, 1991), 6.

[46] Alex von Tunzelmann, *Fallen Idols: History is Not Erased When Statues Are Pulled Down: It Is Made* (London: Headline, 2021), 6.

[47] Jerome de Groot, *Remaking History: The Past in Contemporary Historical Fictions* (Abingdon: Routledge, 2016), 17.

Other Uses of History in the Theatre

Even with these parameters in place, it is necessary to acknowledge from the outset that 'the history play' has many overlaps with other kinds of playwriting. The history play can never be a sealed category, since other types of stage drama, beyond those understood as 'new writing', also make use of history. These include adaptations, which are usually set in the past; revivals, which frequently are either set in the period of the play's first staging or transposed to other periods ('Shakespeare in suits'); and the history musical, of which recent commercial successes such as *Hamilton* (2015) and *SIX* (2017) are prominent examples. The 'new writing history play', then, sits in a Venn diagram of other evocations of the past. In practice, it may well have very similar research-and-development and dramaturgical processes to adaptations and revivals: for example, research and practical exercises that facilitate an intellectual, emotional or somatic connection with the period setting. In a previous article, Rebecca Benzie and I sought to distinguish between the history play as new writing and adaptations.[48] This book maintains that distinction in order to retain consistent terms of reference and comparison, although there is certainly a case for considering literary adaptations such as that of Andrea Levy's *Small Island* at the National Theatre in 2019 (scripted by Helen Edmundson) as both a history play and an adaptation. History musicals are discussed in the book where they contribute to the reception context. Revivals, when staged some time after their first production, in effect become period dramas, costumed and designed to reflect the 'past present' in which they were written. Often, part of the critical reception of the revival consists of reflection on the historical conditions to which the play was

---

[48] Rebecca Benzie and Benjamin Poore, 'History Plays in the Twenty-First Century: New Tools for Interpreting the Contemporary Performance of the Past', *Studies in Theatre and Performance* (2023), doi: 10.1080/14682761.2023.2266205.

a response or reaction.[49] Such productions can invite multiple layers of historical interpretation, as for example when a 2021 revival of William Shakespeare's *Measure For Measure* at the Sam Wanamaker Theatre (the indoor theatre at Shakespeare's Globe) advertised its specific relocation to London in 1975.[50] This meant that – following Vera Cantoni's model of different 'time planes' at Shakespeare's Globe – a 2021 audience was watching a 1604 play in a candlelit theatre based on one used by Shakespeare's company from 1609, designed for this revival to evoke 1975.[51] The past, then, is always multi-layered in the theatre, with each performance setting in motion a different combination of the play's historical provenance, the production's design or setting, its musical score or sound design, its sources, and the building and location in which it is staged. These different ways of reading time in historical performance are considered further in Chapter 4.

Other Historical Fictions

As I indicated at the opening of this Introduction, the history play is also closely connected to other forms of historical fiction in contemporary culture, although theatre is usually somewhat neglected in this context and is frequently crowded out by historical novels, films and television series. Theatre, in common with other historical fictions, can 'challenge, "pervert", critique, and queer a normative, straightforward, linear,

---

[49] For example, a review by Hailey Bachrach of the revival of Larry Kramer's *The Normal Heart* at the National Theatre in London reflects on how the play, originally produced in New York in 1985, responded to the AIDS epidemic as it grew at that time. Bachrach asserts that '*The Normal Heart*, at this point, is a historical play' (Hailey Bachrach, 'Review: *The Normal Heart* at National Theatre', *Exeunt Magazine*, 1 October 2021. Available online: https://exeuntmagazine.com/reviews/review-normal-heart-national-theatre/ (accessed 1 November 2021)).

[50] As the Globe's production blog stated: 'It's 1975. Britain is on the verge of financial and political crisis. Inflation has soared, unemployment is at an all-time high, and political polarisation is continuing to rupture the country into two halves' ('A Glimpse into our 1970s Measure for Measure.' Available online: https://www.shakespearesglobe.com/discover/blogs-and-features/2021/11/10/a-glimpse-into-our-1970s-measure-for-measure/ (accessed 8 December 2021)).

[51] Vera Cantoni, *New Playwriting at Shakespeare's Globe* (London: Methuen, 2017), 31–3.

self-proscribing History', as Jerome de Groot argues in his valuable exploration of historical fictions in contemporary culture, *Remaking History*.[52]

Like scholars of theatre who make distinctions between 'serious' history plays and those that are mere entertainment, film scholars have also sought to distinguish between the treatments of history that they consider rich, rewarding and worthwhile, and those derivative, generic films set in the past. Robert Rosenstone separates '"mainstream" or "standard" films from "serious", "experimental" or "postmodern" historical films"', the latter being 'intellectually dense'.[53] Fredric Jameson argues that the historical film should not be confused with the 'nostalgia film'.[54] Pierre Sorlin, likewise, seeks to put distance between historical films and 'costume' films,[55] and de Groot identifies 'a strand of dissident heritage film-making' including deliberate anachronisms and additional story-telling.[56] Such categorizations may be reflections of critics' own cultural prejudices; or, they may be more pertinent to film, where mimetic realism in acting and production design frequently holds sway.

In terms of cultural esteem, while many of the plays under discussion in this book are examples of prestigious new writing at flagship national venues such as Shakespeare's Globe, the Royal Court and the National Theatre, I am not seeking to identify the best or most outstanding examples, rather to highlight patterns and convergences in the stage representation of history. However, the question of cultural prestige also operates somewhat differently in theatre, as the next section will explore.

---

[52] De Groot, *Remaking History*, 2.

[53] Marnie Hughes-Warrington, 'Introduction: Theory, Production, Reception', in *The History on Film Reader*, ed. Marnie Hughes Warrington (Abingdon: Routledge, 2009), 3.

[54] Hughes-Warrington, 'Introduction', 3.

[55] Pierre Sorlin, *Revisioning History: Film and the Construction of a New Past* (Princeton, NJ: Princeton University Press), 116, 144, 208.

[56] Jerome de Groot, *Consuming History* (Abingdon: Routledge, 2008), 212.

New Writing and the History Play

Herbert Lindenberger, surveying the European history play over several centuries, avers that history was the predominant mode of writing for almost all canonical playwrights from Marlowe to Brecht: 'every major dramatist ... was also a writer of history plays.'[57] As noted in the opening of this Introduction, plays based on historical material remain a popular form of new writing but are rarely referred to as 'history plays.'[58] This may be partly for programming reasons: 'new writing' has a certain cachet, emphasizing a theatre's status as a producing house that is taking artistic risks and investing in emerging talent; it may also make it easier for theatres to narrativize a track record of such innovation when applying, for instance, for Arts Council, local authority or central government funding, or for corporate sponsorship. 'New writing' now dominates British theatre, according to the most recent *British Theatre Repertoire* report, 'constituting 62 per cent of all theatre productions, 63 per cent of all box office income and 64 per cent of all theatregoing.'[59] By contrast, 'the history play' smacks of dusty, conservative theatre; the 'history lesson' play, as D. Keith Peacock names it,[60] that combines a modicum of entertainment, along with a Reithian mission to inform and educate. Mark Berninger usefully outlines this familiar understanding of the history play in the following account:

> Interest in the central (mostly male) figures of history, concentration on political and military events ... Eurocentrism, use of stage realism (in the paradoxical form of 'historical realism'), chronological

---

[57] Herbert Lindenberger, *Historical Drama: The Relation of Literature and Reality* (Chicago: University of Chicago Press, 1975), x.

[58] To give an indication of the centrality of plays with historical settings to the dramatic canon in the United Kingdom, we might note that of the sixteen productions streamed by London's National Theatre during the initial Covid lockdown period in spring and summer 2020, five were history plays, whether classical, modern or contemporary. The plays were Shakespeare's *Coriolanus* and *Antony and Cleopatra*, Alan Bennett's *The Madness of George III*, Peter Shaffer's *Amadeus* and James Graham's *This House*.

[59] British Theatre Consortium, SOLT/UKTheatre and BON Culture, *British Theatre Repertoire 2014* (report), 3.

[60] D. Keith Peacock, *Radical Stages: Alternative History in Modern British Drama* (Westport, CN: Greenwood, 1991), 25.

presentation of events, adherence to documented history but with
the addition of fictional elements (which do not undermine the plays'
claim of historical authenticity), and a subscription to the dominant
view of history and the prevailing interpretation of the historical
events presented.[61]

Similarly, Peacock identifies Terence Rattigan's *Adventure Story* (1949),
Norman Ginsbury's *The First Gentleman* (1945) and Joan Temple's *The
Patched Cloak* (1947) – biographical history plays about Alexander the
Great, the Prince Regent and Henry VII respectively – as perpetuating
'a type of theatrical realism that had evolved during the 1920s and
which reflected in its characterization and action on the social and
ethical values of the predominantly middle-class audiences of that
period', well into the post-war era.[62] As Chapter 2 will discuss in more
detail, these biographical plays reflect not only a dominant type of
theatrical realism but also, in their focus on exceptional individuals,
a particular conception of history. Content and form are thus, in these
cases, aligned and codified: a conventional realist dramaturgy to convey
a conventional understanding of historical events and causality, and
their relationship to the present (what Peacock calls 'agreed history').[63]
Certainly, there were exceptions in this period; Bernard Shaw is the
most obvious example. But I would suggest that Shaw's history plays,
from *Caesar and Cleopatra* (1898) to *Saint Joan* (1922) and *In Good
King Charles's Golden Days* (1939), are able to subvert and surprise
because they are able to rely on audience familiarity with the pervasive
model of historical realism.

Other reasons for theatre-makers' avoidance of the phrase 'history
play' may be linked to the iconoclasm with which new writing in
England has been associated since the founding of the English Stage
Company at the Royal Court Theatre in 1956, and its central mythology

---

[61] Berninger, 'Variations', 39.
[62] Peacock, *Radical Stages*, 19.
[63] Ibid., 2.

of the playwright as untutored outsider,[64] regardless of the 'New Wave' of playwriting's own experimentation with historical narrative in such plays as Arnold Wesker's *Chicken Soup with Barley* (1958) and John Arden's *Serjeant Musgrave's Dance* (1959). According to the English Stage Company's self-presentation, playwriting should not be about painstaking 'technique', but should be fired by passion and inspiration: the tone was set by the much-reported fact that John Osborne had written *Look Back in Anger* (1956) in seventeen days.[65] Such a process would offer any playwright following in Osborne's footsteps little room for research and rumination. The Royal Court's Literary Office continues to offer a play reading service to unsolicited manuscripts, but in 2021 was still insisting, 'We do not read musicals nor historical/ biographical plays as we so rarely have an opportunity to produce this work.'[66] Similarly, Aleks Sierz writes dismissively of the history play when he surveys the 2000s and notes that 'many of the most popular, award-winning plays … were history plays … All very interesting, but hardly the raw gristle of the contemporary.'[67] Later, he adds that these history plays 'represent a flight from the contemporary, a refusal to look reality in the eye'.[68] While he concedes that 'history plays can certainly have a contemporary resonance', he counters that more often they are 'costume dramas with little relevance to today'.[69]

Moreover, as Marvin Carlson argues in *The Haunted Stage*, the theatre itself is saturated with history: it literally frames the stage in dozens of theatres with eighteenth-, nineteenth- or twentieth-century proscenium arches, and metaphorically frames theatrical practice

---

[64] Dan Rebellato, *1956 and All That: The Making of Modern British Drama* (London: Routledge, 1999), 8–9, 77.

[65] Ibid., 76.

[66] 'Script Submissions', https://royalcourttheatre.com/script-submissions/ (accessed 8 December 2021). In 2017, when I began work on this monograph, the phrasing was the even more forbidding, 'We will not read historical or biographical plays and we are unlikely to programme new musicals' ('Literary Office', *Royal Court Theatre*. Available online: https://royalcourttheatre.com/literary-office (accessed 29 April 2017).

[67] Aleks Sierz, *Rewriting the Nation* (London: Bloomsbury Methuen, 2011), 64.

[68] Ibid., 64.

[69] Ibid., 64.

in its reuse of props, costumes, revivals and repeat performances.[70] In this sense, especially in older theatre buildings and institutions, history might be seen as something to escape, to break away from, in order to produce 'new work'. Finally, as indicated at the beginning of this Introduction, Shakespeare's history plays cast a long shadow over conceptions of what history on stage is and does, and this effect has been exacerbated by the loss of other older plays from the repertoire, increasing Shakespeare's dominance of 'classic drama' production. As the *British Theatre Repertoire* report states, 'What we have called the classical canon – from the birth of drama to 1850 – is increasingly dominated by Shakespeare and, in terms of numbers of productions, is in decline.'[71] The fact that two of the English theatre institutions that have most consistently programmed new plays set in the past – the RSC and Shakespeare's Globe – stage them in repertory with Shakespeare revivals, creates a further framing effect: new history plays, sponsored by Shakespeare. For all these reasons, I suggest, among theatre-makers, critics and scholars there is little sense of the history play as a new-writing category, and the wider industry, including playwrights, has a vested interest in not reifying the history play as a concept. The ambition of the present study is to reorientate the idea of the contemporary history play towards open form and theatrical experimentation, and away from notions of the dutiful, the didactic and the generic. To quote Suzan-Lori Parks again, in a 2007 interview: 'Well, I'm known for history plays, but actually, the plays were never "history plays" … So my plays often feature historical figures. But they're all "now" plays …'[72] Or, as she puts it even more pithily later in the same interview, 'It's cool how plays can re-make history. But, my plays are not the History Channel.'[73]

[70] Marvin Carlson, *The Haunted Stage: Theatre as Memory Machine* (Ann Arbor: University of Michigan Press, 2001), 3.

[71] *British Theatre Repertoire 2014*, 48.

[72] Suzan-Lori Parks and Kevin Wetmore Jr, 'It's an Oberammergau Thing: An Interview with Suzan-Lori Parks', in *Suzan-Lori Parks: A Casebook*, ed. Kevin J. Wetmore Jr and Alycia Smith-Howard (New York: Routledge, 2007), 133–4.

[73] Ibid., 139.

History Plays, Past and Present

Nevertheless, there have certainly been times in the recent past when explorations and reimaginings of history were understood as a vital form of new writing. As documented by Palmer, Peacock and Harben, and more recently by Anthony P. Pennino,[74] the emerging political playwrights of the 1960s and 1970s were steeped in historical consciousness and were often formally experimental in ways that anticipate the dramaturgies examined in this book. For example, Caryl Churchill's *Vinegar Tom* (1976) is set in the seventeenth century but features contemporary songs and, in the original production by Monstrous Regiment, includes two characters – the witchfinders Kramer and Sprenger – who appear in 'top hat and tails as performers in a music hall'.[75] David Edgar's *Maydays* (1983) and *Destiny* (1976) are set in different countries and across time spans of around thirty years. Howard Barker's dramas, from *Claw* (1975) and *Crimes in Hot Countries* (1978), to his more 'anti-historical' history plays of the 1980s such as *The Power of the Dog* (1983) and *The Castle* (1985), can be seen as precursors to some of the fantastic and alternate histories discussed in the present volume. Howard Brenton's *The Churchill Play* (1974) is a 'future history' that can be read productively alongside the numerous plays in this book that catapult the action into the future. *Hitler Dances* (1972), also by Brenton, mixes documentary drama, personal memories by the company, masks and multi-rolling, elements of the fantastic (children bringing to life the corpse of a Nazi solider) and a play within a play (the story of Violet Szabo, an undercover operative during the

---

[74] Anthony P. Pennino, *Staging the Past in the Age of Thatcher: 'The History We Haven't Had'* (Cham, Switzerland: Palgrave Macmillan, 2018).
[75] Caryl Churchill, *Vinegar Tom*, in *Plays: One* (London: Methuen, 1985), 132.

war).[76] Pam Gems's *Queen Christina* (1975) explores 'the dilemma of the real Christina', a seventeenth-century monarch 'reared and educated as a man for the Swedish throne, and then asked to marry and breed for the succession'.[77] It uses contemporary language and an episodic structure to critique expectations of women in the 1650s and in the 1970s. After the ground-breaking *Early Morning* (1968), Edward Bond continued to expand the possibilities of the history play in the 1970s and 1980s, with works like *The Fool* (1976) and *Restoration* (1981).

What the study of history plays over time reveals is that forms and patterns often recur and are revisited. The surrealist dramaturgy of Bond's *Early Morning* finds echoes in Janice Okoh's *The Gift* (2020); Brecht's *Mother Courage and Her Children* (1941) is reimagined as a phantasmagoric journey through the wars of the twentieth century by Zinnie Harris in *The Wheel* (2011); the stretched human lifespans of May and Amy in Ella Hickson's *Oil* (2016) expand upon the temporal logics of Churchill's *Cloud Nine* (1979), August Wilson's 'century cycle' plays and O'Hara's *Insurrection: Holding History* (1996);[78] and plays that trace historical change by setting acts and scenes in different periods like, for example, *Loveplay* (2001) by Moira Buffini, deploy similar strategies to Thornton Wilder's *The Long Christmas Dinner* (1931) or Bernard Shaw's *Back to Methuselah* (1922). The most inventive works covered in this volume are as much about repurposing the history of playwriting as they are about imagining past events.

[76] As Paola Botham has discussed, Brenton has returned to the history play in the present century with popular works including *In Extremis* (2006) and *Anne Boleyn* (2010) at Shakespeare's Globe, in which the playwright tempers his 1970s Brechtian anti-humanism with the use of dialectics 'not to confirm a philosophy of history but as a method for open argumentation' (Paola Botham, 'Howard Brenton and the Improbable Revival of the Brechtian History Play', *Journal of Contemporary Drama in English* 2, no. 1 (2014): 170–84, 182).

[77] Pam Gems, *Queen Christina* in *Plays One* (London: Oberon, 2004), 179.

[78] In *Cloud Nine*, the action moves forward nearly a century, but the characters have only aged by twenty-five years. In *Insurrection: Holding History*, a PhD student, Ron, travels back in time with his 189-year-old great-great-grandfather. August Wilson's character Aunt Ester is 'as old as the African American presence in America' and is around 285 years old when she appears in *The Gem of the Ocean* (2003) (Harry Elam Jr, *The Past as Present in the Drama of August Wilson* (Ann Arbor: University of Michigan Press, 2006), 184).

However, to understand the development of contemporary history plays in the twenty-first century, we should also look beyond the national flagship institutions and to companies such as Talawa (founded 1986), 'the UK's outstanding Black British theatre company', Tamasha (founded 1989), which set out to bring 'contemporary work of South Asian influence to the British stage', and Tara Arts (founded 1977). Such companies have presented historical dramas, including migration and diasporic stories, that often break with the expectations of historical realism.[79] To take the example of Tara Arts, the company's three-part twenty-fifth anniversary production, *Journey to the West* (2002) followed an Indian diaspora from Kenya to the UK, starting in 1896 and concluding in 2002. The 'Binglish' performance style developed by company founder Jantinder Verma is intended to 'directly challenge or provoke the dominant conventions of the English stage.'[80] As Dominic Hingorani writes of *Journey to the West*, 'The overt theatricality of the Binglish performance is realised through the use of music, stylised movement and stage imagery as well as the text. This performance style can also utilise mask, a sutradhar (narrator), a chorus and it allows the actors to directly address the audience and play multiple characters.'[81] These approaches to staging historical stories in an epic style are deployed by many of the recent history plays discussed in this book; Vinay Patel's *An Adventure* (analysed in Chapter 4) itself traces a couple's journey from India to Kenya to the UK. In contemporary history plays, such features as direct address, an epic presentational style and multi-rolling may, therefore, be as likely to stem from Binglish as from Brenton.

[79] 'About', *Talawa*. Available online: https://www.talawa.com/about (accessed 29 April 2023). 'History', *Tamasha*. Available online: https://tamasha.org.uk/history/ (accessed 29 April 2023). For instance, Tamasha first staged Ayub Khan Din's *East is East*, set in 1970s Salford, in 1996. Tamasha's 1997 play *A Tainted Dawn* by Sudha Bhuchar and Kristine Landon-Smith was created to mark the fiftieth anniversary of the Partition of India and Pakistan. Talawa have produced Archie Maddocks's migration epic *A Place for We* (2021) and also revived George C. Wolfe's 1986 play *The Colored Museum* in 2011. Tara Arts relaunched as Tara Theatre in 2021.

[80] Jatinder Verma, 'The Challenges of Binglish: Analysing Multi-Cultural Productions', in *Analysing Performance: A Critical Reader*, ed. Patrick Campbell (Manchester: Manchester University Press, 1996), 193–202, 194.

[81] Dominic Hingorani, 'Binglishing Britain: Tara Arts: *Journey to the West Trilogy*', *Contemporary Theatre Review* 14, no. 4 (2004): 12–22, 17.

Tony Kushner's *Angels in America* (1991–3) is also a clear influence on the contemporary plays discussed in this book. In addition, it serves as a further example of the circulation of ideas in historical playwriting. Although the historical period covered by the two parts, *Millennium Approaches* and *Perestroika*, runs only from 1985 to 1990, the coordination of different groups of characters who gradually come to know each other, the play's length and its conscious fashioning of 'A *Gay Fantasia on National Themes*' (the play's subtitle) contrive to give the work an epic quality, revisiting and making sense of very recent history in the United States, even without Prior Walter's angelic and ghostly visitations. Theatre critics Terry Teachout and Frank Rich have both made the claim that *Angels in America* is a history play, the latter commenting, 'the sense of the sweep of the country over roughly a century, going back to immigration in the nineteenth century. It's all there.'[82] *Angels* appears to have had particular influence on history plays that explore the fantastic, as discussed in Chapter 5. Kushner's staging advice for these 'moments of magic', that they 'ought to be fully imagined and realized, as wonderful *theatrical* illusions – which means it's OK if the wires show, and maybe it's good that they do' speaks to the self-awareness of contemporary history plays' evocations of the past.[83] In fact, *Angels in America* began life at Eureka Theater in San Francisco, where according to company member Richard Seyd, 'The intention was to link it to the Caryl Churchill, David Edgar way of working, to write a play for the company of actors.'[84] Tony Taccone, Artistic Director at Eureka, recalls, 'We felt like imitators. We were doing the best of the Brits', while Brian Thorstenstein, an intern at the company, recalls that the company was doing 'a bunch of Caryl Churchill'.[85] Hence, we can see the transatlantic influence of historical playwriting travel back and forth; Churchill herself commended Kushner's writing on *Angels* as

---

[82] Isaac Butler and Dan Kois, *The World Only Spins Forward: The Ascent of Angels in America* (New York: Bloomsbury, 2018), 405, 43.
[83] Tony Kushner, *Angels in America* (London: Nick Hern, 2017), 313.
[84] Butler and Kois, *The World Only Spins Forward*, 34.
[85] Ibid., 30, 79.

presenting 'politics, imagination, and passion, and on a grand scale'.[86] Particularly since the acclaimed National Theatre revival of *Angels* in 2017, we might go on to read the prevalence of large-scale plays on national themes in English theatres, mixing historical and fictional characters, as having been shaped by the scope and ambition of Kushner's play.[87]

Put concisely, then, my argument is not that the contemporary history play is an unprecedented development in new writing staged in England, but that the present century has seen a revival of interest in its aesthetic and political possibilities. As this book will demonstrate, the key features of this revival which differentiate it from the wave of history plays in the later twentieth century are:

1. In plays from England, a focus on the British Empire and its legacies rather than on post-war Britain and Europe, raising questions about the coherence of England as a nation, post-Empire.

2. An emphasis on issues of identity, especially race and experiences of migration, over a singular concern with class politics.

3. A foregrounding of embodied, emotional experiences of the past, unfolding live and in the acknowledged presence of an audience, rather than privileging the play as argument or thesis.

4. Work that is often the product of collaborations between playwright, director and dramaturg, where movement, music and scenography are as prominent, as conveyors of meaning, as dialogue and narrative.

5. Dialogue that, rather than searching for an 'authentic historical language', uses emphatically contemporary speech patterns.

---

[86] Ibid., 400.

[87] It is also possible to see the influence of *Angels* on *The Inheritance,* a two-part play by Matthew Lopez that adapts E. M. Forster's *Howard's End,* filtered through the experiences of gay men in New York in the present generation and in the generation before, who faced the AIDS crisis at its height. It premiered at the Young Vic in London in 2018 before transferring to the West End, and then to Broadway in 2019.

6. A dramaturgy that tends to be consciously 'scuffed' and showing its seams and stitches, drawing our attention not only to the play as a fiction, but to the contingent nature of any kind of knowledge of the past. Sometimes, the staging of the past itself is made to look like a faintly absurd thing to attempt, even as the imperatives to do so are presented as urgent.

7. More hybridized theatrical forms that combine older history-play conventions in new ways, and which work through the challenges of navigating the past in our mediatized and historicized culture.

Contemporary history plays are likely to have three or more of these characteristics, though several of the works covered in this book have all seven. The above list does have some overlaps with Palmer's definition of the concerns of the 'New Historians' that informed the historical drama of the post-1956 playwriting generation. For example, Palmer discerned, as patterns in the historical playwriting of this period, a rejection of the ideal of objectivity and of military history, a de-emphasizing of chronology and narrative, a questioning of 'great man' narratives and a repudiation of Eurocentrism.[88] However, as Paola Botham argues of the twenty-first-century history play, 'While the suspicion over recorded historical material remains a core feature, the alternative provided is a set of questions and/ or possible directions rather than the certainty offered by modern teleologies', such as Marxism.[89] Moreover, I would add, the previous, 'Old History' conventions take a long time to shift because they are so powerfully established and reiterated by the 'historical realism' that dominates fiction, television and film.[90] Inevitably, twenty-first-century

---

[88] Palmer, *Contemporary British History Play*, 12–13. Incidentally, Palmer observes that in contrast to the UK, 'history plays by Americans appear much less frequently in professional theatre, being relegated largely to television, film, or outdoor summer theatres' (Palmer, *Contemporary British History Play*, 2). As the selections in the present study indicate, this situation has certainly changed in the last quarter-century, with history plays by writers from the United States strongly influencing the development of the form.

[89] Paola Botham, 'The Twenty-First Century History Play', in *Twenty-First Century Drama: What Happens Now*, eds. Siân Adiseshiah and Louise LePage (Cham: Palgrave, 2016), 89.

[90] Palmer, *Contemporary British History Play*, 12; Berninger, 'Variations', 39.

playwrights' choices of form, content and perspective will be different because the way they present history reflects how they are thinking about the present. Writing and making plays amidst the 'culture wars', in a society saturated with old and new media, and 'heritage' versions of the past, will produce new dramaturgies even as their creators draw on earlier techniques.

In seeking to establish these points of difference, the present book is indebted to the ideas in Sarah Grochala's *The Contemporary Political Play* (2017) and its identification of 'liquid dramaturgies' as a key means of interpreting contemporary playwriting. The 'liquid' plays that Grochala discusses tend to experiment with form, to collapse space and to move towards a simultaneous understanding of time.[91] Here, as a prefatory note to the chapters that follow, I want to elaborate on Grochala's formulation using some examples from John Potts's *The New Time and Space* to suggest what might be different about liquid dramaturgies when applied to history plays. In his dissection of the networked nature of postmodern spatio-temporal dynamics, Potts echoes David Harvey, who is also central to Grochala's thinking. Potts's sense that 'time has become a montage of fractures' corresponds to Harvey's identification of cultural forms shifting towards fragmentation and indeterminacy;[92] Potts's phrase 'the big now' reflects Harvey's idea that 'time horizons shorten to the point where the present is all there is'.[93] Furthermore, Potts argues that in the twenty-first century, people have rapidly become accustomed to 'telematic communication: co-present at a distance, often a great distance'.[94] In such situations, 'the private is super-imposed onto the public (often to the annoyance of fellow citizens)' as individuals conduct conversations via phone or video-conferencing on trains, in cafes and on the street.[95]

---

[91] Sarah Grochala, *The Contemporary Political Play: Rethinking Dramaturgical Structure* (London: Bloomsbury Methuen, 2017), 17.

[92] John Potts, *The New Time and Space* (Basingstoke: Palgrave, 2015), 51; Harvey, quoted in Grochala, *The Contemporary Political Play*, 81.

[93] Potts, *The New Time and Space*, 94; Harvey, quoted in Grochala, *The Contemporary Political Play*, 80.

[94] Potts, *The New Time and Space*, 57.

[95] Ibid., 58.

Such everyday examples of a 'contemporary hybrid space' that enables a simultaneity – a layering of time that would previously have been impossible – suggest potential ways of describing how contemporary history plays can cut through the prevailing culture using its own communicative channels. After all, the practice of presenting private and domestic scenes in public was a theatrical convention long before it was an irritation on public transport. In addition, as Grochala explains, '[d]ramatic time moves at a faster rate than lived time'; it is subjective, and it normatively presents events as taking place simultaneously.[96] Of course, unlike much entertainment in the new space and time, live, in-person theatre cannot usually be 'time shifted' or viewed on-demand: it requires mutual scheduling to achieve shared space and time ('7.30 pm. Latecomers may not be admitted'). And yet its potential, for history plays in particular, for bringing together action in widely different times and places in order to place them in dialogue, anticipates in some ways the virtual or networked time in which we now live. Contemporary history plays make creative use of the sense that 'time has become a montage of fractures', but in order to invite audiences to make connections between them rather than to have their attention further atomized.[97] The immediacy of this connection – in the most successful examples of history plays that this book highlights – can help to guard against the conception of the past as merely marketable nostalgia.[98] In other words, history plays can use our familiarity with compressed, fragmented, overlapping and collapsed space and time as a performance language to speak to now, but in so doing they can subvert the 'big now', the perpetual present that is an effect of networked time and space as experienced in consumer society.[99] I return to questions of how history play audiences might experience time and causality in Chapter 4.

---

[96] Grochala, *The Contemporary Political Play*, 92–3.
[97] Potts, *The New Time and Space*, 51.
[98] Ibid., 104.
[99] Ibid., 94.

Another strong influence in my understanding of the possibilities of the history play is Maurya Wickstrom's *Fiery Temporalities in Theatre and Performance* (2018), and its contention that 'Theatre may offer a means, in treating history, to avoid being buried in an avalanche of historical ruin, and to instead seek in the past for emancipatory presents and stage them as such.'[100] Wickstrom draws on the thought of Walter Benjamin, for whom 'Historical events are conceived as a kind of mass production of the new, making all events the same, and this projection regularizes and regulates disruption.'[101] As Wickstrom does, I want to identify plays and performances that resist being recuperated into 'processional history', which she describes as 'an inseparable substructure that motors us along the path of serial succession. It seems to exclude intervention, or else to be capable of restoring any intervention that happens back to its unalterable flow.'[102] To me, this 'serial succession' is the continually reinforced chronicle of the past – in the case of England, it is the familiar litany of Romans, Vikings, Normans, Tudors, Victorians and the Second World War – that in its selectiveness presents history as progress and England as, somehow, invulnerable and unchanging, despite its succession of invasions and transformations. Any 'disruption', in the form of reinterpretations of periods or events, or challenges to Malik's 'myth of virtuous origin', are recuperated, distorted or ignored to suit this dominant order, and to suit the genres of historical narrative that we are used to consuming. Wickstrom's idea of 'initiations of history' that resist the 'tragic mode' of historical drama is one that I return to in relation to biographical plays in Chapter 2.

---

[100] Maurya Wickstrom, *Fiery Temporalities in Theatre and Performance: The Initiation of History* (London: Bloomsbury Methuen Drama, 2018), 113.
[101] Ibid., 25.
[102] Ibid., 19.

Dramaturgies of the History Play

In order to navigate a course through a range of recent productions in English theatres, I have structured the book around different dramaturgies of contemporary historical playwriting. 'Dramaturgy' may be an unfamiliar term to some readers. In the theatre, dramaturgy can have several meanings; in Theresa Lang's definition, to dramaturg is nothing less than 'to curate an experience for an audience', and the term has been used to describe a range of activities in theatre companies and institutions, from literary management to the design of lobby displays.[103] A key question that dramaturgs involved in commissioning and programming plays may ask is 'why this, here, now?' or, put another way, 'why this play, for this audience, at this moment?'[104] This emphasis on the timeliness or urgency of a proposed theatrical production, and how it speaks to a particular audience in a specific locale and venue, has clear implications for the analysis of history plays: why invoke this vision of the past now, and what are the resonances of doing so in this place?

In this book I use the word 'dramaturgy', in the sense of a detailed understanding of how any given play works: its internal logic, the 'rules' of the play-world, including how time and space operate, and how its theatrical form and its content respond to each other. Michael Chemers refers to this kind of dramaturgy as the 'aesthetic architecture of a piece of dramatic literature'.[105] In the words of Cathy Turner and Synne K. Behrndt, 'in looking at a work's dramaturgy, we need to consider how all elements interact ... dramaturgical analysis regards the performance as a complex web of elements, and aims to identify the ways in which these connect (or fail to connect)'.[106] The dramaturgical analysis of

---

[103] Theresa Lang, *Essential Dramaturgy: The Mindset and Skillset* (New York: Routledge, 2017), 7.

[104] Ibid., 80.

[105] Michael Chemers, *Ghost Light: An Introductory Handbook for Dramaturgy* (Carbondale, IL: Southern Illinois University Press, 2011), 3.

[106] Cathy Turner and Synne K. Behrndt, *Dramaturgy and Performance* (Basingstoke: Palgrave, 2008), 33.

playscripts (as opposed to performances) may be undertaken initially by an institution's literary manager, its artistic director or play-readers; it might be carried out by a specific named person who is dramaturg for the play's production, or by a company or institutional dramaturg.[107] In some production models this dramaturgical analysis of the text is also part of the 'table-work' of initial rehearsals and may be led by the director. For scholars, by contrast, a *post hoc* dramaturgical reading of a play text may reveal patterns or performance possibilities that were not obvious from a given production – the latent potentialities of the script – and it facilitates the kind of detailed comparison between history plays that is not available when a performance is being experienced live.

Grouping plays, for the purposes of analysis, on the basis of their dramaturgical patterns – and specifically, their manipulation of historical time – will, I hope, avoid the pitfalls of attempting a narrative history of the history play over the last twenty-five years. The narrative approach would, I suspect, conceal as much as it would reveal, especially given the inclusion of plays originating in both the UK and the US which have been staged in England. This is not to downplay the usefulness of other groupings and orderings of history plays, however. Palmer's analysis of history plays groups them by their relationship to emerging patterns of historiography in the twentieth century, the work of what he calls the 'New Historians'.[108] Ian Brown and Barbara Bell order Scottish history plays on the principle of their functions.[109] And most saliently for this monograph, Mark Berninger's five-part typology of the history play captures the dynamic relationship with historical forms of knowledge that the texts in this study exemplify in his last two types, the metahistorical play and the posthistorical play.[110] Nevertheless, the distinctions that I draw in *The Contemporary History Play* between different modes of refashioning the past – single lives, and lives in tandem; parallel and generational timelines; history that

---

[107] Lang, *Essential Dramaturgy,* 34.
[108] Palmer, *Contemporary British History Play,* 13–20.
[109] See Ian Brown, *History as Theatrical Metaphor* (Cham, Switzerland: Palgrave, 2016), 26.
[110] Berninger, 'Variations', 41.

didn't happen and history that *couldn't* happen – are the most useful for grouping together the key strategies for representing the past in twenty-first-century English theatres. Moreover, it is the increasing hybridity between these categories in the last decade that indicates where the history play might be heading.

In the first chapter, 'History versus Dramaturgy', I investigate the many tensions and trade-offs between history and dramaturgy in historical playwriting: when and how playwrights might opt to depart from recorded history in the service of a cohesive theatrical work, and when and how they might opt to place a premium on the historical record, even when this is in conflict with how the play works as a text or a performance. I consider the influence of Shakespeare on contemporary history plays in more detail and set out my argument that history plays are most productively considered as a constructed, provisional version of the past – that is, history in the act of being assembled. To illustrate this idea, I offer an analysis of Jackie Sibblies Drury's 2012 play, *We Are Proud to Present a Presentation about the Herero of Namibia, Formerly Known as Southwest Africa, from the German Sudwestafrika, between the Years 1884–1915* and Marek Horn's *Wild Swimming* (2019). I then focus on the example of language as a dramaturgical choice that works to support different treatments of the past in *The Whip* by Juliet Gilkes Romero (2020) and *Common* by D. C. Moore (2017). Thereafter, the book considers a number of relationships between history and dramaturgy in turn.

In Chapter 2, I explore the biographical history play, the most well-established and popular type of historical drama. My aim here is to defamiliarize its assumptions and conventions. 'Biodramas' have a tendency to reinforce the emphasis put on the exceptional individual in culturally hegemonic narratives, thus downplaying collectivist and communitarian efforts and making them less visible. They often imitate the 'historical realism', causality and storytelling of film and TV biodrama, given the cultural dominance of period drama in the UK. The focus on the individual, on roots and origins, privileges a psychological reading of the subject, and their drives and their contradictions, that favours Naturalism and a balance-sheet approach to characterization, where we are encouraged to weigh up the central figure's virtues and vices.[111] I investigate how these dramaturgical conventions are expanded and resisted using five 'modes' – those of recuperation, fragmentation, duplication, competition and iteration – which appear in different combinations in my case studies, *Red Ellen* by Caroline Bird (2021), *I, Joan* by Charlie Josephine (2022), *Handbagged* by Moira Buffini (2013/22), *The Father and the Assassin* by Anupama Chandrasekhar (2022) and *Marys Seacole* by Jackie Sibblies Drury (2022).

As investigated in Chapter 3, the intergenerational family drama follows the fortunes of a single, fictional family across two or more generations and several decades. Its antecedents are to be found in the 'time plays' of J. B. Priestley, such as *Time and the Conways* (1937) as well as the conservative narratives of nation offered by Noël Coward in *Cavalcade* (1931) and *This Happy Breed* (1942). For all its 'writerly' qualities in disrupting the Naturalistic expectations of linear, 'real-time' action, the multi-generational history play can still veer towards the formally conservative, presenting a series of kitchen-table scenes simply separated by time. The multi-generational history play often also foregrounds the Naturalist preoccupation with family life and problems of nature-versus-nurture and does not always engage actively with its historical settings. At its best, however, I maintain that the intergenerational family drama can be powerfully anti-nostalgic. My examples in this section range from Richard Bean's *Harvest* (2005) to Vinay Patel's *An Adventure* (2018), Samuel Adamson's *Wife* (2019) and Beth Steel's *The House of Shades* (2022).

The polychronic history play, discussed in Chapter 4, follows two or more distinct story strands. The most common form of this is a dual timeline history play, consisting of a present-day strand and a historical strand. The strands cross over at some point, and we discover the play's implied relationship between past and present. This type of history play

---

[111] This invitation to view the character 'objectively' is, of course, rendered moot by the fictional nature of the depiction, by the selection and reshaping of characters and events, and by the other multi-layered and interacting representational practices of theatre.

is useful for thinking about how historical causality and analogy are suggested or asserted in writing about the past. Polychronic history plays have a distinctive dramaturgy and set of tropes, linking them to wider questions of whether history 'teaches lessons', whether knowledge of the past empowers us for the future, and hence whether theatre can use the past to effect change. The examples that the chapter explores feature increasingly complex timelines, beginning with *The Pride* by Alexi Kaye Campbell (2008), and moving on to Anders Lustgarten's *The Seven Acts of Mercy* (2016), Bruce Norris's *Clybourne Park* (2012), *Love and Other Acts of Violence* by Cordelia Lynn (2021), and Hannah Khalil's *A Museum in Baghdad* (2019) before ending with Winsome Pinnock's astonishing *Rockets and Blue Lights* (2020).

The final part of the book is a Coda, exploring the dramaturgy of alternate and fantastic histories. These are plays which imagine what did not happen or what might have been; sometimes this is made clear from the start, and sometimes the line between what is presented as either factual, or historical fantasy, is deliberately blurred. These examples provide an opportunity to reconsider 'facticity' in history plays – the ways that such writing makes various truth-claims in a performance medium that is self-evidently 'not real'. The contemporary plays considered are *A Very Very Very Dark Matter* by Martin McDonagh (2018), *The Glow* by Alistair McDowall (2022), *Rapture* by Lucy Kirkwood (2022) and *Mr Burns* by Anne Washburn (2013). In bringing these disparate plays together, I aim to make comparisons in how each conveys, and undermines, the impression of a historical encounter. These examples all push in various ways at the limits of what a history play might be, and all evince a hybridity between the different categories of history play explicated in this book. Together, they suggest that the future of staging the past will be ever more layered and ludic. Nevertheless, the chapter argues that McDonagh's play, in particular, returns us *in extremis* to the ethical problems of representing the past – problems that gave rise to the history play's many breaks with realism over the last century.

Scope and Limitations

With such a broad definition of the contemporary history play, it is inevitable that I have had to leave out much more than I have been able to include in this study. I began compiling a spreadsheet of new contemporary history plays of the post-2000 era in 2019, and quickly had over 200 examples. Hence, there are whole categories of history play that are under-represented in the corpus of plays that is used in this book. Notable omissions include the community history play, the autobiographical history play, the memory play and the group or ensemble history play (examples of this last category would include *Scuttlers* by Rona Munro (2015), *The Sweet Science of Bruising* by June Wilkinson (2018), *Blue Stockings* by Jessica Swale (2013) and *The Welkin* by Lucy Kirkwood (2020)). Also absent, but important to the recent development of contemporary history plays as new writing, are play seasons and cycles on historical subjects commissioned by theatres. This category would include the series of multi-play events, featuring short plays from numerous writers, that was programmed by the Tricycle Theatre (now the Kiln) in the early 2010s, for example *Afghanistan: The Great Game* (2009), *Women, Power and Politics: Then and Now* (2010) and *The Bomb: A Partial History* (2012).

Because of my selection of plays by dramaturgical approach, I have not been able to include nearly as many plays originating in English regional theatres as I had originally intended. Many of the plays subjected to close reading come from what Aleks Sierz referred to in 2012 as the 'Big Six' new-writing venues,[112] as well as the National Theatre in London. In addition, as noted earlier, the representation of the RSC and Globe, where new historical dramas and Shakespeare revivals rotate in repertory, is inevitably dense given the nature of this project. Another book could certainly be written about the new history plays produced in the period at theatres such as Manchester

---

[112] These are (or were at that time) the Royal Court, Bush, Hampstead and Soho theatres in London, the Live Theatre in Newcastle and Edinburgh's Traverse Theatre (Sierz, *Rewriting the Nation*, 28).

Royal Exchange, Leeds Playhouse, Sheffield Crucible, Northern Stage, Nottingham Playhouse and many others.

Finally, it seems apt to include some remarks on the relationship between text and performance as I represent it in the present study. I have used the term 'new writing' rather than 'new work', because the focus of the book is on single-authored, scripted drama rather than devised work.[113] 'Single-authored' is perhaps an especially misleading designation in the case of play scripts, however. Printed scripts in contemporary UK theatre are almost always composite artefacts, resulting from multiple readings, conversations, workshops, talkback sessions and rehearsals. We need look no further than the early history plays of Caryl Churchill with Joint Stock Theatre Company (*Light Shining in Buckinghamshire* (1976), *Cloud Nine* (1979)) to recall that the singular playwright's name on the text has long been a fiction, with multiple sources and improvisational practices feeding into what constituted the published text. Nor are published play texts the end of a play's development, as the examples of Moira Buffini's scripts for *Loveplay* and *Handbagged* illustrate. Both exist in at least two published forms, having been revised for each edition or revival.[114]

However, *The Contemporary History Play* limits itself to the comparison and analysis of products – public performances and published scripts – rather than processes. In the majority of cases, I have attended the first UK production of the plays discussed here. Where the performance created a notable effect or gave rise to a particular response that was quite distinct from, or over and above, what could be gleaned from the play text, I describe and interpret it. There is a great deal of potential for further scholarship on how history plays are conceived, written, workshopped, redrafted, rehearsed and staged, and

---

[113] By contrast, Catriona Fallow uses the more inclusive 'new work' more frequently than 'new writing' in her article 'New Work in and Beyond Repertory' (2022). (Catriona Fallow, 'New Work In and Beyond Repertory at the Royal Shakespeare Company and Shakespeare's Globe,' *Early Theatre* vol. 25, no. 2 (2022). doi:doi10.12745/et.25.2.4739.)

[114] Compare, for instance, the 2010, 2013 and 2022 editions of *Handbagged*, and for *Loveplay*, the Samuel French edition, Faber single edition and the version included in *Plays 1*.

in what creative, financial and organizational circumstances in each case. *The Contemporary History Play*, therefore, is not based primarily on playwrights' views and experiences of making historical drama, although it has benefited from many conversations with individual practitioners, as noted in the acknowledgements.

This book sets out to examine what it means to stage plays set in the past, in a particular cultural and political moment in England. It therefore seems appropriate to at least acknowledge at the outset some of the processes and material circumstances of which play scripts are a product. As unitary artefacts, sitting innocently on bookshelves, they may look deceptively 'finished'; their open, contingent qualities are well concealed between soft covers. What I hope to show in this book is how these latent qualities of all play texts are made unusually visible – indeed, often rendered as spectacle – by the staging of contemporary historical drama. As the first chapter will explore, history plays remake the past in order to make history in the present.

1

History versus Dramaturgy

Introduction

In this chapter I take a more detailed look at the tensions and contradictions of attempting to stage history. I highlight some of the many dramaturgical factors that are consistently in play when writers imbue their plays with historical material, and when audiences encounter these play-worlds. The chapter begins with an exploration of the influence that William Shakespeare, and Shakespearean institutions, continue to have on the contemporary history play and its conditions of production. Then, using the example of Shakespeare as a springboard into the dramaturgy of the history play and some of its taken-for-granted assumptions, I indicate how contemporary theatre stages the constructed nature of history through metatheatrical and other dissonant strategies. By metatheatre, I mean plays or performances that reveal their status as artworks, through self-reflexive practices such as direct address to the audience, stepping 'out of character' or staging a play-within-a-play.[1] I develop this investigation using the example of Jackie Sibblies Drury's *We Are Proud to Present a Presentation about the Herero of Namibia, Formerly Known as Southwest Africa, from the German Sudwestafrika, between the Years 1884–1915* (2012). To illustrate further the contingent, provisional history that contemporary theatre constructs and enacts, I take Virginia Woolf's

---

[1] See 'metatheatre' in *The Companion to Theatre and Performance* (Oxford: Oxford University Press, 2010). Available online: https://www.oxfordreference-com.libproxy.york.ac.uk/view/10.1093/acref/9780199574193.001.0001/acref-9780199574193-e-2606 (accessed 3 February 2023).

mock-biography *Orlando* as a model and map various recent history plays onto its subversive and self-conscious features. This establishes the process of 'Orlandification' that I will use in the chapters that follow; I then draw detailed connections between *Orlando* and Marek Horn's *Wild Swimming* (2019).* Taking language as a key example of how playwrights use 'then' to address 'now', I discuss two more plays, *The Whip* by Juliet Gilkes Romero (2020) and *Common* by D. C. Moore (2017). Finally, I return to the idea of the posthistorical play, and make my case for the dramaturgical distinctiveness of contemporary history plays.

Playwrights and critics all seem to agree that, when staging a history play, there is an implied conflict between the demand that it should 'be true to history' and the demand that it should work effectively as drama. Herbert Lindenberger, in a transhistorical study of the history play, notes that historical drama implies a tension between fact and fiction: 'the first word qualifying the fictiveness of the second, the second questioning the reality of the first'.[2] Nilhoufer Harben warns against making the mistake of 'stressing the historical element to the detriment of the dramatic or the dramatic element to the detriment of the historical. What has to be achieved is a fine balance ...'.[3] Paola Botham puts the problem more succinctly when she calls the twenty-first-century history play '[a] genre that operates on a tightrope between truth claims and dramatic convention'.[4] Ian Brown, in his study of recent Scottish history plays, also acknowledges the way that 'the process of historical thought is one that can be seen to parallel dramaturgical thought, the shaping of a narrative, plot and action to develop meaning determined by an author'.[5] Reviewing a 2018 revival of Caryl Churchill's landmark 1976 play about the English Civil War, *Light Shining in Buckinghamshire*, Jesse Green provides a more concrete

---

* The term 'Orlandification' was coined and developed by Varsha Panjwani in our conversations on Woolf.

[2] Lindenberger, *Historical Drama*, 7.

[3] Harben, *English History Plays*, 14.

[4] Paola Botham, 'The Twenty-First Century History Play', 87.

[5] Brown, *History as Theatrical Metaphor*, 40.

example: '[I]t's an anticlimax built into the aftermath of the English Civil War, and into Ms. Churchill's construction, that all the shaking ends up changing little. The men who fought to help the gentry supplant the throne wind up no better off than when they started ... That's true of history but taxing as dramaturgy.'[6]

What each of these quotations indicates is that working with historical material brings advantages – for instance, a character's actions and events may have added resonance because we know what their long-term results will be – but also disadvantages, in that no chronicle of actions or events is dramatically interesting in and of itself. Swamp the play with historical detail and verbatim recitals of primary sources and audiences will likely become bored; favour the theatrically engaging over the archivally authentic, and some will cavil that the play has taken liberties. A history play is a lot like a stage adaptation of a classic novel: the key difference is that history plays tend to have multiple non-fiction sources where a literary adaptation is usually of a single, fictional source. As with a literary adaptation, many of those who know the source material feel invested in it and want the theatre production to 'get it right'. Yet, since all texts require interpretation, no two people will agree exactly on the *meaning* of the source text(s) – on what the 'it' is that the production should get right. As this chapter will demonstrate, the solution that some contemporary playwrights find to this problem is to take this recurring tension between fact and fiction – between archive and art, history and dramaturgy – and make it the action of the play.

History Plays and Shakespeare

It is impossible to talk about the dramaturgy of contemporary history plays in England without acknowledging the influence of Shakespeare

---

[6] Jesse Green, 'Review: When the "Light Shining" on Revolution Falters', *New York Times*, 7 May 2018. Available online. https://www.nytimes.com/2018/05/07/theater/review-light-shining-on-buckinghamshire-caryl-churchill.html (accessed 3 February 2023).

on ideas of what a history play is or 'should' be. This is partly because of Shakespeare's cultural ubiquity, and hence the visibility of revivals and adaptations of his historical dramas in the theatrical landscape. The flagship national producing houses regularly stage new versions of what have been conventionally considered 'the histories' (chronologically, from *King John* to *Henry VIII*) in various combinations (for example, the 'Henriad', which is understood by some to run from *Richard II* through the six plays about Henrys IV, V and VI, to *Richard III*). These plays have also been reshaped and adapted to reflect more modern dramaturgies, for instance in the *Wars of the Roses* (1964), the Plantagenets plays at the RSC (1988) and *The Hollow Crown* (1961; later adapted for BBC television in 2012–16).[7] *Titus Andronicus, Coriolanus, Julius Caesar* and *Antony and Cleopatra* – usually bracketed under 'tragedies' but more recently repackaged by the RSC as 'The Roman Plays' (2017–18) – can also lay claim to being history plays in the contemporary playwriting sense, as indeed can *Macbeth, King Lear* and *Cymbeline*, however mythical their treatment of these historical British kings. In addition, of course, past productions of these history plays are available as educational resources and for home consumption, to stream or buy, making up a secondary historical 'archive' of historical performances.

Most saliently for the present study, it is crucial to note that the producing houses most closely associated with the Shakespearean and early-modern repertoire, the RSC and Shakespeare's Globe, have a longstanding investment in new writing that is programmed alongside the historic 'histories' and which are frequently new history plays themselves, responding to some aspect of the current season. As Catriona Fallow argues, 'both the RSC and the Globe place new work in a supposedly positive, reciprocal relationship with the early modern canon, thereby positioning contemporary writers as direct "descendants" of Shakespeare'.[8] This results in staff from both institutions making the

7   See Colin Chambers, *Inside the Royal Shakespeare Company: Creativity and the Institution* (Abingdon: Routledge, 2004), 33–40, 97.
8   Fallow, 'New Work', 173.

claim that Shakespeare was once a 'new writer', too.[9] Fallow identifies a tension in this rhetoric, 'between a desire to de-centre Shakespeare, while also calling upon his significant cultural authority'.[10] For example, I have discussed in a previous article the 'This Other Eden' season of new plays that was staged as a counterpart to the 'This England' history plays at the RSC under Adrian Noble.[11] At the Globe, it was the practice in the 2010s under Dominic Dromgoole's artistic directorship to pair new works with a Shakespeare production each year, creating cross-casting opportunities such as when Miranda Raison played Anne Boleyn in *Henry VIII* and also in Howard Brenton's new play *Anne Boleyn* in 2010.[12] In 2018 Morgan Lloyd Malcolm's *Emilia* was originally programmed in a season of Shakespeare revivals that each featured a character named Emilia; Tom Stuart's *After Edward* (2019) was written as a response the Globe's revival of Marlowe's *Edward II* in the same season (Stuart played the title role in both); and Hannah Khalil's 'collaboration', as it was framed, with Shakespeare and Fletcher, *The Life of King Henry VIII, or All Is True,* was staged at the Globe in the summer 2022 season.[13] Given this interplay and circulation between the symbolic economy of Shakespeare and that of new history plays, the impact of Shakespeare on the landscape of historical drama is worth further examination.

As Kate McLuskie and Kate Rumbold observe in their book *Cultural Value in Twenty-First Century England: The Case of Shakespeare,* theatres can count on the 'familiarity with Shakespeare assured by over a century of compulsory education'.[14] For many taught in English schools, their first encounter with Shakespeare will come via set texts at

[9] Ibid., 174.
[10] Ibid., 177.
[11] Benjamin Poore, 'Before the Fall: Looking Back on the Royal Shakespeare Company's "This Other Eden" Season (2001)', *Journal of Contemporary Drama in English* 6, no. 1 (2018): 176–90. doi:10.1515/jcde-2018-0019.
[12] Fallow, 'New Work', 181.
[13] Hannah Khalil, 'Collaborating with Shakespeare and Fletcher on Henry VIII' (blog), *Shakespeare's Globe,* 17 May 2022. Available online: https://www.shakespearesglobe.com/discover/blogs-and-features/2022/05/17/collaborating-with-shakespeare-and-fletcher on-henry-viii/ (accessed 3 February 2023).
[14] Kate McLuskie and Kate Rumbold, *Cultural Value in Twenty-First Century England: The Case of Shakespeare* (Manchester: Manchester University Press, 2014), 121.

Key Stages Three and Four, and if the set play is a 'history' (in the broad definition discussed in the previous paragraph) then this may also be students' first encounter with a representation of that historical period, too. For instance, it has been unusual for school history syllabuses to devote much time to the reign of Richard II or Henry IV, still less to the ancient world of Titus Andronicus or Coriolanus, regardless of the standing of these eponymous plays as historical drama. Thus, schoolchildren are often learning about a Shakespeare play, for the first time, in tandem with the historical material that he adapts. It is worth noting what is at stake in claiming a proportion of Shakespeare's plays as 'histories' rather than 'adaptations', even when they are predominantly drawn from one source of narrative history. As mentioned earlier, history plays and adaptations have much in common, but a cultural investment in the idea of the 'creative genius' of Shakespeare requires that educational and theatre institutions de-emphasize the craft-based work of adaptation in favour of the notion of an artist responding to inspiration. The way to square the inconvenient details of Shakespeare's sources – be they historical chronicles like Holinshed, or theatrical precursors like the anonymous *True Chronicle History of King Leir* – is to insist on the transformative nature of Shakespeare's work on such materials. As such, it follows that if Shakespeare's 'timeless genius' was applied to historical material, his history plays should be the model of how a 'great' history play should be.

To take some of the most obvious dramaturgical choices as examples, history plays as written under the long cultural shadow of Shakespeare might be expected to make use of a prologue, chorus or commentator characters (such as gardeners or gravediggers) to explicate the action. Such history plays might be expected to focus predominantly on 'great men', thus interpreting history through a biographical lens rather than explicitly through class, gender, sexuality, geopolitics or ecology, for example. The assumption would be that they would follow a linear chronological order, that time is unidirectional, that each main character represents an individual historical personage rather than being multiplied and replicated, and that despite the existence of ghosts, there is only one shared reality, not a multiverse of possibilities. The Shakespearean history play further models the comfortable coexistence of tragic and comic perspectives on events, the centrality of speech, argument, rhetoric and dialogue to moments of historical change, and a discernible relationship between cause and effect which drives the action. None of these assumptions is to be taken for granted in the contemporary history plays discussed in this book. Nevertheless, it must be acknowledged that even as they argue with the Shakespearean history formula, many are still indebted to it in numerous ways. Khalil's *Henry VIII* is an obvious example, as is Jeannie O'Hare's *Queen Margaret*, produced at the Manchester Royal Exchange in 2018, or even the 'future history' of Mike Bartlett's *King Charles III* (2014), written in verse. I will return to Shakespeare in connection with language, as a specific example of a dramaturgical choice, towards the end of the chapter. First, we need to examine more thoroughly how the past as history is framed by contemporary theatre.

The Past on Stage is Constructed, Provisional History

The literary scholar Hayden White, in a series of publications beginning with *Metahistory* in 1973, elaborated his theory that historical narrative is as much a literary construct as prose fiction. In this reading, 'the historical work' is 'a verbal structure in the form of a narrative prose discourse that purports to be a model, or icon, of past structures and processes in the interests of *explaining what they were by representing them*' (emphasis in original).[15] White began by enumerating the elements of this 'poetics of history', arguing that, like novels, works of history rely on certain genres, or modes of emplotment (the Romantic, Tragic, Satirical or Comical), which are combined with certain modes of argument (the Formist, Mechanist, Organicist or Contextualist theories

---

[15] Hayden White, *Metahistory: The Historical Imagination in 19th-Century Europe* (Baltimore, ML: Johns Hopkins University Press, 2014), 2.

of history), resulting in historiography that has particular ideological implications (which he classifies as Anarchist, Radical, Conservative and Liberal).[16] These historiographical genres and modes are, in turn, mediated by tropes which further represent the events that are being narrated in specific ways: 'Metaphor is essentially *representational*, Metonymy is *reductionist*, Synecdoche is *integrative*, and Irony is *negational*.'[17] Given that none of these choices is transparent or neutral when encountered in historical writing, it follows that '[t]here does, in fact, appear to be an irreducible ideological component in every historical account of reality'.[18] As Keith Jenkins and Alun Munslow remarked in 2004, 'it would be difficult to overestimate the influence of White on thinking about the nature of history such that, for us, there is "no going back"': that is, we cannot return to a naive supposition that history simply reports a series of factual events without the use of imagination or aesthetic devices.[19] Of course, the right-wing 'culture war' attack on historical enquiry, on 'bias' and 'rewriting history', is founded, in part, on precisely this nostalgia for an imagined time when historical writing was simply the relaying and trading of 'facts'. But to take any version of events at face value, without an awareness of how its version of reality is constituted by language for ideological as well as aesthetic purposes, is to lay oneself open to the manipulations of propaganda.[20]

If we take White's insights and apply them to theatrical representations of the past, we can see that the transfiguration of textual and material fragments of the past into a more or less fictive set of texts called 'history' – which is then read and reimagined by playwrights and companies, and replayed for particular audiences, in a slightly different

---

[16] White, *Metahistory*, 29.

[17] Ibid., 32.

[18] Ibid., 21.

[19] Jenkins and Munslow, *The Nature of History Reader* (Abingdon: Routledge, 2004), 198.

[20] See historian Alan Lester's response to the formation of the 'History Reclaimed' pressure group. (Alan Lester, 'History Reclaimed – But from What?', *Snapshots of Empire* (blog), *University of Sussex*, 15 September 2021. Available online:. https://blogs.sussex. ac.uk/snapshotsofempire/2021/09/15/history-reclaimed-but-from-what/ (accessed 3 February 2023).

way every night – is hardly conducive to a stable, neutral or transparent iteration of historical events. History plays, by the time they reach an audience in the theatre, have been re-narrativized at least five times already: by their historical sources, by the interpreters and stitchers-together of those sources ('historians'), by their playwrights, by their creative teams and by the specific circumstances of each individual performance. Even the model that I have just outlined makes the wildly unlikely assumption that no processes of rewriting, research and development, or dramaturgy have taken place with the play text before going into production. It also makes the gross oversimplification of implying that the playwright's reading of historical sources is itself a bounded and neutral activity, rather than an ongoing process shaped and informed by personal, political and artistic investments. As Alexander Feldman proposes, 'The theatre is a locus of transformation, its representative strategies are forms of illusion and its productions are subject to the contingency of innumerable mediating effects … [hence] attempts to discuss drama within the context of postmodernism are fraught with difficulty.'[21] He goes on to cite Daniel Jernigan's argument that drama's 'inherently postmodernist characteristics – self-reflexivity, provisionality, polyvocality' meant that theatre was postmodernist *avant la lettre*.[22] In this sense, then, theatre's treatment of history exemplifies and enacts White's theories of the historiographical process especially vividly, because of stage drama's inherent instability as an art form. Jerome de Groot notes this quality of theatre in his survey of historical fictions, commenting, 'Drama's ability to be momentary, dismissive, brief, enigmatic and intangible means that plays relating to history can be more ephemeral and therefore more challenging than, for instance, film or even novel versions.'[23]

Moreover, staged history is never completely illusionistic, even when it tries to be; it always shows signs of its constructedness, of being

---

[21] Alexander Feldman, *Dramas of the Past on the Twentieth-Century Stage: In History's Wings* (Abingdon: Routledge, 2013), 26.

[22] Feldman, *Dramas of the Past*, 26.

[23] De Groot, *Consuming History*, 229.

a made – in the collaborative, creative sense, a *made-up* – version of the past. In *Performing History* (2000), Freddie Rokem notes that the performance of history is 'a transposition of the historical past on stage, and also the story of their production process'.[24] Josy Miller extends this thought in her examination of 9/11 plays:

> The medium of the theatre, through its long loaded, provocative, semiotic history, constantly invites its audience to imagine, in large part due to the failure of the stage to recreate reality despite phenomenal technical resources that are currently being employed. We are always being asked/asking to go on an imaginative journey, be it one of fictive titillation or critical projection.[25]

Or, to cite Julia Head's 'Director's Note' on Marek Horn's play *Wild Swimming*, 'We believe there are always two plays being performed. One is the play *Wild Swimming* by Marek Horn, and the other is two actors attempting to perform the play *Wild Swimming* and ultimately failing. These two worlds should be constantly present and not always in agreement'.[26] While this pattern is arrestingly evoked in Horn's published script, to some extent all history plays have this inbuilt element of inadequacy; it is just that sometimes the 'actors failing to perform the play' is more or less foregrounded – and is sometimes layered amid actors *playing* actors failing to perform the play (as, for example, in Moira Buffini's *Handbagged*, which I discuss in Chapter 2).

As writing for and in performance, history plays embody and literalize that 'constructedness' through such tropes as multi-rolling, direct address, songs announcing an idea or theme, onstage costume changes, deliberate anachronisms, clashes of acting style or language, the manipulation and repurposing of props, onstage musicians, framing devices (e.g. the play-within-a-play in Richard Bean's *England*

---

[24] Freddie Rokem, *Performing History: Theatrical Representations of the Past in Contemporary Theatre* (Iowa City: University of Iowa Press, 2000), 202.

[25] Josy Miller, 'Performing Collective Trauma: 9/11 and the Reconstruction of American Identity', in *History, Memory, Performance*, ed. David Dean, Yana Meerzon and Kathryn Prince (Basingstoke: Palgrave Macmillan, 2015), 191.

[26] Julia Head, 'Director's Note', in *Wild Swimming* by Marek Horn (London: Nick Hern, 2019), no pagination.

People Very Nice (National Theatre, 2009)) and non-realistic elements of production design such as miniature sets (Rory Mullarkey's *Saint George and the Dragon* (National Theatre, 2017)) or the boxed, framed silhouettes of women workers that featured at the start and end of Lucy Kirkwood's *The Welkin* (National Theatre, 2020). Although clearly influenced by Bertolt Brecht's treatment of history in works such as *Mother Courage and Her Children* and *Life of Galileo*, this is evidently different from the kind of 'rational'[27] epic theatre, the 'theatre for a scientific age' that Brecht proposed in his theoretical writings. In a sense, in its refusal of the radical separation of elements, its fusing together of music and song, choreography, scenography, writing and acting, productions of these plays veer closer to the 'magic' of the *Gesamtkunstwerk* that Brecht contested and urged audiences to abandon.[28] Where Brecht saw 'the historical play' as not a 'fabrication',[29] the contemporary epic revels in its fabricated and partial qualities.

In our present environment of repeated, interrelated and disorientating national and global shocks, historical narrative as conventionally conceived becomes suspect, both within and beyond the world of theatre. Miller regards the proliferation, in post-9/11 theatre, of what Jean-François Lyotard calls 'thousands of uncomfortable little stories' as indicative of the 'impossibility of reconstructing the master narrative' of America, the story that the United States told to itself and to the world.[30] In his bleaker moments, Rokem too adopts a scepticism towards the idea of a didactic or 'usable' historical narrative: 'Finally, the only thing we can learn from history is probably that it is impossible to learn from history.'[31]

---

[27] Bertolt Brecht, *Brecht on Theatre*, ed. Marc Silberman, Steve Giles and Tom Kuhn (London: Bloomsbury, 2015), 72–3.

[28] Ibid., 75.

[29] Ibid., 210.

[30] Miller, 'Performing Collective Trauma', 188.

[31] Freddie Rokem, 'Discursive Practices and Narrative Models: History, Poetry, Philosophy', in *History, Memory, Performance*, ed. David Dean, Yana Meerzon and Kathryn Prince (Basingstoke: Palgrave Macmillan, 2015), 23.

Rather than providing or reinforcing stable narratives, then, we might usefully think of the history play as rendering history 'subject to the logics of poetics', as Soyica Diggs Colbert describes the climax of Katori Hall's play *The Mountaintop* (2009).[32] Aristotle contrasted history with poetry – counterintuitively, according to our present-day cultural hierarchy – by saying that history 'treats of particular facts' but that poetry is more philosophical and worthy of serious attention.[33] Rokem identifies another key line of the *Poetics*: '[The] distinction between historian and poet … consists really in this, that the one describes the things that have been, the other a kind of thing that might be.'[34] This seems like an apt description of the provisional, contingent history that theatre offers.[35] In contemporary history plays, we are often midway between things that have been and things that might have been; such is the nature of our encounter with an imagined past. The plays' dramaturgy is the poetics to which dominant versions of history are subjected.

Reading History in Performance

The coexistence of a dramatic narrative with a historical narrative gives the history play distinctive storytelling challenges. As audiences experiencing a production of a new-writing history play, it is likely that we do not know at the outset what will happen to the characters (unless we have read the script in advance). Depending on the historical setting(s), however, we may know what the historical events around which the action takes place are; and then, depending on the play's dramaturgical choices, we may expect to be able to slot the play's

---

[32] Soyica Diggs Colbert, 'Black Leadership at the Crossroads: Unfixing Martin Luther King Jr. in Katori Hall's *The Mountaintop*', *The South Atlantic Quarterly* 112, no. 2 (2013): 261–83, 279. doi:10.1215/00382876-2020199.

[33] Quoted in Davies, *Historics*, 52.

[34] Rokem, 'Discursive Practices', 24.

[35] See also Howard Barker: '[t]he theatre is not a disseminator of truth but a provider of versions. Its statements are provisional' (quoted in Feldman, *Dramas of the Past*, 26).

narrative – for instance, its introduction of fictional characters with their own desires and social or political situatedness – around the broader historical narrative. This leads to what I refer to as the 'double burden of exposition' in many history plays: the necessity to convey at least two levels of backstory and narrative causality, without the dramaturgy becoming static, or reliant on narrator figures, or overly dependent on the linguistic and narrative tools of the theatre at the expense of its other expressive possibilities. In the understanding of dramaturgy proposed by Theresa Lang and quoted in the Introduction, then, the challenges of how 'to curate an experience for an audience' are especially acute with the history play, since it relies on the interaction between knowledge generated by the performance and knowledge that is familiar from pre-existing historical narratives. This pre-existing knowledge is what Davies calls 'affirmative' history or 'knowledge that is already known',[36] and what Anthony P. Pennino interrogates as 'heritage culture'.[37]

Audience expectations can also place certain demands on the kinds of historical narrative that are presented (or considered presentable) on stage. As Frances Babbage notes of adapting unhappy endings in literature, 'We must also ask whether theatre as a medium *can* close its tellings on so bitter a note, should its creators desire, or whether the very qualities that make performance uniquely suited to popular storytelling – animation, collectivity, spontaneity, participation, connectedness – are also those that make genuinely dark and unsettling conclusions unsustainable'.[38]

---

[36] Davies, *Historics*, 5–6, 1.

[37] Anthony P. Pennino, *Staging the Past in the Age of Thatcher: The History We Haven't Had* (Cham, Switzerland: Palgrave, 2018), 4. Rokem, too, calls for a critical account of how this kind of familiar history contributes to audiences' experiences and expectations: 'I think we have reached a point in time where our knowledge and understanding of the historical past has already, to a large extent, been created through exposures to aesthetic representations of history ... This certainly calls for a deepened understanding of how such representations are constituted' (Freddie Rokem, 'Discursive Practices and Narrative Models: History, Poetry, Philosophy', in *History, Memory, Performance*, 24).

[38] Frances Babbage, *Adaptation in Contemporary Theatre: Performing Literature* (London: Bloomsbury Methuen Drama, 2018), 98.

We Are Proud to Present

To see many of these contradictory impulses and imperatives in action, we might usefully consider Jackie Sibblies Drury's *We Are Proud to Present a Presentation about the Herero of Namibia, Formerly Known as Southwest Africa, from the German Sudwestafrika, between the Years 1884–1915*. The play was performed at the Soho Rep theatre in New York in 2012, and was produced in the UK at the Bush Theatre in 2014. Its lengthy title, usually abbreviated to *We Are Proud to Present*, signals the work's metatheatrical intentions whilst also, perhaps, alluding to an earlier metatheatrical historical drama, Peter Weiss's *The Persecution and Assassination of Jean-Paul Marat as Performed by the Inmates of the Asylum of Charenton Under the Direction of the Marquis de Sade* (1964), conventionally abbreviated to *Marat/Sade*. As Emma Willis explains in her article 'Metatheatre and Dramaturgies of Reception', Drury's play depicts a company of six young actors, three Black and three White, attempting to devise a performance about the little-known genocide of the Herero by German colonizers.[39] Willis explains that metatheatre can be serious or comedic – pointing to Moliere's *Rehearsal at Versailles* (1662) and Michael Frayn's *Noises Off* (1982) as examples of a comedic use of the form; it is 'to the tradition of the bumbling yet endearing troupe of actors that the play is most closely related'.[40] However, in Drury's play, spectators go from being 'in on the joke' to becoming self-conscious witnesses to an act of 'real' violence.[41] Nevertheless, because of the framing device, 'In Drury's play, any semblance of the historical real is endlessly problematized and ironized'.[42] Drury has described the interpretive and expressive struggle of the actors as mirroring her own struggles as a writer, and her

[39] Emma Willis, 'Metatheatre and Dramaturgies of Reception in Jackie Sibblies Drury's *We Are Proud to Present*', *Journal of Contemporary Drama in English* 4, no. 1 (2016): 197. doi:10.1515/jcde-2016-0015.

[40] Ibid., 201.

[41] Ibid., 199.

[42] Ibid., 205.

'well-meaningness' in approaching the subject, commenting that the 'actors [are] failing to make the same kind of play that I failed to make'.[43]

Willis concludes her analysis with an especially notable phrase: 'metatheatre, Drury's play in particular, stages the unfolding of thought'.[44] Like Katori Hall's *The Mountaintop*, mentioned earlier, *We Are Proud to Present* contains a moment right at the end where the logics of its own construction collapse. As the opening stage directions warn: '*The presentation sections and the process sections are distinct at the start, but over time process becomes presentation, the spaces aren't what they appear to be and boundaries are broken.*'[45] In the play's final scene, 'Processtation', the White actors playing the colonizing Germans and the Black actors playing the Herero become more and more like Americans re-enacting their history, throwing in American slang and racist jokes. As Leonor Faber-Jonker puts it, 'The final scene is the dehumanization of the Herero, the Jim Crow South and slavery all rolled into one. It is the universal terrorizing of the Other.'[46] As with all Drury's plays, the stage directions are precise but unprescriptive. When Actor 2 has a noose put around his neck, terrifying him, the actors break character; Actors 2 and 6 leave, and the remaining actors '*process what has just happened … Which might lead to a smile. Which might lead to laughter*'.[47] Drury explains what happens if the actors find laughter, and how the remaining Black actor, Actor 4, '*cannot laugh*', but is instead watched by the others as he '*cleans up the space*', '*takes down the noose*' and '*tries to speak* [to the audience], *but he fails*'.[48] As Willis argues, in the play 'The fact that we retain the memory of the unseen – that it shocks and traumatizes us – demonstrates the very close relationship between the metatheatrical game and that which

[43] 'Interview with Jackie Sibblies Drury', *InterAct Theatre Company*, YouTube. Available online: https://www.youtube.com/watch?v=D6pkEYpoL3M (accessed 28 June 2022).

[44] Willis, 'Metatheatre', 209.

[45] Jackie Sibblies Drury, *We Are Proud to Present* …(London: Methuen Drama, 2021), no pagination.

[46] Leonor Faber-Jonker, 'Introduction', in *We Are Proud to Present* … by Jackie Sibblies Drury (London: Methuen Drama, 2021), xx.

[47] Drury, *We Are Proud to Present*, 97.

[48] Willis, 'Metatheatre', 98.

is felt as a real effect ensuing from it.'[49] The suggestion of a terrified actor with his head in a noose, which in turn suggests a lynching in the Deep South, which in turn suggests the genocide of the Herero, is more powerful than the direct, separate depiction of all of these. And while on one hand critics of the play's dramaturgy might argue that it does the Herero a disservice by universalizing their suffering ('the universal terrorizing of the Other'), my perspective is that it illustrates the uncomfortable truth that we do understand history in our own terms, by making it 'about us', and that this is not necessarily a lazy or a narcissistic practice. As Rebecca Schneider's theories of re-enactment,[50] and Diana Taylor's concept of 'the repertoire' indicate, sometimes a repeated movement or gesture can be very powerful in citing the non-verbal history that eludes or is excluded from the archive.[51] In one of his final actions, Actor 4 puts the noose 'in or on the box of letters, the archive' on which the actors' show is meant to be based, and 'closes the box' before looking out into the audience. As with the controversial ending to Drury's *Fairview* (2019), *We Are Proud to Present* lodges these uncomfortable, unresolved feelings about Black history and agency with the audience rather than offering platitudinous lessons or warnings 'from history'. Everyone in the theatre, and everything about the theatre, is implicated.

Virginia Woolf's *Orlando* and the Contemporary History Play

In many respects, contemporary history plays that eschew the realist mode owe much to Virginia Woolf's 1928 mock-biography *Orlando*, conceived as a tribute to her lover Vita Sackville-West and to Knole

---

[49] Ibid., 99.
[50] Rebecca Schneider, *Performing Remains: Art and War in Times of Theatrical Reenactment* (Abingdon: Routledge), 9–40.
[51] Diana Taylor, *The Archive and the Repertoire: Performing Cultural Memory in the Americas* (London: Duke University Press, 2003), 16–17.

House, home to Vita's family since the Elizabethan era. In this section, I want to draw particular attention to how this form of mock-history finds echoes in contemporary history plays, before focusing on Horn's *Wild Swimming* as a prime example of this process of 'Orlandification'.

The first key feature that Woolf's *Orlando* and contemporary history plays share is their treatment of time. Like Amy and May in *Oil*, like Oscar and Nell in *Wild Swimming*, like August Wilson's Aunt Ester in *The Gem of the Ocean* (2003), and like Chris Bush's Johanna Faustus, Orlando lives well beyond a natural lifespan, and like some of the roles and characters in Caryl Churchill's *Cloud Nine*, she transforms from man to woman in the process. Like the multi-era history play, Orlando notes and represents the difference between time on the clock and time of the mind, between subjective and objective notions of the passing of time: 'Some weeks added a century to his age, others no more than three seconds at most.'[52] With a distortion of time comes a distortion of space, as when Orlando is able to see 'on a clear day … perhaps forty' English counties from the top of the oak tree in Knole's grounds.[53] This becomes even more pronounced at the end of *Orlando*, where the landscape at Knole 'shook itself, heaped itself, let all this encumbrance of houses, castles and woods slide off its tent-shaped sides. The bare mountains of Turkey were before her.'[54] Here we might think of the miniature houses arranged on rolling green countryside that formed the stage design for Rory Mullarkey's *Saint George and the Dragon* (2017). By the time Orlando reaches the twentieth century, 'Nothing is any longer one thing'; objects remind her of people and Oxford Street omnibuses could be ice blocks on the Elizabethan Thames.[55] The palimpsestuous city of London through time is a trope that recurs in *Saint George and the Dragon* (2017), in Chris Bush's *Faustus: That Damned Woman* (2020) and in Moira Buffini's *Loveplay* (2001).

---

[52] Virginia Woolf, *Orlando* (London: Penguin, 1993), 68.
[53] Ibid., 14.
[54] Ibid., 226.
[55] Ibid., 210.

The second connection I want to highlight is that both *Orlando* and the contemporary history play communicate the strangeness of the past. In *Orlando*, rather than suggesting that the people in the past were just like us, the voice of the biographer is at pains to demarcate the fantastical *difference* of previous eras. She claims that each century had its own ecosystem: 'Everything was different. The weather itself, the heat and cold of summer and winter, was, we may believe, of another temper altogether.'[56] Where the eighteenth century was bright and clear, the nineteenth century existed under a 'bruised and sullen canopy' and was suffused with damp.[57] The anecdotes of 'a young countrywoman' turning to powder and 'unfortunate wayfarers' being transformed 'literally to stone' in the Great Frost conveys the impression of a fairytale.[58] Indeed, anticipating Hayden White, Orlando's biographer adopts different forms with each century: fairy tale, mock epic[59] and satire.[60] Like Johanna Faustus, and Oscar and Nell, Orlando encounters the great literary figures of his/her day, including Shakespeare, Addison, Dryden, Pope and Swift; like *Wild Swimming*, which will be analysed later in this chapter, Woolf's book plays with anachronism, bringing together writers who didn't quite live contemporaneously, as a footnote slyly indicates.[61] Its narrative voice is supremely confident but historically 'unreliable'.

Thirdly, both *Orlando* and the contemporary history play adopt an interventionist stance as shapers of time. In a theatrical manner, Orlando's biographer announces: 'With the twelfth stroke of midnight, the darkness was complete. A turbulent welter of cloud covered the city. All was darkness; all was doubt; all was confusion. The Eighteenth century was over; the Nineteenth century had begun.'[62]

---

[56] Ibid., 19.
[57] Ibid., 157.
[58] Ibid., 24.
[59] Ibid., 96–7.
[60] For example, when the biographer discusses nineteenth-century gender roles (Woolf, *Orlando*, 131–3) or Victorian clutter (Woolf, *Orlando*, 160).
[61] Woolf, *Orlando*, 119.
[62] Ibid., 157.

Such self-conscious historicism, giving the change in calendar date the dramatic momentousness of instant epochal change, with all the suddenness of an act-drop curtain, recalls the injunction 'Die, old century, die' from the stage adaptation of Angela Carter's *Nights at the Circus* (2006), or Mary's announcement at the end of D. C. Moore's *Common* that 'There is a City to Run. Century to Forge' – in both cases, referring to the nineteenth century.[63] In these texts and productions, period is announced and presented rhetorically, and at best with a playful self-awareness of the arbitrariness of periodization and the absurdities of historical hindsight.

My fourth and final connection is that Woolf was invested as a writer in family histories and histories of women, bringing 'the obscure' figures of the past into view,[64] and numerous contemporary history plays attempt similar correctives to the 'Lives of Great Men' model, from Jessica Swale's *Blue Stockings* (2013) and *Nell Gwynne* (2015) to Morgan Lloyd Malcolm's *Emilia* (2018) and Breach Theatre's *It's True, It's True, It's True* (2018), to the imagined women at the centre of Lucy Kirkwood's *The Welkin* (2020). Woolf's method can even be read as a defence of theatre as historiography, since she observed some years later that 'it would be far easier to write history [but] that method of telling the truth seems to me so elementary, and so clumsy, that I prefer, where truth is important, to write fiction'.[65] Fiction thus becomes an alternative, more sophisticated means of telling the truth, not an escapist, trivialization of truth.

However, we might consider whether it is really the case that Orlando is always 'on the margins of history' and only 'glimpses' the influential and celebrated.[66] Orlando's wealth, aristocratic birth and social connections enable him/her to live without having to work to earn a living for several centuries, to mix with royalty and to nurture a single long poem all this time, honed by contact with the 'spirit of the

---

[63] D. C. Moore, *Common* (London: Methuen Drama, 2017), 118.
[64] Woolf, *Orlando*, xxii.
[65] Ibid., xxiii–xxiv.
[66] Ibid., xxvi.

age' but also by conversations with London's pre-eminent men of letters. Most strands of historical playwriting struggle with this tension, too: presenting underdog or subaltern narratives that nevertheless feature exceptional people. Perhaps the difference is that Emilia Lanier, Artemisia Gentileschi, Nell Gywnne or undergraduates at Cambridge did not have the head start of being a man for 200 years first.

Wild Swimming

In *Wild Swimming*, we can see the influence of *Orlando* particularly strongly, in terms of both content and form. Oscar and Nell are both described in the text as 'an ageless, time-travelling water sprite'.[67] The action takes place between the Elizabethan era and the present day, where the characters meet repeatedly on 'A deserted beach in Dorset';[68] the sea is a key symbol in Woolf's fiction as well as the setting for the play. Like *Orlando's* lovers and suitors, Oscar and Nell also transcend normal human lifespans. Oscar does not turn into a woman in the play; in the FullRogue production of 2019, however, he was played by a woman (Annabel Baldwin), since, according to director Julia Head, 'when a man played Oscar, Marek's voice became too loud, too important'.[69] Like Orlando, Oscar has ambitions to be a 'Great Poet' and namedrops Philp Sidney, Lord Byron and Percy Shelley,[70] while Nell reads *Jane Eyre* (the meeting between Orlando and Marmaduke is an echo of the meeting between Jane and Rochester in the novel).[71]

Unlike *Orlando*, which skips over wars and ends – with the benefit of our own historical hindsight – with Orlando and Marmaduke safely ineligible for service between the world wars, Oscar serves at Gallipoli during the First World War (whereas Orlando had served as Turkish Ambassador). This changes his perspective on poetry and the

---

[67] Marek Horn, *Wild Swimming* (London: Nick Hern, 2019), 4.
[68] Ibid., 6.
[69] Julia Head, 'Director's Note', in Horn, *Wild Swimming*, no pagination.
[70] Horn, *Wild Swimming*, 35, 15, 33, 35.
[71] Woolf, *Orlando*, 257, n.22.

value of art, a position that is roundly critiqued by Nell, who is now a published poet and who travels with a companion named Sasha (in Woolf, the name of the young Orlando's companion during the Great Frost).[72] The play's final sequence does away with dialogue for a time, instead describing the dialogue in stage directions in a way reminiscent of Drury's *Fairview* and *We Are Proud to Present*. Like *Orlando*, *Wild Swimming* plays with form, subverting the idea that a play text is a reliable set of instructions for communicating the playwright's settled intentions. Instead, the stage directions come with their own directions, which decode the 'must', "might", could' and 'should' of the section that follows.[73] *Orlando* ends with a fantastical, sweeping convergence of Knole, the oak tree, Orlando's poem, Marmaduke and Orlando herself (along with a goose). Conversely, *Wild Swimming* does not end with a sense of closure and completion, but with Oscar, in particular, feeling displaced by the changing mores of recent decades: 'I always say something wrong because the goalposts of what is and isn't appropriate keep moving.'[74] Nell becomes the more Orlando-esque figure, in tune with the spirit of the age and ready to appear on *Question Time*, but she warns Oscar not to panic and try to push her down like a person who is drowning.[75]

Like *Orlando*, too, *Wild Swimming* revels in playful anachronisms, with combinations such as 'period-specific swimwear and modern reading glasses'.[76] Indeed, to disable a reader's anachronism-detector, the play text refuses to specify single dates: 'It is 1810 ... or 1811/It is also 1843 *and* 1847.'[77] The characters, or the actors playing them, also communicate their historical inauthenticity by admitting, for instance, 'I don't know what crinoline is.'[78] In some ways it plays the 'what happens next?' game with Woolf's mock-biography, imagining a couple

---

[72] Horn, *Wild Swimming*, 48–9.
[73] Ibid., 54.
[74] Ibid., 56.
[75] Ibid., 58.
[76] Ibid., 29.
[77] Ibid., 28.
[78] Ibid., 30.

who are even more 'ageless' negotiating the gender and sexual politics of the twenty-first century and its foreclosure of the future. Rather than the triumphant reception of Orlando's poem 'The Oak Tree', *Wild Swimming*'s collapsing of time in an English landscape tells us: '*The rules are broken. The play is ending. The world is dying*'; yet like Woolf's wild satire, it also nods to its own constructedness as an ending: 'the playwright has cleverly problematised the resolution of his play'.[79]

Language and the History Play

The final aspect of *Wild Swimming*'s gleeful historical inauthenticity that I want to analyse is language, and in doing so I aim to develop an understanding of what is at stake in the stylistic selection and crafting of language for the dramaturgy of the history play. In keeping with the patterns identified above, the approach to language in *Wild Swimming* is one in which the historicity and credibility of diction is overtly disregarded. Not only is contemporary lexis like 'PTSD' used,[80] but Oscar and Nell bicker using modern cadences, for instance when Nell mocks Oscar's fanboyish, undergraduate pretentiousness with her line, "'I've just been … like … reading a lot of Philip Sidney actually? // I just think he's like … sort of amazing?'", with the question-mark punctuation suggesting the 'upspeak' that is now associated with younger generations.[81] The characters also express themselves in terms of present-day feminist politics: 'Because you know "nice guys", Oscar? // You know like … "nice guy" syndrome?'[82] Naturally, as each is an ageless, time-travelling water

[79] Ibid., 59.
[80] Ibid., 11.
[81] Ibid., 17.
[82] Ibid., 20.

sprite, Oscar and Nell cannot be charged with historical inaccuracy; yet undoubtedly part of the comic enjoyment of the play comes from the breaking of the conventional sign-system of the history play. The Prologue begins with '*Historically appropriate music*' and Oscar and Nell wearing '*the clothes of the Renaissance*'.[83] The first few lines imply a mock-Shakespearean idiom:

— We begin our poor play in the late sixteenth century
— Or perhaps 'tis the early *seventeenth* century
— Time is elastic in the theatre
— And of all such possibilities
— Our little 'O' encompasseth them all.[84]

— before phrases like 'into the mix' and then '"*Gap*" "*Yah*"' [gap year] and '"*Rich*" "*Bitch*"' supplant them.[85] By the end of the Prologue, the style can no longer hold as the two sprites 'laugh heartily' at their modern phrasing as applied to Elizabethan England.[86]

As this chapter has already amply demonstrated, a high proportion of historical drama in English theatres situates itself in relation to the Elizabethan and Jacobean periods; it might even be said that in the theatre, the 'Jacobethan' stands in for the idea of 'history' in general, thanks to its association with Shakespeare.[87] Hence, characters in contemporary dramas only have to adjust their verb endings ('encompasseth') and introduce archaic contractions (''tis') and a jokey idea of pastness (and perhaps also of cultural prestige, and of 'great acting') is swiftly conveyed.[88]

---

[83] Ibid., 6.
[84] Ibid., 6.
[85] Ibid., 6–7.
[86] Ibid., 7.
[87] See Ella Hawkins, *Shakespeare in Elizabethan Costume: 'Period Dress' in Twenty-First-Century Performance* (London: Arden, 2022) for an exploration of the iconography of Shakespeare and how it is used as visual shorthand in twenty-first-century culture.
[88] McLuskie and Rumbold discuss the value ascribed to Shakespeare in the traditional model of cultural authority, whereby his plays were valuable *because* their language required close study and academic interpretation. Yet, paradoxically, the decentring

If we extend our purview beyond *Wild Swimming*'s pastiche of Early Modern English, we can discern that most contemporary history plays tend to avoid archaic, 'fustian' or even poetic language, but instead seek the 'immediacy and accessibility' of having historical characters speak just like us.[89] As Mark Berninger explains, archaic speech is associated with the genre model of the 'traditional history play',[90] and so modern-sounding dialogue becomes crucial for the contemporary history play in asserting the 'new writing' credentials of the work. It acts as the guarantor of a 'fresh, modern take' on the historical material, and yet it implies a certain irreverence, since using modern language is in itself a form of anachronism. Through its twenty-first century dialogue, the contemporary history play cannot, at any given moment in performance, be mistaken for, say, a historical melodrama in the style of Henry Irving, or a play by Shakespeare and/or his contemporaries, or a literary biodrama of the mid-twentieth-century variety (for instance, Rudolf Besier's *The Barretts of Wimpole Street* (1930)).

The use of modern language in history plays has a history in itself. As Harben explains,

of language in contemporary revivals of Shakespeare only holds – is only considered 'permissible' – if that language is perceived to be 'intact'. Even though it is widely acknowledged that directors and dramaturgs will edit Shakespeare's plays for performance, if that editorial work is at any point noticeable, if Shakespeare's words are seen to have been 'tampered with', then the revival becomes open to charges of 'dumbing down' and of insufficiently respecting the playwright's 'timeless genius'. Hence, the 'immediacy and engagement' model that McLuskie and Rumbold discuss has the double effect of implying that Shakespeare can be enjoyed *despite* the 'difficulty' of the language, yet also treating that language as sacred and something that must be seen to be left completely undisturbed by the engagement with the contemporary that applies to acting, scenography, sound design, costume and so on.

[89] Stephen Jeffreys, in his playwriting manual, urges that 'even if you are writing a play set in biblical times, the characters will still feel themselves to be modern … as far as they are concerned, they are at the forefront of history and technology, and you have to write them accordingly' (Jeffreys, *Playwriting: Structure, Character, How and What to Write* (London: Nick Hern, 2019), 212). Though Jeffreys is not here suggesting that dialogue in history plays should be modern, this seems to be the preferred solution for contemporary writers of history plays – a feature that Berninger would class as 'posthistorical' (Berninger, 'Variations', 40).

[90] Berninger, 'Variations', 39.

A pronounced feature of the twentieth-century English history play is the overt treatment of the past in terms of the present. This approach can be seen to stem from Shaw. He audaciously challenged the conventions of nineteenth-century historical drama which attempted to create a semblance of historical reality in the form of the 'right' historical atmosphere through elaborate costumes and sets, artificial speech and sentiments.[91]

This outlook has been highly influential; as D. Keith Peacock argues, by the 1960s 'all history plays were now to become contemporary history. It was to be employed primarily as a means of discussing the present.'[92] However, I am sceptical of how far the use of modern language necessarily goes hand-in-hand with radical or oppositional treatments of history. As Palmer and Peacock agree, Shaw 'successfully bent history to serve his social philosophy', which 'emphasised the importance ... of exceptional individuals such as St Joan or Caesar, and exhibited little concern for the masses'.[93]

For a later generation of historical playwrights, the challenge of language was often to find a specific idiom that would somehow evoke the distinctiveness of the period. For Stephen Jeffreys, 'I felt that writing plays set in the past could liberate language from the straitjacket of TV-soap-opera-style realism ... [audiences would accept] a more extravagant style of language.'[94] Jeffreys' advice to playwrights is that 'the most important thing is to capture the appropriate flavour' and he indicates a preference for immersing himself in 'literature and poetry as a way into the creative style of the times'.[95] He adds that 'I personally dislike inaccuracy and anachronism' and cites Timberlake Wertenbaker as another playwright who studied period language in order to get the late eighteenth-century working-class idiom of *Our Country's*

[91] Harben, *English History Plays*, 6.
[92] Peacock, *Radical Stages*, 30.
[93] Palmer, *The Contemporary British History Play*, 3; Peacock, *Radical Stages*, 23.
[94] Jeffreys, *Playwriting*, 206.
[95] Ibid., 209.

Good 'right'.[96] This method appears to take a middle course, avoiding contemporary usages that might be perceived as jarring, whilst feeding in idioms that will serve as markers of immersive research in the writing of the period.

The Whip

A recent play like *The Whip* is an example of work that has strong affinities with the Jeffreys approach to historical language. Juliet Gilkes Romero's drama, staged at the RSC's Swan Theatre in 2020, shows how the abolition of the slave trade within the Empire was only achieved in the British parliament by making a deal to compensate slave owners with millions of pounds of public money. The UK government only finished paying off this debt in 2015, and many wealthy families in England today owe their fortunes to the slave trade, slave owning, and its compensation scheme upon abolition. The play therefore works as a historical exposé where the uncomfortable truth of the material requires that the world of the play be consistent and plausible. Several scenes are based on the parliamentary debates recorded in Hansard, and the conversations that take place outside the Commons remain in a semi-formal early nineteenth-century style, whether uttered by servants or aristocrats. An example is this exchange between Alexander Boyd MP and Horatia Poskett, his housekeeper:

> BOYD: (Gesticulating.) Did no one think to tell me that the nation's coffers were about to be ransacked!
> HORATIA: I have not stood here idle, Sir. It's why I brought [the papers] in.
> BOYD: In Jesus' name! Where are my boots?[97]

It seems clear that to undermine the 'historical realism' of the dramaturgy, through overt anachronisms of language or by other

---

[96] Ibid., 209.
[97] Juliet Gilkes Romero, *The Whip* (London: Oberon, 2020), 94.

theatrical means, would run the risk of undermining the credibility of the historical claims being made in *The Whip*, claims which have been little discussed in our wider politics and culture. Content and form work together; but insofar as the archaic diction of parliamentary speeches must carry across to private spaces, Romero's play aims for a documentary precision that limits the scope for linguistic invention. As future chapters will explore in more detail, this model of apparent transparency, which is overtly based on the historical record and which occludes the element of creative licence, is increasingly rare in the contemporary history play.

In terms of the dramaturgy of these plays, deliberately anachronistic language is a feature that makes it more 'writerly' in the Barthesian sense, as the writer draws attention to the constructedness of their text, making it more open to interpretation. The more 'historically realistic' the dialogue seeks to be, the more the play rhetorically gestures towards being a neutral relaying of documentary truth rather than a 'made' artefact, an assemblage. Linguistic verisimilitude performs the self-absenting of the playwright, partially obscuring their presence in the work.[98] By contrast, the more the dialogue tilts towards anachronistic usages, the more it foregrounds the writer's presence in the work; it becomes a writerly text, and thus more strongly aligned with 'new writing' rather than 'historical drama'. As we have seen in connection with *Orlando*, this writerly presence is also generated and sustained by discursive and self-aware stage directions, such as those found in *Oil*, *Wild Swimming*, *Swive [Elizabeth]* and *Marys Seacole*. Through unconventional uses and chronologies of history, through stage directions acquiring a discursive voice and through language that doesn't 'fit' with the purported setting, the play text foregrounds the *process* of historical playmaking.

---

[98] See Dan Rebellato, 'Exit the Author', in *Contemporary British Theatre: Breaking New Ground*, ed. Vicky Angelaki (Basingstoke: Palgrave Macmillan, 2013), 11.

The dominant style of television and film historical drama is to update the dialogue's grammar, vocabulary, syntax and idiom in such a way that most viewers, it is hoped, will not notice. Relatively rare is the screen period drama that either seeks to conjure a sense of historical difference through a stylized form of speech (like the BBC/Amazon drama *Ripper Street* (2012–16)) or that revels so overtly in the modernity of its dialogue, like Netflix's 2022 adaptation of *Persuasion* (directed, perhaps significantly, by Carrie Cracknell, who worked with Ella Hickson on *Oil*). A similar argument might be made for adaptations, too – that language is now, as much as possible, modernized in an attempt to collapse the distance between stage world and audience. Yet while there is considerable variation in the dramaturgies of language in the contemporary history play, many do deliberately seek to make language a marker of *in*authenticity, an ironic manicule pointing towards the production's metatheatrical attempt to stage history – and to inevitably fail in that attempt.

Common

My final example of language and its contribution to dramaturgy is D. C. Moore's *Common*, produced on the Olivier stage at the National Theatre, London, in 2017. The playwright has clearly gone to some lengths to devise a distinctive set of speech patterns for the world of the play. On the printed page, what is noticeable is, firstly, the running together of words, for example: 'I was the rebornspiritghost of his longdeaddaughter.'[99] Sometimes such compound words are nouns that suggest a single idea or object, after the German model. At other times, they produce the effect of a surreal composite image, as when London is referred to as 'that vastchimneycoffin where all evil is born & most goodness dies'.[100] It is also notable that, as in the previous quotation, the text makes liberal use of ampersands, and initial capitalization: '(*Aside.*)

---

[99] Moore, *Common*, 8.
[100] Ibid., 8.

I said before, use That They Most Desire. It is often That They Most Fear too.'[101] In this way, the published play script seems to mimic early nineteenth-century typographical conventions in a manner that is (except in a surtitled performance) not legible in the moment of performance. On the other hand, these typographical idiosyncrasies might be taken as an invitation to give these compound words, metaphors and capitalized words specific types of emphasis, or perhaps to invite a declamatory style of delivery in the style of a Romantic-era tragedian.[102]

Also notable is the fact that stage directions adopt the same language as the dialogue: '**Villagers** *gather from shadow, lustrous lit, maskdressed as animaltypes or devilfolk or somepartboth, on edge of their vast Common*.'[103] In contrast to the somewhat tonally flat stage directions of most history plays, or the knowing quality of Shavian stage directions that comment on the action from a modern point of view, the stage directions on *Common* are of a piece with the dialogue. This shared style implies that the text is somehow a 'found item', a document uncovered from the past, rather than a new play. Its eccentric visual presentation suggests that this is a story about the nineteenth century that we are unused to hearing, and indeed this can certainly be said of the English Clearances, which are not part of traditional history teaching in schools nor of historical drama. On the other hand, the play text insists in its notes – and this is a point backed up by the protagonist Mary – that 'we are not here for reasons of dry historical accuracy', a line which received laughter and applause on the night I attended.[104] Paradoxically, then, the play presents itself as both immersed in the Napoleonic era's language and style, and yet potentially unreliable and inauthentic as history, a historical fantasia, even. In the Coda, I

---

[101] Ibid., 31.

[102] When I attended the National Theatre production in 2017, I found the language difficult to follow since some of the words got lost in the Olivier's vast auditorium, and unfamiliar rhythms of speech and syntax meant it was hard to mentally 'fill in' any missed words.

[103] Moore, *Common*, 5.

[104] Ibid., 60.

consider the possible impulses that lie behind alternate or fantastic treatments, where other histories are told 'straight'.

Common serves to illustrate the challenges of going against the conventions of modern speech in history plays. It seems that in our consumption of contemporary drama, we have collectively agreed that 'difficult' language outside of Shakespeare needs to be defused and even mocked. *Common's* generally negative critical reaction was based on a number of factors, but the play's language was a recurring objection.[105] However, it is too limiting to conclude from this that using contemporary language instead is simply a pragmatic choice on the part of twenty-first-century playwrights, a weary or unimaginative compromise. Rather, language isn't *doing* the same things in Shakespeare's or Shaw's histories as it is in contemporary history plays like those of Drury, or Horn, or Lynn, or Hickson, or Parks. Individual speeches from these writers can rarely be taken out of context and admired as poetry, as is routinely done with Shakespeare's verse, or

---

[105] For example, Andrzej Lukowski reported that 'my best guess is it exists because Moore found the language interesting and went from there. Which is fair enough, but his odd stew of ornate sentences and outlandish compound words peppered with modern swears often serves to distance us from a convoluted plot that often seems to be aggressively challenging us to give a shit' (Andrzej Lukowski, review of *Common* by D. C. Moore, directed by Jeremy Herrin, National Theatre, London, *Time Out London*, 7 June 2017, reproduced in *Theatre Record* 37, no. 11–12 (2017): 609). Similarly, Susannah Clapp complained that 'from my close-to-the-stage position I could not hear half these words: so many lines were swallowed. Those I caught were so contorted that getting to the nub was like parsing Latin. Sentences turned back to front, pronouns missing: long straggles of words flailing around in search of significance' (Susannah Clapp, review of *Common* by D. C. Moore, directed by Jeremy Herrin, National Theatre, London, *Observer*, 11 June 2017. Available online: https://www.theguardian.com/stage/2017/jun/11/common-olivier-anne-marie-duff-theatre-national-review (accessed 3 February 2023)). Natasha Tripney notes that the play's language is 'full of clunky compound adjectives' and that Moore 'pulls the *Deadwood* trick of swapping out blasphemy for profanity' (Natasha Tripney, review of *Common* by D. C. Moore, directed by Jeremy Herrin, National Theatre, London, *The Stage*, 7 June 2017. Available online: https://www.thestage.co.uk/reviews/common-review-at-national-theatre-london–ambitious-but-impenetrable (accessed 3 February 2023)). Only Alex Sierz seemed to find in Moore's text 'a poetic language that reads beautifully', which 'pulses with the rhythms of the past' (Aleks Sierz, review of *Common* by D. C. Moore, directed by Jeremy Herrin, National Theatre, London, *Tribune*, 16 June 2017, reproduced in *Theatre Record* 37, no. 11–12 (2017): 611).

celebrated for their contrarian wit and pith, as monologues by Shaw were throughout the twentieth century.[106] Since it downplays the heroic and the rhetorical modes, the language of the contemporary history play might seem flat by comparison – although its playfulness in slipping in and out of 'official' historical registers can be a pleasure to behold in the hands of a writer like Drury. I maintain that this is not an error or a missed opportunity. Language is only one tool for theatrical expression, only one element of its dramaturgy. As Dawn Walton observes in a conversation with Maddy Costa, 'text is broader than just words'; as Costa paraphrases Walton's meaning: 'the text of a play is also its movement, its lighting, its design, the dramaturgy of performance and production'.[107] The play says what is says and does what it does when all of those elements work together. The same can be said of narrative: if a history play can be communicated adequately only by relaying the narrative, then it is not a drama that has been fully realized for theatre. It has *told a story* about the past rather than created the conditions for an imaginative encounter with it. It does not need to be a play.

All History Plays are Posthistorical

A consideration of the work that language does in supporting and generating the impression of historical realism leads me to a further conclusion, however. If historical realism is a carefully crafted illusion, based on meeting an audience halfway in their expectations of a history play, then all history plays are, to a greater or lesser extent, 'posthistorical'.

---

[106] Maggie Inchley implies an inheritance from Shaw in the extended discussion and complex ideas presented in plays by David Hare and David Edgar, which is defended in these playwrights' own essays on drama (Maggie Inchley, *Voice and New Writing, 1997-2007: Articulating the Demos* (Basingstoke: Palgrave Macmillan, 2015), 41). This reinforces the idea that, until recently, 'new writing' had been primarily conceived as language-driven rather than as writing for the full resources of the stage, a point emphasized by Maddy Costa ('The Well-Made Play'.).

[107] Costa, 'The Well-Made Play'.

As mentioned in the Introduction, Mark Berninger's classification of history plays in the 1990s places them on a spectrum based on their relationship to the historical record. At one end we have the documentary history play, then the realistic history play. The revisionist history play, in the middle of the spectrum, tends to follow the conventions of the realistic history play but challenges and revises elements of its content.[108] Finally, the metahistorical play and then the posthistorical play are at the increasingly self-reflexive, metatheatrical and experimental end of the spectrum. Berninger's is the most flexible and convincing account of the contemporary history play I have yet encountered, and it has had a substantial impact on the development of this book. And certainly, Berninger's characterization of the different categories as a spectrum implies a difference in degree rather than kind. However, looking back on the definition of a posthistorical play in the light of the examples discussed here – and the collective agreement that productions and their audiences make to not 'notice' modern language when it suits us – I wondered how many of the other defining features of the posthistorical play are actually features of the realistic history play, the artifice of which is obscured by familiarity.

So, for example, Berninger's definition calls the posthistorical play 'the most problematic type of history play … It contains a high degree of fictionalized history … the posthistorical play thrives on unrecorded "gaps of history"'.[109] As this chapter has shown, through its application of Hayden White's theories, history itself is already a deployment of the techniques of literature in order to assemble documentary fragments into a narrative. As previous work has suggested, playwrights' accounts of writing history plays consistently identify historical 'gaps' as being their creative way into a project.[110] If history plays only included events

---

[108] Berninger, 'Variations', 40.
[109] Ibid., 40.
[110] See Benzie and Poore, 'History Plays': 'the playwright's prefatory notes, in a programme or published text for a history play, frequently assert the writer's use of the historical record and then identify the point at which they began to invent and imagine'. In the article, we selected accounts from June Wilkinson, Lucy Kirkwood and Helen Edmundson, but there were many other examples from 'Author's Notes' and prefaces to published plays.

that could be verified by documentary and archival sources, they would be heavily skewed towards accounts of the rich and powerful. The posthistorical play also 'uses various forms of non-mimetic drama such as symbolism, non-mimetic language … a nonrealistic setting, and undefined or unfixed identities of the characters'.[111] As this chapter has sought to establish, 'mimetic' language is in the ear of the listener, and in a similar way, the realism of theatrical settings is perceived differently by each generation. The free-floating furniture, in the suggestion of a room without doors or walls, that we might find in a revival of Ibsen or Shaw at in-the-round venues like the Manchester Royal Exchange or the Orange Tree in Richmond upon Thames, for example, would strike a nineteenth-century audience member as quite bizarre.[112] As for unfixing the identities of historical characters, that most avowedly is the case in contemporary history plays, as I have charted through my discussion of 'Orlandification'; Chapter 2 will investigate that 'unfixing' in more detail. My last example is Berninger's observation that in the posthistorical play, 'The logic of time is secondary to and shaped by the dramatic logic.'[113] This absolutely and clearly applies to the examples of *We Are Proud to Present* and *Wild Swimming*, but it is also true of *The Whip*, which manipulates time using the accepted realist conventions of flashbacks, beginning scenes *in medias res*, and telescoping and combining of events. The logic of realism is only one among many – the culturally dominant one. As Colbert proposed, it *is* possible, instead, to render 'history subject to the logic of poetics'.[114]

---

[111] Berninger, 'Variations', 40.
[112] See Roman Jakobson for a further discussion of how realism needs to constantly redefine how it is being more 'realistic' than conventional representation. (Roman Jakobson, 'On Realism in Art', in *Readings in Russian Poetics: Formalist and Structuralist Views*, ed. Ladislav Matejka and Krystyna Pomorska (Chicago: Dalkey Archive, 2002), 38–46.)
[113] Berninger, 'Variations', 40.
[114] Colbert, 'Black Leadership at the Crossroads', 279.

Conclusion

The idea of history and dramaturgy being locked in some epic battle over control of the contemporary history play – which is perhaps implied by this chapter's title – evidently does not bear much scrutiny. Both 'history' and 'dramaturgy' are ways of talking about disparate things that are woven together to form a moving, breathing whole.[115] Certainly, both are interdependent in contemporary history plays, but in combination, they are challenges to the 'common-sense' assumptions that history consists of verifiable facts, and that drama's job is to give a credible, realistic account of how these things happened, like a time machine with a picture-window. Starting with the decidedly non-realist model of the Shakespearean history play, this chapter has sought to defamiliarize the practice of putting on plays about the past, both by enumerating some of its challenges – such as audience expectations, exposition and narrative – and by foregrounding plays that represent its processes. In establishing the connections between *Wild Swimming* and Woolf's *Orlando*, I have proposed that we can usefully think of the contemporary history play as an 'Orlandification' of theatre. I have drawn attention to the selective nature of claims to verisimilitude in the theatre, using language as a prime example. This has pointed to the insight that language behaves differently in contemporary history plays because of the other dramaturgical elements with which it now combines. Finally, I have used the definition of a posthistorical play to defamiliarize its purported opposite, showing historical realism to be simply a 'posthistorical' dramaturgy that happens to be codified and orientated towards the status quo.

---

[115] To paraphrase Magda Romanska, 'dramaturgy' derives from the Greek compound word 'dramatourgos' which meant a play maker, or play composer (that is, a playwright, a composer of drama); 'drama' meant 'action', and the 'ergo' meant 'working together', so 'dramatourgos' meant someone who worked together actions in a meaningful way. (Magda Romanska, 'Introduction', *The Routledge Companion to Dramaturgy*, ed. Magda Romanska (Abingdon: Routledge, 2014), 1.)

2

The Biographical History Play

Introduction

Biographical narratives continue to dominate historical drama, whether on stage or screen. Surveying historical fictions in the first decade of the twenty-first century, Jerome de Groot sees British historical film as obsessed with biography, and regards such films as Shekhar Kapur's *Elizabeth: The Golden Age* (2007) and Stephen Frears's *The Queen* (2006) as 'reading political, cultural and historical events through the lens of the royal personage'.[1] Such films are 'companion pieces of sorts' to television's own focus on dramatizing royal biographies, especially those of the Tudors and the Stuarts.[2] For Ursula Canton, writing in 2011, the increased number of recent plays that use characters based on historical figures, 'seems to be part of a wider phenomenon, the omnipresence or seemingly un- or little mediated representation of reality in nearly all media', including the rise of reality television and YouTube.[3] In common with film and television, as de Groot notes, theatre 'is often interested in understanding through personality', be that the outspokenness of Joan of Arc or the quietism of Albert Speer.[4] Moreover, since the mid-2010s, the global success of Lin-Manuel Miranda's stage musical *Hamilton* has reinscribed and recentred the biographical drama as a study of the character of 'Great Men'. In this reading, as Waldstreicher and Pasley

---

[1] De Groot, *Consuming History*, 214.
[2] Ibid., 213–4.
[3] Ursula Canton, *Biographical Theatre: Re-Presenting Real People?* (Basingstoke: Palgrave, 2011), 2.
[4] De Groot, *Consuming History*, 230.

argue, 'Personality shapes destiny and makes history'.[5] The cultural phenomenon of *Hamilton* has led to the musical being co-opted for educational purposes with the #EduHam Project offering 'deeply discounted tickets to high school juniors in New York and Chicago' and 'a ready-made curriculum for teaching *Hamilton*'.[6] Biographical stage drama, then, is even more deeply embroiled than other kinds of history play in education and the pervasive idea that theatre is 'good for you'; D. Keith Peacock identified this pattern when surveying the biographical dramas of the mid-twentieth century (in this case, Terence Rattigan's *A Bequest to the Nation* (1970)):

> Here was a play written in what might be described as the 'history lesson' tradition of historical drama. This consisted of deftly but simply drawn characters, each of whom was employed to convey, with apparent realism, a number of facts and dates from the past. It was primarily contrived to ensure that an audience, while adding a little to its knowledge of history, would also experience an entertaining evening's theatre.[7]

Alan Bennett makes this Reithian urge to educate, inform and entertain explicit in his introduction to *The Madness of George III*: 'As I struggled to mince these chunks of information into credible morsels of dialogue … I often felt it would have been simpler to call the audience in a quarter of an hour early and give them a short curtain lecture on the nature of eighteenth-century politics before getting on with the play proper.'[8] The tension between the transmission of information and

[5]   David Waldstreicher and Jeffrey L. Pasley, 'Hamilton as Founders Chic: A Neo-Federalist, Antislavery, Usable Past?' in *Historians on Hamilton: How A Blockbuster Musical is Restaging America's Past*, ed. Renee C. Romano and Claire Bond Potter (New Brunswick, NJ: Rutgers University Press, 2018), 141–2.
[6]   Romano and Potter, 'Introduction', in *Historians on Hamilton*, 9. See also Jim Cullen, 'Course Syllabus', in *Historians on Hamilton*, 351–60.
[7]   Peacock, *Radical Stages*, 25. We might compare this definition with the notable irritation of critics in response to Morgan Lloyd Malcolm's *Emilia* – discussed later in the chapter – that it was not a history (or literature) lesson (see Laura Kressly, '"There's Only So Much Work Our Imaginations Can Do": *Emilia* and London's Privileged Theatre Critics', in *Notelets of Filth: A Companion Reader to Morgan Lloyd Malcolm's Emilia*, ed. Laura Kressly, Aida Patient, and Kimberly A. Williams (Abingdon: Routledge, 2023),154–5).
[8]   Bennett quoted in Palmer, *Contemporary British History Play*, 46.

creative license – between dramatic action and historical precision – is an issue that I explored in the previous chapter, and it resurfaces in contemporary biodrama with a vengeance.

In terms of its dramaturgical profile, the biographical history play tends to reinforce the emphasis placed on the exceptional individual in culturally hegemonic narratives. It promotes a conventional view of historical events and causality because these are the backdrop to the biographical content; destabilizing them destabilizes the 'exceptional' qualities of the subject. Conventional characterization and conventional historical narrative are thus mutually reinforcing. Unlike the more 'liquid' plays discussed in later chapters of the book, most biographical history plays reinscribe the individual's human lifespan – rather than the life of a collective, a movement, a group or an idea – as the marker of achievement, inviting us to reach a 'verdict' on whether someone was on 'the right side of history'. The focus on the individual, on roots and origins, privileges a psychological reading of the subject – their drives, their contradictions – that tends to favour Naturalism over any disruption of theatrical form. There is often a vast amount of material to manage in the representation of a historical individual's life set against their times. Rather than distilling it, the usual practice is to lean heavily on exposition and narration, telling its audience things rather than inviting an encounter with an imagined past. It is often burdened with expectations to rehabilitate or 'do justice to' the subject, a pressure highlighted, in some cases, by the input of relatives, descendants and those who knew the subject.[9]

In this chapter, I want to propose that the positioning of biodrama as a history lesson does theatre no favours as a contemporary art form. Reaffirming the idea of the individual of special character as the determining force in history has both political and dramaturgical

---

[9]   See, for example, the musical *Mandela* (music and lyrics by Greg Dean Borowsky and Shaun Borowsky, book by Laiona Michelle), which ran at the Young Vic Theatre in 2022–23; *Get Up Stand Up: The Bob Marley Musical* by Lee Hall, which ran at the Lyric Theatre in 2021–23; and the Michael Jackson musical running since 2022 at the Neil Simon Theatre on Broadway, *MJ the Musical* by Lynn Nottage.

consequences. It is not sufficient, I suggest, to 'reform the system from within' by staging oppositional biographies of rebels and outlaws. Rather, the concept of any historical person being consistent and whole unto themselves without context or circumstance needs to be dismantled, because its repetition wears out the resources and potential of theatre on activities that television and film already do, on forms that they already handle and in which they are culturally dominant.

So many history plays are biographical dramas – and so many biographical dramas are historical – that I have had to be highly selective in organizing this chapter, discussing a larger number of plays more briefly instead of analysing four or five works at greater length as I do in the book's later chapters.[10] Palmer's helpful chapter on stage biodrama in *The Contemporary British History Play* identifies four main patterns: 'traditional shaker and mover plays, psychohistories that apply the methods of Freudian analysis to historical figures, domestic history that shows the interest of twentieth-century historical studies in the private life even of public figures, and alternative histories [focusing] on the victims rather than the agents of historical change' – what he later calls 'losers' biography'.[11] By contrast, I will propose five biographical categories, starting with recuperation and fragmentation, then duplication and competition, and finally iteration. These categories are not wholly discrete, and contemporary biographical history plays are often at their most inventive when these patterns overlap and interact. As such, these dramaturgical strategies can challenge the historically bounded, individual humanist subject upon which biodrama has traditionally modelled itself. This chapter will begin by sketching a history of biographical drama on English stages and will examine the problem of what I call 'monumentalism': the tendency to treat stage biography as a tribute or memorial that must be depicted

---

[10] The dominance of the biographical drama is illustrated by its prominence in critical studies. Of the 'four crucial texts', for example, that Michael Y. Bennett identifies in *Narrating the Past Through Theatre*, all are to some degree biographical (*Danton's Death, Life of Galileo, A Man for All Seasons, Salome*) with the mode of biography and historiography being dictated by the subject matter and treatment.

[11] Palmer, *Contemporary British History Play*, 23, 75.

in concrete, literal terms, rather than as a metaphor. The chapter then analyses in turn the different ways that 'Great Men' monumental biodrama has been challenged, whether by a focus on two figures rather than one, by a dramaturgy of competition or by feminist and queer recuperation of historical figures. I should note here that I use the term 'recuperation' throughout this chapter to refer to the imaginative recreation of biographies that have been lost, taken or previously rendered invisible through dominant historiographical paradigms. My case studies are Morgan Lloyd Malcolm's *Emilia* (2018), Caroline Bird's *Red Ellen* (2021), Charlie Josephine's *I, Joan* (2022), Moira Buffini's *Handbagged* (2013/22), and finally Jackie Sibblies Drury's *Marys Seacole* (2016/22), which I analyse to highlight the possibilities of the iterative biodrama that stages historical patterns and legacies, rather than life stories. With the exception of *Emilia*, all of these plays were staged in English theatres within twelve months of each other, between September 2021 and September 2022, meaning that this chapter can be read as a snapshot of the range of biodrama approaches on offer at any one time.

Biodrama in English Theatre: A Brief Biography

Biographical drama is so ubiquitous that it may be helpful to establish some historical context in order to draw out how this kind of history play is changing, and how, in most cases, it has *not* adapted to the changing status of the theatre in the last century. As Richard Palmer remarks, 'From the sixteenth century, the principal course of historical drama was biographical, with an underlying assumption that a few important individuals shaped major events'; furthermore, in 'episodic chronicle plays' of the Early Modern period, the central figure of a monarch, like Shakespeare's Henry VI or Marlowe's Edward II, 'often provided the only source of unity'.[12] Palmer notes, 'The ingredients of mainstream

[12] Ibid., 21.

historical drama emerged early on: important historical figures whose actions, both private and public, have political consequences and portray an overriding message to the watchers of the drama.'[13] Moreover, Herbert Lindenberger observes that private experience has become more prominent than public events in historical biodrama over the last two centuries,[14] a point picked up by Palmer,[15] as well as Peacock.[16] The focus on a single, complex individual whose actions cause momentous change in their time, but whose consequences may be unforeseeable to them, means that historical biodrama has often been rendered as tragedy,[17] in accordance with Hayden White's modes of emplotment, discussed in Chapter 1. This has led to biodramas sometimes being praised or damned for not conforming to tragic expectations. The underlying assumption seems to be that, in rare cases, a successful biodrama is able to transcend the mediocrity of the history play and achieve the status of tragedy.[18] However, as Maurya Wickstrom rightly cautions, 'It is easy, it seems, to use the theatre as a form that seems so readily to offer its tragic formula to simplify and reduce historical fieriness, temporal novelties, to extinguished ash … the theatre can offer other, much less formulaic and predictable means by which to explore what happens when history is initiated, not finished.'[19]

In the twentieth century, biodrama changed in content but, mostly, not in form. Harben notes the 'powerful nature of Shaw's impact on

---

[13] Ibid., 22.
[14] Lindenberger, *Historical Drama*, 122.
[15] Palmer, *Contemporary British History Play*, 22.
[16] Peacock, *Radical Stages*, 17.
[17] See Palmer: 'Biographical plays and tragedy have always crossed over, though critics have disagreed over whether one is public and the other private, and whether they are included in the category of history plays' (Palmer, *Contemporary British History Play*, 6).
[18] Palmer quotes Philip Hope-Wallace's review of Bolt's *A Man for All Seasons*: 'The piece, so well-imagined and neatly contrived, remains a decent, modern example of the historical costume play and never moves even momentarily into the greater field of tragedy' (Palmer, *Contemporary British History Play*, 28). As Waldstreicher and Pasley note with regard to *Hamilton*, the repeated foreshadowing of the protagonist's assassination helps to create the impression of 'a tragedy of Shakespearean proportions … This is Great Man history with a vengeance' (Waldstreicher and Pasley, 'Founders Chic', 144).
[19] Wickstrom, *Fiery Temporalities*, 61.

modern drama' as reflected in 'the fact that the penchant throughout the century is for a debunking of the heroic. The hero is often viewed as an ironic, equivocal compound of body and spirit, instinct and intellect, blindness and imagination'.[20] Nevertheless, in Shaw's history plays, 'the great man is the agent of civilisation's advance; he prefigures the superhumanity of the future. In holding to this view Shaw was very much a Victorian.'[21] Even though the dramaturgy of biodrama remained undisturbed in this formulation, it was still felt to be more modern and credible than the romantic historical dramas of the previous century. Peacock cites a review of Rubenstein and Bax's biodrama *Shakespeare* (1921) which opines: 'it raises the hope that the English drama may escape from the monotony of artificial plots into the rich variety of human life by becoming biographical'.[22] According to Palmer, it was not until the English premiere of Brecht's *Life of Galileo*, at the Mermaid Theatre in 1960, that this 'biographical bias' was challenged; Brecht 'invited us to see how social forces shaped that individual's actions'.[23] Palmer suggests that it was Robert Bolt's superficially 'Brechtian' but ultimately more conservative *A Man for All Seasons* that was more influential: it is 'in many respects the major impetus to postwar historical drama ... Bolt, not Brecht, is in the mainstream of English historical drama'.[24]

In addition to its formal conservatism, post-war English biodrama was also very male-dominated. As Peacock comments, the post-1956 generation of playwrights (itself a mostly male coterie) had little interest in women as protagonists, making the period even less progressive in this respect than the 1920s and 1930s.[25] As the historian Hallie Rubenhold argued in her 2020 Baillie Gifford Prize lecture, 'The Problem with

[20] Harben, *English History Plays*, 27.
[21] Ibid., 29.
[22] Peacock, *Radical Stages*, 20.
[23] Palmer, *Contemporary British History Play*, 25.
[24] Ibid., 25, 27.
[25] Peacock, *Radical Stages*, 153.

Great Men', this bias towards men as the shapers and defining figures of each epoch runs deep in our culture: 'The reason that Great Man Theory has persisted for all these years, is because he has faded into the background. History feels inactive and dead, and so we have left him standing, a rusting monolith, unmolested, unacknowledged, but continuing to cast a long shadow over how we view our history.'[26] Many of those writing on historical biodrama note this pattern, which has its roots in Thomas Carlyle's 1840 lecture series *On Heroes, Hero-Worship, and the Heroic in Human History.*[27] Carlyle insisted that 'In all epochs of the world's history we shall find the Great Man to have been the indispensable saviour of his epoch: – the lightning without which the fuel never would have burnt.'[28]

The Great Man Theory that influences whom we centre as historically significant is also, of course, very White. For Rubenhold, 'The world of Great Man Theory regarded the destitute as lazy, women as physically and intellectually weaker than men, and the dark-skinned as inferior to the light-skinned.'[29] It is only in the last two decades that people of colour have been the subjects of biodrama on main stages and at commercial venues, as in the cases of, for instance, *Lions and Tigers* by Tanika Gupta, about the anti-colonial revolutionary Dinesh Gupta, produced at Shakespeare's Globe in 2017, or *The Meaning of Zong* by Giles Terera, about the abolitionist Olaudah Equiano, and first staged at

---

[26] Hallie Rubenhold, *The Problem with Great Men* (Edinburgh: Edinburgh International Book Festival, 2020), 6.

[27] For a sense of how hero-worship continues to inform biodrama, we might compare Robert Bolt's thoughts on Thomas More with Lin-Manuel Miranda's on Alexander Hamilton. Bolt says: 'What's amazing about More is the perfection of his behaviour – both in detail and overall. A nearly faultless performance ... He was a perfect gentleman – a breathtaking performance as a human being' (quoted in Harben, *English History Plays*, 172). Similarly, Lyra D. Monteiro quoted Miranda as saying, 'When I encountered Alexander Hamilton I was immediately captivated. He's an inspirational figure to me. And an aspirational one. Elsewhere, it had been reported that "Hamilton reminded him of his father"' (Lyra D. Monteiro, 'Race-Conscious Casting and the Erasure of the Black Past in *Hamilton*', in *Historians on Hamilton*, 65). As Monteiro suggests, 'It is hardly surprising that someone who displays this kind of adoration of a founding father would find it difficult to truly incorporate slavery into the story of his life' (Monteiro, 'Race-Conscious Casting', 65).

[28] Quoted in Harben, *English History Plays*, 29.

[29] Rubenhold, 'Great Men', 5.

Bristol Old Vic in 2022. In the years prior to this, biodrama had become one way for actors of colour to find significant roles for themselves in a theatre industry that had rarely reflected more than an all-White version of the past. *Red Velvet*, Lolita Chakrabarti's highly successful biodrama about the African American nineteenth-century actor Ira Aldridge, premiered at the Tricycle in 2012, starring Adrian Lester. Paterson Joseph premiered his solo show *Sancho: An Act of Remembrance* – about composer, actor and anti-slavery campaigner Charles Ignatius Sancho – at Wilton's Music Hall in 2018. And Cush Jumbo starred in a one-woman show about Josephine Baker, *Josephine and I*, at the Bush Theatre, London, in 2015, which subsequently transferred to New York.

The Biographical Play as Monumentalism

To help frame what follows, we might usefully compare the longstanding presence of the single biographical play in theatre culture to the presence of statues in the built environment. The historian Alex von Tunzelmann writes in her book *Fallen Idols* that statues are 'icons of individuals: their symbolism may cross the line between secular and religious. They are held to represent those individuals and, at the same, time, national, cultural or community identity'.[30] While they may stand unnoticed and unremarked upon in cities as people go about their everyday business, some people become very upset when statues are defaced, damaged or pulled down, as happened famously with the statue of the slave trader Edward Colston in Bristol in 2020, the statue of the imperialist Cecil Rhodes at the University of Cape Town in 2015 and many other examples throughout human history. As with biodrama and 'historical realism', what we think of as 'statues' are usually the most conservative representational type, 'portrait statues: the figurative representations of individuals that are put up to celebrate and promote their virtues'.[31]

---

[30] Von Tunzelmann, *Fallen Idols*, 4.
[31] Ibid., 7.

While both biodrama and statues might appear timeless, each is the product of specific circumstances, and specific political and aesthetic contexts. In the former case, as we have seen, the biodrama as we know it emerged from the chronicle plays of the Renaissance and was adopted and adapted centuries later by German Romanticism. In the latter case, von Tunzelmann points to a similar history: 'a nineteenth-century revival of the Renaissance revival of the classical style', responding to the Carlylean enthusiasm for Great Men.[32]

However, as *Fallen Idols* argues in its conclusion, it does not have to be this way. Sculpture as a way of remembering and reflecting on the past does not need to follow the 'individual on a pedestal' formula. Public art in memory of individuals can be street art, like murals, instead: 'less burdened with classical allusions, less permanent, more dynamic, more democratic'.[33] There are plenty of examples around the world of dismantled, reconfigured or recontextualized statues that invite imaginative engagement, along with statues that place individuals on a larger historical canvas or which present multiple figures and a space for the visitor to interact with them. Among von Tunzelmann's instances are the broken-up statue of the Paraguayan dictator, Alfredo Stroessner, which is now a memorial to his victims; the headless statue of Kwame Nkrumah, Ghana's first prime minister, at Kwame Nkrumah Memorial Park (the statue was beheaded after the 1966 coup that overthrew Nkrumah); and the 800 steel columns suspended from a roof at the National Memorial for Peace and Justice in Montgomery, Alabama, each of which represents a county in the US where lynchings took place, with the names of victims engraved on each one.[34] This chapter's typology of approaches to biodrama – recuperation and fragmentation, duplication and competition, and iteration – aims to highlight how playwrights are exploring alternatives to the equivalent of the Great Man statue. At the same time, I am mindful of von Tunzelmann's caution that '[s]upplementing the Great Men theory with a few Great

[32] Ibid., 13.
[33] Ibid., 207.
[34] Ibid., 212–14.

Women represents a cosmetic change, not a meaningful change, to how we think about history'.[35]

Recuperation and Fragmentation: The *Emilia* Effect

I want to begin this exploration of the possibilities of biodrama with Morgan Lloyd Malcolm's *Emilia*, since all biodrama on English stages in the 2020s is to some extent a response to the success of this play, both as theatre and as a cultural phenomenon. First staged at Shakespeare's Globe in 2018, *Emilia* proved to be so popular that it secured a West End transfer to the Vaudeville Theatre in 2019. It was also streamed to a global online audience in November 2020 during the first waves of the Covid pandemic. *Emilia* has since been the focus of several academic articles and books; the published play text has been through three editions, including a Methuen Student Edition, and has become a set text in schools, where it has also been widely licensed for amateur performance. For the purposes of this chapter's argument, I want to touch on the play's content briefly in order to highlight how its dramaturgy works to recuperate the historical figure through a strategy of fragmentation. This fragmentation strategy is, of course, not unprecedented; as Ursula Canton notes, there are several plays from the 1980s on wards that deploy a fracturing of their biographical subject so that, '[i]nstead of echoing the idea that human beings are unique individuals with a relatively coherent and continuous personality, this unity is visually deconstructed on stage'.[36] Rather, it is the impact of Lloyd Malcolm's use of the technique, and its distinctive hybridity with other biodrama approaches, that I want to explore here.

As Laura Kressly summarizes, '*Emilia* is an imaginative retelling of the life of English Renaissance poet Aemilia Bassano Lanyer, who, in addition to being one of the first women in England to write and

---

[35] Ibid., 213.
[36] Canton, *Biographical Theatre*, 99–100.

publish her own poetry (*Salve Deus Rex Judaeorum* in 1611), is a chief contender for having been the "Dark Lady" of Shakespeare's sonnets.[37] It was a landmark production at the Globe, in terms of the production team (which consisted predominantly of women), the processes (collaborative rather than hierarchical) and the inclusivity of the event itself, which was made accessible through a cheap tickets scheme and performances for parents and carers, 'with babies and small children welcome'.[38] As Kressly et al. note, Lloyd Malcolm's intentions are explicitly recuperative: 'For every Emilia there are hundreds of other talents and voices lost to history. We must seek them out and amplify them. Let's stop re-reading the same old narratives.'[39] *Emilia* also set out to be intersectional in its feminist act of recuperation; Lloyd Malcolm specifies that the play 'was written to be performed by an all female cast of diverse women' and in the Globe production Emilia is 'played at different life stages by three different visibly racialised women'.[40] In the play's final scene, Emilia is named as 'Italian. Jewish probably but you hid it. And likely of North African Descent [*sic*]', but the production's representation of her as three different bodies enables her to stand in for an idea of 'diverse women' and thus for the play to speak directly to some of the contemporary experiences of women of colour: of anti-immigration rhetoric, of the experiences of Black women and 'misogynoir', of the #MeToo movement and its backlash.[41]

As Eleanor Chadwick points out, Emilia being embodied by a trinity of women of colour is a symbolic move on the part of the play, which allows for several seemingly contradictory ideas to be present simultaneously.[42] We are told that the play 'takes place in several time zones at one time', that it 'isn't an accurate representation of Renaissance

[37] Kressly et al., 'Introduction', in *Notelets of Filth: A Companion Reader to Morgan Lloyd Malcolm's Emilia*, ed. Laura Kressly, Aida Patient, and Kimberly A. Williams (Abingdon: Routledge, 2023), 2.

[38] Ibid., 4.

[39] Morgan Lloyd Malcolm, quoted in Kressly et al., 'Introduction', 5.

[40] Kressly et al., 'Introduction', 3.

[41] Ibid., 6–7.

[42] Eleanor Chadwick, 'History, Her Story, or Our Story? Navigating the Tensions of Historically-Responsive Storytelling in *Emilia*', in Kressly et al., *Notelets*, 110.

England, it isn't a historical representation. It is a memory, a dream, a feeling of her.'[43] Yet, as previously noted, the play specifically wants to draw our attention to a historical oversight; it is difficult to see how this might be done without representing history. The three Emilias (played in the Vaudeville Theatre performance that I saw by Saffron Coomber, Adelle Leonce and Clare Perkins) represent 'the three ages of her', and yet 'everyone except Emilia3 is a Muse. The Muses are the embodiment of Emilia's will. It is up to you how you show this.'[44] In effect, then, everyone on the stage is either Emilia or an aspect of her, meaning the play is in the tradition of the 'studio psychodrama', a term I have previously applied to stage adaptations of nineteenth-century novels.[45] The studio psychodrama often features a younger and an older version of the character, and the action is understood to be taking place inside the protagonist's head, making it a kind of memory play where characters can come and go fleetingly and actors can multi-role, as the story becomes subject to dream logic ('a memory, a dream, a feeling of her'). Perhaps, then, the dramaturgy of *Emilia* represents a new hybridity where the studio psychodrama meets the performance logics of the Globe's 'new writing' tradition.[46] This 'collage of a life', as the critic Hailey Bachrach puts it, creates an 'impressionistic and highly subjective feel'.[47] In order to make objective political points about the present *without* making any claims on historical representation, *Emilia* puts pressure on the transmissibility of that 'feeling of her', urging, as Isabel Stuart argues, that audiences experience the story viscerally.[48] Yet in its explicit invocation of Black strength, solidarity and love, it invites an identification with women of colour that is eroded by the

---

[43] Morgan Lloyd Malcolm, *Emilia* (London: Oberon, 2019), vii.

[44] Ibid., viii.

[45] Benjamin Poore, *Heritage, Nostalgia and Modern British Theatre: Staging the Victorians* (Basingstoke: Palgrave, 2012), 81–3.

[46] This spatial dramaturgy then had to be re-adapted for the much more conventional proscenium-arch configuration of the Vaudeville.

[47] Hailey Bachrach, 'Quilted History: Emilia and Swive' (blog), *Hailey Bachrach*, 22 January 2020. Available online: https://hbachrach.com/ (accessed 21 March 2023).

[48] Isabel Stuart, 'Feeling Collectives: Emotions, Feminist Solidarity, and Difference in *Emilia*', in Kressly et al., *Notelets*, 185.

final, rousing speech's emphasis on 'every woman'[49] (but 'You don't need to be a woman to know what is coming').[50] As Stuart observes, in the production, 'She is a kind of Everywoman (though this is problematised within the play through explicit attention to race and class in particular).'[51] In the advertising for the Vaudeville Theatre transfer, the 'Everywoman' angle is made plain with the following text: '1609. I AM EMILIA. Writer. Wife. Lover. Mother. Muse. ... 2019. WE ARE EMILIA.'[52] These lines also allude to the play's opening, where Emilia3 announces 'For centuries these are the words they have used to describe me. Not anymore ... I am Emilia', and the other two Emilias join her to add, 'We are Emilia.'[53] In Stuart's estimation, this 'we' avoids 'the tempting trap of universalism' since it 'enables a held space for audiences to express their feelings in response to the patriarchal systems that oppress *all* women, while recognising the difference in these struggles'.[54]

The representational logics of *Emilia*, then, embrace everything from a dreamlike subjectivity to an inclusive solidarity based on shared (and also distinct) material conditions of oppression. In addition, the splitting of Emilia into three suggests a psychoanalytical interpretation. Lloyd Malcolm states in the 2018 edition of the play that the older Emilia, 'Emilia3', '*directs and encourages and instructs. She is like a ring master, a gang leader, a mother*'.[55] For Catherine Quirk, the three Emilias reflect the 'triple-layered scheme' of the witnessing of trauma theorized by the psychiatrist and psychoanalyst Dori Laub. In this model, applied to *Emilia*, '[t]he first layer, the experiencing witness, is taken on by each Emilia in turn. The audience takes on the part of tertiary witness, the interlocutor of the testimonial. And in between, until she steps

---

[49] Stuart, 'Feeling Collectives', 187–8.
[50] Lloyd Malcolm, *Emilia*, 75.
[51] Stuart, 'Feeling Collectives', 184.
[52] Vaudeville Theatre flier (author's personal collection).
[53] Lloyd Malcolm, *Emilia*, 1.
[54] Stuart, 'Feeling Collectives', 188, 189.
[55] Quoted in Catherine Quirk, 'We Are Emilia: Emilia as Witness, Witnessing Emilia', in Kressly et al., *Notelets*, 132.

into her own past, Emilia3 serves as secondary witness, narrating her testimony to us.'[56] The play is therefore a playing out of Emilia3 merging progressively with that past; and because the audience is implicated by being 'active participants in the story' and in sharing the same theatrical and psychic space, it provides another sense in which 'We are Emilia', concludes Quirk.[57] However we might analyse and interpret it, it seems clear that the intention of the triple-casting of Emilia is to be inclusive, to stimulate the sense of the collective: it splits the character because the movement of the play is then to unify.[58]

My focus is not so much of the success or failure of this strategy, and more on the question of how the biographical narrative works when the 'story' of the play becomes a transhistorical invocation of female collectivity. Rosemary Waugh, in her review of the production for *Exeunt* magazine, objected that 'I want, most of all, to be told a story.'[59] My reservation tends in the opposite direction: that there is *too much* story in *Emilia*, and the way that the narrative is left hanging in Act 2 undermines some aspects of the play's politics. As I hope this book thus far has made clear, I am not objecting, as some mainstream critics did, to the play's dramaturgy because I find it 'patchy', 'odd' or too polemical, and therefore not a 'quality' history play.[60] Rather, I question the necessity of the play jumping through so many narrative hoops – creating a new 'Shakespeare authorship theory' along the way – when the very rubric of 'memory' and 'dream' licenses freedom from these

---

[56] Quirk, 'We Are Emilia', 131.

[57] Quirk, 'We Are Emilia', 131, 137.

[58] Rebecca Benzie further explores the notion of the three Emilias as a representation of shared experience in her book *Feminism, Dramaturgy and the Contemporary History Play*, Methuen Drama Engage (forthcoming).

[59] Rosemary Waugh, review of *Emilia* by Morgan Lloyd Malcolm, directed by Nicole Charles, Shakespeare's Globe, London, *Exeunt Magazine*, 16 August 2018. Available online: https://exeuntmagazine.com/reviews/review-emilia-shakespeares-globe/ (accessed 21 March 2023).

[60] See Kressly, 'There's Only So Much Work', 154–7.

constraints.[61] For example, the play ends with Eve being burned at the stake, having been accused of witchcraft. The stage directions give us: '*We see EVE being placed on a pyre. Music. Build. Horror and sadness.*'[62] While Emilia3 addresses the audience directly ('This is what happens when we speak'), '*we see EVE go up in flames*'. A song is sung for her, and then we are transported to a dreamlike encounter with Shakespeare.[63] Considering that the play is 'For Eve. For every Eve', the character of Eve herself – one of the Bankside washerwomen who pay to be taught by Emilia and with whom she publishes seditious pamphlets – is given remarkably little stage time.[64] Likewise, the women who support Emilia in her writing, like Lady Katherine and Lady Anne, appear and disappear from the story but have no independent life in Emilia's head-canon. In a sense, then, the feeling of community and collectivity in the auditorium comes at the expense of the collective narrative on stage: it remains all about Emilia because, as the 'Introduction to the Poems' states, 'Our Emilia spoke through the ages to us and I hope we have done her proud with this play. She's our hero.'[65] Either Emilia is every woman, or Eve is; the play tells us whose experience is meant to be emblematic.

Red Ellen

The breathless, headlong rush through history and personal narrative is also a feature of *Red Ellen* by Caroline Bird, a co-production between Northern Stage, Nottingham Playhouse and the Royal Lyceum

---

[61] Ironically, the play centres Shakespeare – through his repeated appearances, especially at the end, and through the interrupted performance of *Othello* at the end of Act 1 – more than any other male character. Of course, on stage Shakespeare's toxic masculinity is lampooned by the casting (Charity Wakefield) and the performance, but it still gives him more presence than all the female characters. As in previous romantic dramas about Shakespeare, *Emilia* imagines the 'real-life' inspiration that brought the plays into existence, only this time it is repositioned as plagiarism of a creatively gifted lover (Lloyd Malcolm, *Emilia*, 29–30).

[62] Lloyd Malcolm, *Emilia*, 72.

[63] Ibid., 72–3.

[64] Ibid., *Emilia*, 75.

[65] Ibid., *Emilia*, 78.

Theatre Edinburgh, which toured England and Scotland in 2022. Here, the feminist, recuperative mode is also deployed, but without fragmentation: the subject, Ellen Wilkinson, is required to do it all herself; indeed, this is made a feature of the play's feminist dramaturgy. In the published play text, Bird's 'Notes on Ellen' emphasize speed, colour and movement, linking these to character but also to gender: 'To inspire action in others, a woman must often duck and weave, switch tones, keep the air around themselves unpredictable.'[66] The play represents the last fourteen years of the life of Ellen Wilkinson, MP for Jarrow in the northeast of England since 1935 and, at the time of her death, Education Secretary in the post-war Labour government. One of the historical centrepieces of the story is the Jarrow March (or 'Jarrow Crusade') of 1936, a protest march to Westminster of some 200 unemployed workers from the northeast of England (Jarrow had an unemployment rate of 80 per cent at the time). The play offers the insight that Wilkinson – who was central to the organization of the march – was able to see it in terms of theatre and spectacle: 'This march is about *dramatizing* the information, into an unforgettable human event that will visually, physically, poetically, once and for all, force the entire country to truly *understand*.'[67] Ellen is shown to have been right about the power of the march, but for the wrong reasons. She is represented as the idealist where Herbert Morrison (later Home Secretary) is the realist ('They will crush those men, fob them off and send them away with nothing but blisters and broken dreams').[68] Her lover Otto Katz dismisses and mocks her 'heroic failure', but years later, Winston Churchill admits that 'Everyone remembers your march', which has been 'romanticised into some sort of heroic folk movement'.[69]

This is the rousing core of the play, underlined by the prominence of the Jarrow Crusade on the production posters – which imitate the aesthetics of socialist realism – and by the play script's blurb that Ellen

[66] Caroline Bird, *Red Ellen* (London: Nick Hern, 2021), 8.
[67] Ibid., 48.
[68] Ibid., 37.
[69] Ibid., 53–4, 62.

was 'Forever on the right side of history, but on the wrong side of life'.[70] Yet underneath the marketing that suggests a twentieth-century, socialist Emilia or Joan of Arc, the portrait of Wilkinson is surprisingly ambivalent. We see her being duped by her Communist friend Isobel, and by Otto, into fundraising for Moscow, and endangering the life of Albert Einstein.[71] When questioned by Morrison about her allegiances, she is witty but evasive; the dialogue is tight, full of one-liners, but her complicity with Stalinism is dismissed as a quirk rather than a terrible miscalculation.[72] Despite the agit-prop staging that would seem to frame her as such, this Ellen is neither an everywoman nor a heroine. In Act 3 Scene 5, her attempts to fulfil her government role managing air-raid shelters during the war are perceived as naive and callous by the working-class Londoners with whom she speaks. In the next scene, Ellen is stoic and accepts that bombs are 'the great leveller', but the tension is never quite resolved.[73] Her decision to drive her car in a blackout two scenes later, resulting in a crash and a serious head wound, smacks of a self-destructiveness driven by guilt, which hardly serves the ordinary Londoners whose disapproval so distressed her in the first place. While Ellen is given several fiery feminist face-offs – especially with Morrison in the break-up scene – in other ways she is presented as volatile, incurious, unperceptive and solipsistic (despite her profession to 'CARE', an insistence that echoes the helpless, wilfully blinkered position of Sarah Kahn at the end of *Chicken Soup with Barley*, discussed in Chapter 3).[67]

The play's Afterword explains how the first draft of the play was 'five hours long, packed with characters, linear, with not a single date altered'.[74] The published and produced version is certainly much tighter, but as a result it creates the impression of rushing at breakneck pace through these encounters and events: the Jarrow Crusade, the

---

[70] Ibid., no pagination.
[71] Ibid., 23, 26.
[72] Ibid., 19–21.
[73] Ibid., 68.
[74] Caroline Bird, 'Afterword', in *Red Ellen*, 103.

Spanish Civil War, the rise of Fascism and Stalinism, the Second World War and the foundation of the Welfare State. Ellen is given a restless energy, drinking coffee and smoking endless cigarettes: 'This should feel real and slightly worrying', warn the notes of the need for her to run wherever possible and to occasionally fall over.[75] This ducking and weaving, dashing and falling expresses on a symbolic level the difficulty that women then (and implicitly, now) faced in public life when it is built around heteropatriarchal assumptions. Yet it also reflects the double-bind of narrative, recuperative biodrama: while the historical timeline gives the personal story its resonance, the biodrama must present both the conventional history *and* its alternative reading, resulting in a surplus of plotlines to chase and resolve.[76] This is embodied by Ellen's exhausting attempts to hold these opposing functions together. It's especially the case when the history in question – the years around the Second World War – is so central to current, contested notions of Englishness (see the Introduction). Additionally, as we have seen, biodrama tends towards either celebration or tragedy rather than ambivalence, and here the dramaturgical motif of workers' solidarity is at odds with the messiness of Ellen's life and actions. 'Oppositional' biodrama gets locked into playing Great Man historiography at its own game, still putting portrait statues on pedestals, only different ones.

I, Joan

I, Joan by Charlie Josephine, staged at Shakespeare's Globe in Autumn 2022, is another example of a recuperative biodrama that followed in the wake of *Emilia*, and indeed, one that was produced at the same venue under the same Artistic Director, Michelle Terry. The play explores the conceit that Joan of Arc – who appears in Shakespeare's *Henry VI*

---

[75] Bird, *Red Ellen*, 7.

[76] Unlike *Emilia*, *Red Ellen* provides a sign-off for each of the supporting characters: the second Act contains a whole series of one-on-one scenes with each of the figures that Ellen had met on her political ascent: her sister Annie, Isabel, Herbert, Otto, Winston Churchill, Annie again and then David, the Jarrow steelworker who becomes an 'angel of death' figure at the end.

Part I – had what we would today call a nonbinary gender identity. Using frequent direct address, Joan (played by Isobel Thom) is able to speak of their feelings of discomfort about being labelled a girl both to a confidant, Thomas, in the historical period of the fifteenth century, and in contemporary terms, to the audience.[77] While, in performance, Thom's Joan did use the words 'queer', 'nonbinary' and 'genderfluid' to describe themself, and was evidently aware of our modern world of 'TERFs and Twitter' as well as their medieval world, they also were able to communicate their bafflement of existing in a binary environment where the language to describe their identity doesn't exist (Joan is shown making use of 'they/them' pronouns, adopted loyally by 'Joan's Army', a peasant militia here reimagined as a queer, nonconforming and exuberant group of outsiders). Hence, to a degree, this Joan is fragmented in that they exist in fifteenth-century France as well as apparently on our temporal plane, although Nick Curtis, reviewing the production for the *Evening Standard*, surmised that '[w]hen Joan chats to us they're conversing with God'.[78]

What sounds complicated to describe textually reads clearly and instinctively in performance. In a programme note, choreographer Jennifer Jackson writes of the battle scenes: 'Looking at the world of battle through an internal lens ... War became a dance'; Joan's Army was 'queering the space with their joy and resilience. Their contemporary movement and perspective, dragging history kicking and screaming

---

[77] The decision to reimagine Joan as nonbinary was initially a controversial move. As the trans writer Shon Faye observes, 'there can be a strong impulse by LGBT people today to understand people in the past through the lens of our own language, and to sketch the lives of these historical figures with the conceptual tools available to us in the present' (Shon Faye, *The Transgender Issue: An Argument for Justice* (London: Penguin, 2021), 200). Citing the controversy over the Anne Lister memorial plaque on Holy Trinity Church in York and whether it should have included the word 'lesbian' – anachronistic for the time – Faye adds: 'The fierce dispute over the precise description of a dead Victorian woman is more about contemporary LGBT politics than it is about history', citing 'the recent disappearance and erasure of lesbian subcultures in Britain' as one reason for question of the plaque's wording being particularly fraught (Faye, *Transgender Issue*, 201).

[78] Nick Curtis, review of *I, Joan* by Charlie Josephine, directed by Ilinca Radulian, Shakespeare's Globe, London, *Evening Standard*, 2 September 2022, reproduced in *Theatre Record* 42, no. 9 (2022). Available online: https://www-theatrerecord-com.libproxy.york.ac.uk/magazine/production/2579 (accessed 3 October 2022).

into 2022.'[79] These sequences were legible as such in the performance I attended, and were augmented by the live musicians' use of percussion and brass – including those conventionally comedic instruments, the tuba and the trombone – which suggested a pots-and-pans, improvised army of unexpected power and cogency, and by an eye-catching set design of playful simplicity, where the floorboards seemed to curve up to the orchestra, literally 'queering the pitch' of the regular Globe stage and providing an extraordinary range of possibilities for entrances. The audience, on the evening I saw it, loudly cheered, clapped and whooped their approval of Joan's speeches; despite – or because of – the deliberate slippage between 'queer', 'trans' and 'nonbinary' in their direct address, the audience seemed to recognize Joan as 'one of us'. *Emilia*'s use of galvanizing rhetoric and multiple perspectives to expose the cruelties and absurdities of patriarchy, then and now, seems an obvious antecedent.

The critical reception of *I, Joan* had none of the disdainful bafflement that greeted Drury's *Marys Seacole*, as discussed later in this chapter. Curtis expressed a widely held positive opinion of the production: 'Experienced live, it strikes me as an expansive, unifying and overall joyful piece of work – baggy at times but too subtle for a hot culture-war take.'[80] Several reviews explicitly disavowed the notion that a history play needed to be a lesson or lecture: 'it's not a lecture, it's a party, and a bloody fun one at that';[81] 'this is no gender studies lecture.'[82] So charmed were the critics by the production that, unusually, they dismissed complaints about historical accuracy as beside the point: 'only

[79] *I, Joan*, Shakespeare's Globe (theatre programme), 2022, no pagination.

[80] Curtis, review of *I, Joan*.

[81] Andrzej Lukowski, review of *I, Joan* by Charlie Josephine, directed by Ilinca Radulian, Shakespeare's Globe, London, *Time Out*, 1 September 2022, reproduced in *Theatre Record* 42, no. 9. Available online: https://www-theatrerecord-com.libproxy.york.ac.uk/magazine/production/2579 (accessed 3 October 2022).

[82] Isobel Lewis, review of *I, Joan* by Charlie Josephine, directed by Ilinca Radulian, Shakespeare's Globe, London, *The Independent*, 3 September 2022, reproduced in *Theatre Record* 42, no. 9. Available online: https://www-theatrerecord-com.libproxy.york.ac.uk/magazine/production/2579 (accessed 3 October 2022).

the unimaginative would quibble over historical accuracy';[83] 'the play is obviously speculative rather than meticulously historical';[84] 'to be frank most people won't be coming to this for the medieval theology'.[85] However, perhaps ultimately it was Joan's Catholicism and foreignness, along with her historical distance, that encouraged critics' generous and open-minded tendencies (catholic with a small 'c', as it were). When the history play touches on British subjects, on Empire or on events within living memory, more is felt to be – shall we say – at stake. Critics suddenly find perceived accuracy all-important, and 'playing fast-and-loose' with history is to be condemned. Joan – French, long dead, not a man, cross-dressing and Catholic, both heretic and saint – can be reimagined because English culture doesn't feel as though it 'owns' her.

Nevertheless, I did find one strand of criticism of *I, Joan* persuasive with regard to this section's concern with recuperation. Lukowski puts it vividly when he avers: 'Josephine's play is timid about depicting Joan as either a killer or a Catholic, and defaults to euphemistic scenes that suggest their success in battle came as a result of progressive values and general fabulousness. Fine, but it's still a three-hour play about a military campaign.'[86] Similarly, Sarah Hemming in the *Financial Times* points out 'some uncomfortable muddiness in the overlaps with the original story: after the first battle, for example, Joan is horrified by

[83] Sam Marlowe, review of *I, Joan* by Charlie Josephine, directed by Ilinca Radulian, Shakespeare's Globe, London, *The Stage*, 2 September 2022, reproduced in *Theatre Record* 42, no. 9. Available online: https://www.theatrerecord-com.libproxy.york.ac.uk/magazine/production/2579 (accessed 3 October 2022).

[84] Susannah Clapp, review of *I, Joan* by Charlie Josephine, directed by Ilinca Radulian, Shakespeare's Globe, London, *The Observer*, 11 September 2022, reproduced in *Theatre Record* 42, no. 9. Available online: https://www.theatrerecord-com.libproxy.york.ac.uk/magazine/production/2579 (accessed 3 October 2022).

[85] Rachel Halliburton, review of *I, Joan* by Charlie Josephine, directed by Ilinca Radulian, Shakespeare's Globe, London, *The Arts Desk*, 2 September 2022, reproduced in *Theatre Record* 42, no. 9. Available online: https://www.theatrerecord-com.libproxy.york.ac.uk/magazine/production/2579 (accessed 3 October 2022).

[86] Lukowski, review of *I, Joan*.

the slaughter, but soon seems to accept it,[87] and *The Arts Desk*'s Rachel Halliburton notes that Josephine's decision to emphasize 'the ecstatic aspect of Joan's religion rather than the theology' makes 'the script teeter towards being over simplistic'.[88] Reviewers thus praised *I, Joan*'s irreverence towards its source material, but mostly stopped short of saying that the historical narrative did not match the 'queer joy' of its presentation.[89,90] Rather than try to square the inherent violence and religiosity of the Joan of Arc narrative with this theatrical event about 'Delicious Fluid Freedom, of Liberation, and Joy', the play might have liberated itself from its own narrative beats, a possibility that I will explore at the end of this chapter.[91]

The recuperative mode, then, whether it offers an oppositional feminist revision or a queer counternarrative, is still usually reliant on rendering history as story, even when that story seems to work against a coherent dramaturgy. In *Red Ellen*, a condensed retelling of fourteen of

[87] Sarah Hemming, review of *I, Joan* by Charlie Josephine, directed by Ilinca Radulian, Shakespeare's Globe, London, *Financial Times*, 8 September 2022, reproduced in *Theatre Record* 42, no. 9. Available online: https://www-theatrerecord-com.libproxy.york.ac.uk/magazine/production/2579 (accessed 3 October 2022).

[88] Halliburton, review of *I, Joan.*

[89] Scott Matthewman, review of *I, Joan* by Charlie Josephine, directed by Ilinca Radulian, Shakespeare's Globe, London, *The Reviews Hub*, 2 September 2022, reproduced in *Theatre Record* 42, no. 9. Available online: https://www-theatrerecord-com.libproxy.york.ac.uk/magazine/production/2579 (accessed 3 October 2022).

[90] I found a similar dissonance between form and content when I saw *Boudica* by Tristan Bernays at the Globe in 2017. *Boudica* was a bold and jubilantly entertaining drama, but like *I, Joan*, it is an example of the double-bind that modern plays depicting events in the distant past are apt to find themselves in. Knowing that it is a new play, an audience might expect the displays of violence to have a modern sensibility; but what is a modern sensibility in new writing staged at a Shakespeare visitor attraction? Does it involve imitating the violence of long-form television and of video games, where much of the sword-and-sorcery genre now resides? Or does that involve evoking the violence of Shakespeare's *Titus Andronicus*, with its sickening acts of rape and tongue-removal? And how does that scorched-earth spirit of vengeance coexist with pleas to live peaceably alongside the occupying forces? At the Globe, the combined armies of the Iceni, the Trinovantes and the Belgics sang victory songs and covers of 'London Calling' by The Clash; we were encouraged to enjoy their destruction of Camulodunum and the upset it causes to the arrogant Romans. We therefore became complicit with the rapists and tongue-removers of the British tribes. The central acts of warfare that define these stories are irreconcilable with their celebratory, revisionist impulse.

[91] Quoted in Halliburton, review of *I, Joan.*

the most tumultuous years of the twentieth century meant Wilkinson was depicted as hurling herself from one vignette to another. In *I, Joan*, Joan apparently breaks free from their own era in order to address the Globe audience but must still prosecute a military campaign against the English. These biodramas are evidently not as free of the idea of the history lecture as they might appear; these compelling characters seem to be struggling to liberate themselves from the narrative hoops that conventional historical playmaking insists on making them jump through. What might they do if the theatrical encounter was allowed to take precedence over the history lesson?

Dual Biodrama: Duplication and Competition

In this section I want to consider two closely related modes that deal in doubling the biographical subject, subjecting the play's central figures to the logics of duplication and competition. For the moment, let's call them collectively 'dual biodramas'. This type of drama, where two historical figures who are profoundly connected yet in conflict with one another, is almost as long-established as the heroic Great Man play. Where the latter positions the exceptional individual as the shaper of history, dual biodramas shift the ground slightly by emphasizing the interaction between two forceful personalities; it is through this dialectic that historical change is enabled. Viewed in this light, we might identify Shakespeare's *Anthony and Cleopatra* (*c.* 1607) as a forerunner of the dual biodrama, with Bernard Shaw's *Caesar and Cleopatra* (1899) its belated and self-consciously satirical prequel. Many historical dramas that develop character beyond hero-and-villain archetypes, and that contain an antagonist who is rounded and given equal weight to the protagonist, can therefore be included in this category, though they may not indicate as much in their titles. Friedrich Schiller's *Mary Stuart* (1800) covers the last days in the life of Mary, Queen of Scots and her execution at the hands of Queen Elizabeth I of England; in a central scene, invented for the purposes of the drama, Mary and Elizabeth meet face to face.[92] Georg Büchner's play *Danton's Death* (1835), set during the French Terror of 1794, is about the rivalry and political and personal differences between Danton and Robespierre more than a portrait of an individual. Peter Shaffer's *Amadeus* (1979) presents the life of Mozart through the eyes of his jealous fellow composer Antonio Salieri. Palmer suggests that this rivalry was manufactured by Shaffer from 'flimsy materials' because it enabled the playwright to explore contrasts and extremes: 'Salieri is worthy but his work mediocre; Mozart is unworthy and his work brilliant.'[93] The play thus becomes a 'dialectic between a disillusioned character and one who embodies some inexplicable power.'[94]

More recently, Michael Frayn's *Copenhagen* – first staged at the National Theatre, London, in 1998, transferring to the West End and then to Broadway in 2000 – imagines what might have happened at the 1941 meeting in Denmark between the physicists Niels Bohr and Werner Heisenberg that caused the permanent breakdown of their friendship.[95] David Edgar's play *Albert Speer* (National Theatre, London, 2000) covered the life of the Nazi architect and his relationship with Hitler, using a lesser-known historical figure to shed light on an infamous one. Tom Morton-Smith's *Ravens: Spassky vs Fischer* (Hampstead Theatre, 2019) depicts the events surrounding the World Chess Championship in Reykjavik in 1972, where grandmasters Boris Spassky and Bobby Fischer became unwilling tools of Russian and American efforts to engineer political advantage during the Cold War. Dual biography has some overlaps with a category of biodrama discussed by Ursula Canton, the meta-biography.[96] This type of play

---

[92] Robert Bolt's *Vivat! Vivat Regina* (1970) is a more recent account of the rivalry between Elizabeth and Mary (see Palmer, *Contemporary British History Play*, 28).

[93] Palmer, *Contemporary British History Play*, 32.

[94] Ibid., 32.

[95] See Steven Barfield, 'Dark Matter: The Controversy Surrounding Michael Frayn's *Copenhagen*', *Archipelago: An International Journal of Literature, the Arts and Opinion* 8, no. 3 (2004), stave 1. Available online: http://www.archipelago.org/vol8-3/barfield.htm (accessed 21 March 2023).

[96] This categorization, in turn, has correspondences with Alexander Feldman's 'historiographic metatheatre' (Feldman, *Dramas of the Past*, 2) and Mark Berninger's 'metahistorical play' (Berninger, 'Variations of a Genre', 40).

uses 'a biographer-character who can explicitly examine our concept
of the past', and can also combine 'the presentation of biographical
processes with implicit formal and structural means that raise questions
about its nature'.[97] Drawing on the work of Stephanie Kramer, Canton
cites Frayn's *Copenhagen* as an example of the explicit approach, and Liz
Lochhead's *Mary Queen of Scots Got her Head Chopped Off* (1985) as an
example of doing so implicitly.[98] *Handbagged* and *The Father and the
Assassin*, considered later in this chapter, use meta-biography explicitly
to present competing versions of the past, with that contestation taking
place as a live encounter in the theatre.

One of the most critically and commercially successful dual biodramas
of the 2000s was Peter Morgan's *Frost/Nixon*, which premiered in 2006
at the Donmar Warehouse in London and subsequently transferred to
the West End and Broadway; it was made into a film in 2008. *Frost/
Nixon* dramatizes the build-up to, and the recording of, the landmark
four-part television interview that former President Richard Nixon
gave to television journalist and celebrity interviewer David Frost in
1977. Nixon – having resigned over the Watergate scandal in 1974 but
having been excused from the Watergate trials due to ill health and
subsequently pardoned by his successor, Gerald Ford – confessed to
his wrongdoing in the final interview in a broadcast that attracted 'the
largest audience for a news programme in the history of American
television'.[99] Against the odds, and at huge financial and reputational
risk, Frost pulls off a tremendous media coup. In meta-biography terms,
Frost/Nixon can be considered an example of the implicit technique: we
are given the impression of multiple sources based on documentary
material, but it is mediated through, and subject to the commentary of,
our narrator figure, the '*liberal intellectual*' Jim Reston.[100]

James Graham's *Best of Enemies* (Young Vic, 2021) is cut from
similar cloth to *Frost/Nixon*. Like Morgan's play, it revels in the rivalry

---

[97] Canton, *Biographical Theatre*, 11.
[98] Ibid., 102.
[99] Peter Morgan, *Frost/Nixon* (New York: Faber and Faber, 2014), 80.
[100] Ibid., 4.

between two figures from different social, cultural and political worlds, played out on television – this time a decade earlier, in 1968. The play takes as its subject the broadcast conversations between Gore Vidal and William F. Buckley Jr, which took place as part of ABC's networked news coverage of the Republican and Democratic conventions of 1968. These spiky, often ill-tempered exchanges were popular with viewers and caught the attention of politicians, giving ABC an unexpected hit despite having a far smaller news budget than its established rivals NBC and CBS. The Buckley/Vidal conversations are credited in the play with ushering in a new age of adversarial politics on television and of politics as entertainment. Where Buckley personifies a populist conservatism, Vidal is presented as a harbinger of the New Left which 'concerns itself less with … social *class*, and more [with] – social *justice*'.[101]

Handbagged

Moira Buffini's *Handbagged* is one of the most popular recent examples of the dual biodrama, to judge by its staging history. It began life a one-act play in the *Women, Power and Politics: Then and Now* festival at the Tricycle, Kilburn, in 2010. In 2013, it was rewritten as a full-length play, and again staged at the Tricycle before transferring to the West End, followed by a UK tour. A production at the New Vic Theatre in Newcastle-under-Lyme went on to tour in 2019, and the play was revived again at the Tricycle – now named the Kiln – in 2022. *Handbagged* traces the history of Queen Elizabeth II's meetings with Margaret Thatcher when she was the UK's Prime Minister between 1979 and 1990, in the imagined words of the monarch and PM at the time (referred to in the character list as Mags and Liz) and as older versions of themselves (called T and Q). It therefore both duplicates the biographical subject – there are two central 'movers and shapers', and the play concerns their relationship – and fragments it, as in *Emilia*, since Q often disagrees with her younger self, Liz, and likewise Mags with T. Inevitably, the two central figures are

---

[101] James Graham, *Best of Enemies* (London: Methuen Drama, 2021), 31.

depicted as in competition for power and popularity, and over control of the stage narrative. Actor 1 and Actor 2 play the supporting roles, from Kenneth Kaunda to Enoch Powell, Arthur Scargill to Nancy Reagan.

The play has a peculiar, troubled history in relation to its biographical subjects. Indhu Rubasingham, director of all three Tricycle/Kiln productions, recalls that three days before Buffini was due to start work on the full-length version, Margaret Thatcher died; 'The timing was extraordinary.'[102] Then, part-way through the run of the 2022 revival, Elizabeth II died. The run was not cancelled; when I saw the production, London was full of mourners queuing to file past the Queen's coffin, but the atmosphere in the theatre was genial and celebratory. Because of its revival history – and Buffini's practice of revising her plays – there are at least three different published versions of *Handbagged*. It is therefore possible to trace the changes made since the staging nine years earlier, which I will indicate at several points in the following analysis. What became clear from these alterations, and also from the play's reception after the Queen's death, is that the *Handbagged*'s seemingly irreverent premise conceals a deferential attitude to the monarch. While Mags and Liz, T and Q contest each other's historical accounts, claims and memories – and Actors 1 and 2 attempt to present counternarratives and oppositional histories – the 'master' narrative of these years remains as immovable as Thatcher's trademark blonde helmet of hair.

Handbagged goes through several transmutations in the first few minutes. In the play's opening sequence, there is something almost mesmeric about the Beckettian repetition and overlapping of lines, a sense reinforced on the page by the lack of punctuation, creating an impression of flatness in the dialogue. A combination of assertion and contradiction is established, often by the younger and older version of the same character:

Liz   Philip and I had put money on the [election] result
Q   No we had not[103]

---

[102] Moira Buffini, *Handbagged* (London: Faber and Faber, 2013), no pagination.
[103] Moira Buffini, *Handbagged* (London: Faber and Faber, 2022), 20.

This initial mood is broken several minutes in by the switch in idiom and audience address brought about by Actor 1, playing the Footman, who begins to explain his role: 'I am a functionary.'[104] A concern then emerges in the play, expressed by the Footman, that the events require contextualizing for the audience: 'Only there's a generation that don't know what [Labour governments before Thatcher] did', he explains. He is reluctantly allowed to provide historical exposition, though with impatience by Liz, who protests wearily, 'Do you have to? I don't want this to get dull and there's a lot to get through before the interval', and, when it comes to the Falklands War, 'It's been gone over again and again in all sorts of other places and I don't want to trudge through it here.'[105] Later, the play mocks its own limitations, with Actor 2 conceding that some of the roles 'are horrible, thin caricatures but times are hard and it's a job.'[106] In this way, *Handbagged* creates the impression that it has somehow been produced against the company's better judgement, both as 'Actors' and as the figures they portray. The effect is rather like music hall, or light entertainment television from the 1970s: Eric Morecambe and Ernie Wise bickering during the introductions; Ernie fretting over the play he's written for the celebrity guest, while Eric gets twitchy that they won't get to sing 'Bring Me Sunshine' at the end. The comedic sequence after the interval, in which the two multi-rolling actors bicker over their parts and co-deliver a speech by Neil Kinnock,[107] is the most extended example of *Handbagged* operating in the genre of *Wild Swimming* and *We Are Proud to Present*, discussed in Chapter 1: events in which 'there are always two plays being performed', the play itself and also 'two actors attempting to perform the play … and ultimately failing.'[108]

---

[104] Ibid., 23.
[105] Ibid., 35, 57.
[106] Ibid., 39.
[107] Ibid., 71.
[108] Head, 'Director's Note', in Horn, *Wild Swimming*, no pagination.

In the first part, Actor 1 has an earnest outburst over the importance of 'telling the story', where Actor 2 is more resigned to the play's biases and omissions: 'It's their story. That's the contract.'[109] Actor 1's objections about the importance of the 1981 riots are dismissed aggressively by Mags ('if you don't like it you can get on your bike') and more mildly by Liz ('One doesn't want to be here all night').[110] Actor 1 is then required, 'in a stroke of casting genius', to play Nancy Reagan.[111] The move both silences Actor 1's 'extradiagetic' voice and humiliates him (in the production, Actor 1, played by Neet Mohan, was obviously uncomfortable playing Nancy, though not so much that he undermined the character's function in the scene). In this way, the play gestures towards other biographies, other experienced realities of life in 1980s Britain – and also towards the inequities at the heart of the theatre industry – but the dramaturgical movement is the repeated action of *containing* those other realities.

Where Actor 1 in the 2013 version is very knowledgeable about the sinking of the *General Belgrano* warship during the Falklands War,[112] these events are omitted from the 2022 version, which makes slightly more of Enoch Powell and his resemblance, as a populist demagogue, to Boris Johnson.[113] In the 2013 text Actor 1 announces that he 'Wiki'd the eighties' and so knows all about the pop group Bucks Fizz, but in the 2022 script he is rather more sympathetic and less of a gauche youth.[114] Queen Elizabeth is given stronger counter-arguments to Thatcher's declinist narrative about post-war Britain, making Liz and Q seem less out of touch.[115] The Thatchers are associated with racist language where Liz and Q are all post-colonial, modern diplomacy;[116] the Thatchers entertain the now-notorious sexual predator and abuser

[109] Buffini, *Handbagged* (2022 edition), 54.
[110] Ibid., 55.
[111] Ibid., 55.
[112] Buffini, *Handbagged* (2013 edition), 65–6.
[113] Buffini, *Handbagged* (2022 edition), 62.
[114] Buffini, *Handbagged* (2013 edition), 54.
[115] Buffini, *Handbagged* (2022 edition), 45; compare with Buffini, *Handbagged* (2013 edition), 43.
[116] Buffini, *Handbagged* (2022 edition), 43.

Jimmy Savile for Christmas ('he's a laugh', says Thatcher's husband Denis), though there is no mention of his close relationship with Prince Charles.[117] The final sequence of the 2022 *Handbagged* removes a reference to a woman crying at the bus stop when Thatcher resigns, meaning the public reaction is presented as purely one of 'Absolute jubilation'.[118] This seems to conveniently edit out the uncomfortable fact of Thatcher's popularity with many voters.

Hence, the play – particularly in its 2022 revision – ends up affirming the Queen's good sense and fortitude, and implying that Thatcher was an aberration, a blip who didn't gain popular support. As Marion Bailey, who played the older Queen ('Q'), said at the time, '[in the play] the Queen is kind of the goodie, compared with Thatcher. She's the one that represents decency, and care for society'.[119] It is therefore little wonder that the play continued with its run after the death announcement and during the week of national mourning and funeral, having had its first preview cancelled, on the day the death was announced. It offers its audience a flattering misremembered view of recent history. Because of its self-imposed parameters, we do not have to face the act that the British public re-elected the Conservatives even after Thatcher, under John Major, for another five years; we don't see the Queen's mishandling of Diana's death or Diana's exposé of the power games in the royal family. And the Actors are not permitted to take over the show. The injustice of this one-sided, 'winners' history' is noted, but neither wiser, older Actor 2 nor his more idealistic colleague are able to change the kind of play it is.[120] That makes it an unusual example in this chapter: a play that performs its own helplessness in the face of biodrama's aesthetic and commercial imperatives, while

---

[117] Ibid., 79. Admittedly, the 2022 edition makes an additional, satirical reference to Queen Elizabeth's supposed favourite child, the disgraced Prince Andrew, saying he looked 'kingly' on his wedding day (Buffini, *Handbagged* (2022 edition), 91).

[118] Buffini, *Handbagged* (2022 edition), 111.

[119] Emine Saner, 'The Audience Want to Connect with Her', *The Guardian*, 14 September 2022. Available online:. https://www.theguardian.com/stage/2022/sep/14/queen-death-handbagged-kiln-theatre (accessed 21 March 2023).

[120] Actor 1 says, 'I just feel there's some massive omission here' when he is silenced over the events of 1981 (Buffini, *Handbagged* (2022 edition), 53).

overwhelmingly benefiting from them, in terms of its subjects' fame and topicality. It stages its own act of recuperation, a strange, inverted Brechtian 'familiarization technique' where the direct address and theatrical self-awareness combine to encourage us to accept things as they are, to naturalize the contradictions.

The Father and the Assassin

Handbagged, pre-dating *Emilia* by five years, offered a combination of duplication, fragmentation and competition in the presentation of a story that had already been exhaustively told and retold. Anupama Chandrasekhar's play *The Father and the Assassin* combines competition with a direct appeal for recuperation from its protagonist, who demands that his story *must* be told. A depiction of the life and death of Gandhi from the point of view of his assassin, Naturam Godse, *The Father and the Assassin* premiered at the National Theatre in London on the Olivier stage in 2022, returning to the same theatre by popular demand in 2023. It is still unusual for a main-stage history play to have an imperial setting and to *not* channel its perspective through a White narrator or protagonist, and for this reason the programming and the success of *The Father and the Assassin* feels like an important development. British India, the independence movement, and Partition and its legacies are, of course, British history too, and need to be told and given prominence as such in theatrical reckonings with the past. As Nesrine Malik argues in *We Need New Stories*, 'This cherry-picking, this confining of history committed by Britain outside of its borders as belonging to the countries which it colonised, leaves us with a heavily editorialised and truncated history … And it is, indeed, Britain's history … British colonies were not administrative outposts, they were British soil, and their residents were British.'[121]

The Father and the Assassin operates on three different time planes, as the published text explains. The first is from the murder of Gandhi

---

[121] Malik, *New Stories*, 176–7.

to the deaths of Godse and his collaborator Apte; the second covers the years 1917 to 1948; and the third strand is the 'now' of performance.[122] This means, in practice, that Godse has many lines of direct address, as he orchestrates the action and goads and taunts the audience, rather like a medieval Vice figure, or like the Vice's more famous descendant, Shakespeare's Richard III. He insists, 'I guarantee, once you get to know my story, once you truly understand me, I know you'll celebrate me. Maybe even build statues in my honour', making the rhetorical move of an appeal for the audience's enlightened judgement (implying, 'if you don't agree, then you don't truly understand me').[123] Yet Godse also tries to 'sell' his version of the historical events to us on entertainment value alone: 'I can promise you a few things straight away: there's a gun in my story, a trigger is pulled, and there's blood and death – it's a potboiler!'[124] He also dismisses, in the first few seconds, 'That fawning Attenborough film! With Sir Ben Kingsley', opening the play with a disavowal of what it perhaps assumes will be a London audience's main reference point for Gandhi's life story.[125] However, I will argue that despite reversing its perspective, *The Father and the Assassin* ultimately reaffirms the values of Richard Attenborough's 1981 film, burnishing Gandhi's reputation as a Great Man and exposing Godse as an unconvincing supervillain.

Born into a family where the previous sons had not survived childhood, Godse was raised as a girl and was a medium for the Goddess Durga, which meant the family had many gifts and visitors. According to the play, it is only when Godse meets Gandhi for the first time, in the midst of a protest over British cotton, that he becomes aware that he is biologically male. His insecurity about his masculinity seems a driving factor in his aggression and attraction to political extremes. Susannah Clapp remarked in her review of *I, Joan* that '[t]here is no better place to see someone making themselves up than in the theatre. You can be with a character step by step, and the self-discovery is wraparound, extending

---

[122] Chandrasekhar, *The Father and the Assassin* (London: Nick Hern, 2022), 11.
[123] Chandrasekhar, *The Father*, 14.
[124] Ibid., 16.
[125] Ibid., 14.

beyond an individual actor'; this is as true of Godse's self-invention as a
swaggering revolutionary as it is of Josephine's Joan.[126] When he is sent
away to school in Pune, Godse meets Mithun, the school watchman,
who is involved in the anti-colonial movement. Mithun tutors him
in how to act the part of a 'man' in speech, movement and posture.[127]
When Godse unwittingly brings about Mithun's death at the hands of
the British police, he projects his guilt onto Gandhi, whom he now
accuses of betraying the people, having fervently admired him before.

By the interval, we have gathered enough clues to understand that
Godse is not really in control of the story he is trying to tell; the closing
line of the first part, addressed to Gandhi, is 'Enough! This is my story
and I'll tell it my way. Why don't you just stay dead?'[128] Yet there is
little at stake dramaturgically: we know the historical end-point (like
Attenborough's film, *The Father and the Assassin* begins with Gandhi's
assassination and then recapitulates in flashback). We also know that
Godse has trouble controlling his own version of events, because he is
so deeply conflicted, still admiring Gandhi and seeing him as a father
figure and needing to reject him for precisely those reasons. Apart from
Gandhi, the most vocal of Godse's internal antagonists is his childhood
friend Vimala. In Act 3 Scene 4, Godse insists, 'She's of no importance,
narratively speaking', and attempts to silence her, perhaps because
she is a more charismatic speaker than him.[129] They have an extended
argument in Act 3 over Gandhi's salt march and the violence of the
British police. The play (as history lesson) needs Vimala's counterpoint,
despite what Godse's head wants, and so the requirements of biodrama
win. The play poses as the work of Godse the trickster, only to reveal
the carefully prepared curtain-lecture underneath. The close of the
play expresses this same pattern, where Godse tries to behave as if he
has triumphed, but Gandhi's laughter indicates that we are only being
invited to read this one way, as the triumph of the *ahimsa* movement;

[126] Susannah Clapp, review of *I, Joan*.
[127] Chandrasekhar, *The Father*, 43.
[128] Ibid., 61.
[129] Ibid., 66.

'the Father' is literally having the last laugh. Hence, despite Godse's menacing final speech, which seems to link him to divisive historical figures of the future, his insistence that at times of strife 'I will rise' has been comprehensively debunked.[130] The play's dramaturgy tells us that his attempt to 'rise' – just like his solo attempt to rehabilitate his reputation – should not be feared, since Gandhi's spirit lives on.

The Father and the Assassin, in its direct-address narration of a life from the subject's point of view, recalls *Emilia*'s 'a dream, a memory' psychodrama strategy. Indeed, with the repeated motif of Gandhi treating Godse like a son, and the latter's murderous rage against this father figure, we are, in some ways, back in the realm of the twentieth-century Freudian psychobiography or psychohistory, as Palmer calls it, such as John Osborne's *Luther*, where motivation is found in sublimated drives, traumas, fetishes and obsessions.[131] Despite the play's title, Godse disavows the idea of a dual biography, yet it's made clear to us that he has fashioned his identity in opposition to, and therefore in a state of dependence on, Gandhi ('Do I begin with him or with me? Is there a difference?', Godse muses).[132] His frustration is that Gandhi won't compete with him for audience approval or for a place in his narrative, and has no need to; as he admits in his imagined conversation with Gandhi before pulling the trigger: 'I don't change lives, I don't make ripples … I don't matter.'[133] If oppositional biodrama is usually about reclaiming and celebrating figures from the past, then this is deliberately The Biodrama That Goes Wrong. In seeking to topple Gandhi's statue, Godse climbs up, accidentally gives it a polish and then falls off the plinth himself.

---

[130] Ibid., 97.
[131] Palmer, *Contemporary British History Play*, 40–2.
[132] Chandrasekhar, *The Father*, 16.
[133] Ibid., 93.

Iterative Biodrama: *Marys Seacole*

Most of the biodramas discussed so far have been, in different ways, metahistorical, to use Mark Berninger's terminology. They are self-reflexive, concerned with 'how history is made'.[134] As such, as Berninger notes, they make use of metadramatic and metatheatrical elements, disputing in their action and their dialogue – as we saw in *Handbagged* and *The Father and the Assassin* – who is the prime mover of history, who gets to tell their story and who gets to play which role. In line with Alexander Feldman's notion of historiographic metatheatre, too, these plays have questioned how history comes to be written, who gets silenced in these processes and where the gaps speak to us: Shakespeare's appropriation of Emilia's poetry is a prime example of this in *Emilia*. In each case, however, the biodrama takes on the tasks of educating and informing, and when it makes a case for the recognition of 'Great' individuals, it saddles itself with narrative responsibilities and an implicit expectation that the subject will be heroic, admirable – cast in the same mould as the statues of ages past.

One way of transcending these expectations is offered by the example of Jackie Sibblies Drury's play *Marys Seacole*, produced at the Donmar, London, in 2022, and previously staged in New York in 2019. It rejects the presumed duty to educate from the outset; the stage directions of the first scene announce:

> *Mary Seacole stands before us.*
> *If you don't know who she is, well,*
> *look her the fuck up.*[135]

---

[134] Berninger, 'Variations', 40.

[135] Jackie Sibblies Drury, *Marys Seacole*, ebook (New York: Dramatists Play Service, 2022), 3. See also the Donmar's production page, which featured this line prominently ('Marys Seacole', *Donmar*. Available online: https://booking. donmarwarehouse.com/events/1801APGQPRKNVLCHGSKJBCTJKDRMGPL NL?_ga=2.138071159.694363853.1654353699-105755424.1654353699 (accessed 28 April 2023)).

The play begins as if it will feature Mary telling her story through direct address, in the language and tone of her autobiography *Wonderful Adventures of Mrs Seacole in Many Lands* (1857). But from the moment another character, Duppy, walks over to her and fits her with a Bluetooth earpiece, the audience is given due notice that the actor (Kayla Meikle) will not stay in her 'canonical' role.[136] She is dressed by Duppy as a contemporary nurse, and we are soon in a modern nursing home. The cast – all women in the Donmar production, three actors of colour and three White actors – multi-role as characters from different periods, all with variations on Mary's name: Mamie, Miriam, Duppy Mary, May and Merry. We move from the nursing home to Seacole's hotel in Kingston, Jamaica, where she cared for English cholera sufferers in the 1850s, and then to a city park where two nannies are watching their charges, and then to a nursing school where a nurse is being trained in how to handle a mass shooting incident, and eventually to the Crimea, even though the Crimea has, in a way, already been present at the nursing school ('*Something that is at once a public place and a battlefield*').[137] In bold opposition to the kind of biodrama that balances its Act 1 and Act 2 with complementary scenes resolving its plotlines, Drury's Act 2 is announced a few minutes before the play's end. It presents a mash-up of the lines and situations that we have already experienced – '*The Crimean battlefield continues to be and also becomes everywhere else and every-when else we have been*' – building in intensity and adding new perspectives and horrors (in the Donmar production, a cascade of body parts tumbled onto the stage, bringing

---

[136] This moment itself might be an iteration of – and a callback to – a consciously anachronistic moment in Robert O'Hara's *Insurrection: Holding History* (1996) where a postgraduate student, Ron, travels back the slave rebellion led by Nat Turner in 1831. The enslaved character Hammet stands next to Nat 'with a modern-day Headgear Walkie-talkie' (309). Earlier in the play, Ova Seea Jones had weighed the slaves' cotton with a digital scale (289). The disruptive potential of untimely objects, and the ways that they imply correspondences between then and now, is an established, but nonetheless theatrically effective, trope. It gains its impact from the normative assumption that all plays are attempting historical realism, and that they are trying hard *not* to 'break period'.

[137] Drury, *Marys Seacole*, 77.

to mind, for me, the grimly comic cannibalism of Edward Bond's *Early Morning* (1968)).[138]

Rather like Ella Hickson's polychronic history play *Oil*, then, *Marys Seacole* seems to present a different play with different rules in every scene, yet it is unarguably a unified work of art, since there are so many call-backs and correspondences which are then brought in to land simultaneously in Act 2. The Bluetooth earpiece continues to activate, sending modern Marys messages from Mary Duppy or Florence Nightingale.[139] At various points, the stage directions in the play text put it, '*Mary Seacole comes alive in Mary*' and she speaks with Seacole's familiar cadences and confidence. The relationship between Mary and Mamie is ambiguous; Mamie is often the junior worker to whom Mary is exacting, undermining, harshly critical and peremptory (in Kingston, Mary demands that Mamie use her handkerchief, a gift from her mother, to look after Miriam, who vomits into it).[140] At one point, Duppy Mary appears as Mamie's mother; the rest of the time she is Mary's mother. Both of the nineteenth-century Marys and Mamies talk of being sent by their mothers to a hilltop house to care for a White woman, a pattern that finds its correspondence in the many ways that women of colour are paid and expected – on and off the clock – to look after White people's bodies and feelings, while being expected never to make themselves fully visible or tangible to them.[141] In these ways, then, *Marys Seacole*, as the title suggests, uses fragmentation to some degree: between different past and present Marys and between Mary and Mamie as different subject positions in the care-work nexus. There is also an element of competition, particularly between Mary and May (as Florence Nightingale) over who gets to care for the wounded of the Crimea, using what methods, and claiming what degree of credit.[142] However, the competition is not the central dynamic, as it is in the plays

---

[138] Ibid., 106.
[139] Ibid., 70–1.
[140] Ibid., 49.
[141] Ibid., 60–1.
[142] Ibid., 93.

considered previously, nor does the fragmentation lead to an affirming unification at the play's end. I suggest that *Marys Seacole* is more aptly considered as an *iterative* biodrama, one where situations and conversations and injuries and antipathies are repeated through time, rippling out from Mary Seacole to the social and racial dynamics of the present day. I have adopted the idea of an iterative structure from Sarah Grochala's analysis of debbie tucker green's *Generations*, in which – in accordance with the word's use by Jacques Derrida – iteration is repetition with variation.[143] As in Grochala's reading of *Generations*, 'each iteration invokes previous iterations' which itself 'generates new meaning'.[144] *Marys Seacole* focuses on what its biographical subject *means*, particularly for women of colour, rather than what she did ('*Look her the fuck up*'). It's about the tension between how a woman of colour sought to represent herself and how others might then insist, and persist, in representing her. Drury's Seacole specifies that 'I am, not to be prideful, the most impressive woman you have ever encountered' and 'I give power to myself'.[145]

Repetition/Reproduction

The fascination of Drury's play is not primarily narrative but situational: we are invited to witness a scenario, and assess what is happening, what the characters see and don't see about the roles that they assign to others and to themselves. It is entirely distinct from the model of biodrama that behaves as if it must follow the historical playbook no matter what. *Marys Seacole* is also situated in a tradition of plays by African American writers that reconfigure history in formally challenging ways. In her book *The African American Theatrical Body*, Soyica Diggs Colbert argues that a characteristic of African American drama is what she calls 'repetition/reproduction',

[143] Grochala, *The Contemporary Political Play*, 165.
[144] Ibid., 169.
[145] Drury, 124, 127.

building on Suzan-Lori Parks' formulation of 'rep and rev'. For Colbert, repetition/reproduction 'creates a structure by which the repetition of performances may find fitting space to reproduce a scene and rework that scene's history'.[146] Such a move 'gives black dramatists and audiences an opportunity to redo the past', or to return to 'the scenes of crimes to interrupt historical processes used to render black people objects'.[147] Colbert works through this idea with regard to Parks's *The America Play* (1994), where an Abraham Lincoln impersonator digs a hole which is an exact replica of the Great Hole of History, and is repeatedly interrupted by paying customers who want to play John Wilkes Booth and assassinate Lincoln. The play is full of copies and replicas (cut-outs, busts and relics) and is both static and full of restless movement (the original Hole of History theme park was 'back East' but the Lesser Known Lincoln is digging a copy Out West). Colbert connects repetition/reproduction to an idea of movement: 'the repetition/reproduction dyad – always in motion – resists oppression'.[148] This theory and tradition seems applicable to *Marys Seacole*, both in the repetition – the iteration – of multiple versions of a character, and the restless movement across continents that characterizes Seacole and the play's modern migrant and diasporic nurses.

As a biodrama, we might also connect *Marys Seacole* to Parks's *Venus*, first staged at the Joseph Papp Public Theatre, New York, in 1996.[149] As Deborah R. Geis summarizes it, *Venus* 'presents a surrealistic

[146] Soyica Diggs Colbert, *The African American Theatrical Body: Reception, Performance, and the Stage* (Cambridge: Cambridge University Press, 2011), 13. doi:10.1017/CBO9781139027243

[147] Ibid., 14, 10. Beth Palmer has also discussed *Marys Seacole* in connection with Colbert's work (Beth Palmer, 'Nineteenth-Century Women's Lives on the Contemporary Stage', Keynote address, University of Valencia, 2022, 9:23. Available online: https://www.youtube.com/watch?v=AxcnmkkBn6A (accessed 9 October 2023)).

[148] Colbert, *The African American Theatrical Body*, 39.

[149] The play remains unproduced in the UK, although Parks's works *White Noise* (Bridge Theatre, London, 2021), *Father Comes Home from the Wars Parts I, II and III* (Royal Court, London, 2016), *In the Blood* (Finborough, London, 2010), and the Pulitzer Prize-winning *Topdog/Underdog* (Citizens', Glasgow, 2009 and Royal Court, London, 2003) have all been staged.

portrait of the historical Venus Hottentot, a Khoikhoi woman named Saartjie Baartman. In Parks's version, we see the consequences of "Venus's" exploitation, first by a sideshow director named the Mother Showman and then by the Baron Docteur who claims to love her but ultimately dissects her to advance his medical career.[150] Heidi J. Holder encapsulates the play's dramaturgy thus: 'Resisting the temptation to be drawn towards synthesis and closure, the dramatist startlingly foregrounds basic elements of structure such as the act of numbering, and then displays the process of building and taking apart narrative. In Parks's history plays, the process is the story.'[151]

We can see this idea of foregrounding process taken a stage further by Drury. In Nadia Latif's production of *Marys Seacole* at the Donmar, characters and set were constantly undressed and redressed to create precisely the anachronistic mix for each stage picture to make it impossible to forget that the history on display was mutable, in motion, Marys echoing through time. My favourite item was a 2D shrub, wheeled on during the scenes set in Jamaica, rendered in the style of a Victorian picture book illustration but mounted on the kind of metal frame used to transport a saline drip in a modern hospital: a beautifully rendered piece of authentic fake theatrical scenery. As the consternation of the critics indicates, *Marys Seacole* refuses to do the educational work of the conventional biodramas of English theatre; indeed, its form rather implies that to do so would be just another instance of (predominantly) White audiences expecting a woman of colour to 'take care' of them, by spoon-feeding the pabulum of an informative 'Great Woman' historical narrative.[152]

[150] Deborah R. Geiss, *Suzan-Lori Parks* (Ann Arbor: University of Michigan Press, 2008), 75–6.

[151] Heidi J. Holder, 'Strange Legacy: The History Plays of Suzan-Lori Parks', in *Suzan-Lori Parks: A Casebook*, ed. Kevin J. Wetmore Jr and Alycia Smith-Howard (New York: Routledge, 2007), 28.

[152] Despite the plural *Marys* of the title, reviewers of the recent UK premiere of the play at the Donmar affected to be mystified by its failure to educate them and to act as a 'fitting tribute' to Seacole – a kind of 'tone policing' for the dramaturgy of biodramas. Arifa Akbar in the *Guardian*, for example, professed to find the play 'mystifying', and complained that

Conclusion

In a video to publicize *Marys Seacole* at the Donmar, director Nadia Latif talks with Jackie Sibblies Drury. She asks, 'How difficult is it to stage a biographical play?' to which Drury replies,

> It's the blessing and the curse, right? … You're sort of dealing with someone's anticipation of what the play is going to be or what it should be or what it should be saying about this person … But then the exciting thing is to get to disrupt that in some way … I'm sure that there are going to be some people that are going to come to the show wanting it to be like *A Man For All Seasons* but Mary Seacole, you know? … wanting to have them sort of celebrated in a way that you've seen other sort of historical characters celebrated.[153]

'the figure of Mary Seacole is a vehicle used to explore our current-day issues too nakedly rather than a study of a singular life and its forgotten achievements' (Arifa Akhbar, 'Marys Seacole Review: Mystifying Drama about Caring Through the Ages', review of *Marys Seacole* by Jackie Sibblies Drury, directed by Nadia Latif, at Donmar Warehouse, *The Guardian*, 2 April 2022. Available online: https://www.theguardian.com/stage/2022/apr/22/marys-seacole-review-donmar-warehouse-london (accessed 21 March 2023)). In a similar vein, Andrzej Lukowski complains of the lack of 'a clear point' and says the play is 'headspinning' and 'starts to bounce around madly', becoming 'messy and diffuse' (Andrzej Lukowski, review of *Marys Seacole* by Jackie Sibblies Drury, directed by Nadia Latif, at Donmar Warehouse, *Time Out*, 22 April 2022. Available online: https://www.timeout.com/london/theatre/marys-seacole-review (accessed 21 March 2023)). Finally, Lizzie Akita in the *Standard* comments ruefully, 'It's such a shame that Mary Seacole's little-known story competes for attention in Jackie Sibblies Drury's muddled time-travelling drama' and concludes, 'Seacole's story probably deserved greater care and respect than this haphazard dramatisation' (Lizzie Akita, 'Marys Seacole review: Muddled Drama Takes Too Long to Make Its Point', review of *Marys Seacole* by Jackie Sibblies Drury, directed by Nadia Latif, at Donmar Warehouse, *Time Out*, 22 April 2022. Available online: https://www.standard.co.uk/culture/theatre/marys-seacole-review-donmar-warehouse-jackie-sibblies-drury-b995683.html (accessed 21 March 2023)). Akita is seemingly unaware of Seacole's resurgent posthumous fame. Examples of this renown include the statue of Seacole outside St Thomas's Hospital in London, the 2005 reprinting in Penguin Classics of *The Adventures of Mrs Seacole in Many Lands*, Jane Robinson's 2005 revisionist biography and Helen Rappaport's biography published earlier in 2022, her presence on the Key Stage 2 National Curriculum in England and Wales, her appearance as a historical character in a 2021 episode of *Doctor Who* ('War of the Sontarans') and her presence in countless children's history books.

[153] Donmar Warehouse, 'How to Stage a Biographical Play', YouTube. Available online: https://www.youtube.com/watch?v=qNX74dAkml8 (accessed 12 June 2022).

Drury adds that part of the challenge for Latif is dealing with Seacole's iconic image in the UK: 'her face, her hair, the statues that are around town'.[154]

This chapter has shown how many possibilities – and combinations of these possibilities – are available to playwrights when working with biographical material; the distance travelled from Bolt's *A Man for All Seasons* and the playwriting equivalent of commemorative portrait statues. The chapter has worked through examples of recuperative biodramas that set out to reassess reputations or to rewrite lost lives into history (*Red Ellen*; *I, Joan*). It has explored the implications of combining this approach with a fragmented biographical subject, as in *Emilia*. It has examined dual biodramas in which the biographical subject is multiplied and vies for control of the narrative and its enactment, as in *Handbagged* and *The Father and the Assassin*. Finally, the chapter has proposed iteration as a powerful way of making connections beyond the model of the historical-realist individual. Ultimately, it has argued for a more 'liquid' form of biodrama that, like *Marys Seacole*, emphasizes simultaneity and transhistorical connection rather than linear narrative: in effect, following the dramaturgy of the situation rather than dramatizing the life. It is in this sense of a live engagement with historical legacies that I have highlighted the value of 'encounter'. No form of historical drama can offer unmediated access to the past, but theatrical biodrama can be live in a way that screen biopics cannot. *Marys Seacole* also speaks, I believe, to Maurya Wickstrom's call, quoted earlier, for 'less formulaic and predictable means by which to explore what happens when history is initiated, not finished'. Drury's play is a series of initiations, even if the results seldom change: '*And then the comforters build up the strength to comfort again*', as the stage directions say of the final tableau where the three women of colour go to the three White women, '*to pet* [them] *and whisper sweet names in* [their] *ear*'.[155] Seacole's

---

154 Ibid.
155 Drury, *Marys Seacole*, 128.

insistence in the play's final moments that 'Me give power to myself', her return feeling like '*a goddess landing on a temple*' is an initiation, an incantation, that resonates through time.[156]

Of course, *Mary Seacole*'s iterative dramaturgy, if adapted across every new biographical play, would become a new orthodoxy; the pertinent qualities of each historical life ought to generate each play's specific form. As a final, related example of new possibilities for biodrama, I want to refer briefly to *Curious*, Jasmine Lee-Jones's solo show that was performed at Soho Theatre in 2021. Lee-Jones plays Jaz, a nineteen-year-old drama school student who feels alienated from the Restoration play that she is meant to be rehearsing. Jaz follows a trail of evidence, from a detail in a Hogarth print to a rare pamphlet in the Black Cultural Archives, and uncovers the story of an eighteenth-century actress, Celia Edlyne. Brought to England as a slave from Nigeria, Edlyne became a professional actress and played Othello, but was captured and executed as a runaway when she lost the protection of her lover, Duchess Blythe Whitmore. At the play's end Jaz tells the audience that

> Celia Edlyne's made up.
> 'Cos when I went to look and see
> There was next to nothing
> No one
> No one like me.[157]

The play's journey of discovery is revealed as an exercise in wish fulfilment, that Jaz eventually lets go of as her disillusionments with a prospective boyfriend ('The Fakedeep'), her best friend Mon and with drama school all progressively mount. In sculptural terms, it's the equivalent of erecting a commemorative statue for a ground-breaking queer, Black actress who didn't exist, in order to provoke discussion of the icons and inspirations that are missing from the historical record. In theatrical terms, it can be read as a nod to those actors of colour

---

[156] Ibid., 126–7.
[157] Jasmine Lee-Jones, *Curious* (London: Methuen Drama, 2021), 101.

who *have* been able to find a professional forbear to celebrate on stage, be it Aldridge, Sancho or Baker.

Like Drury's Marys rippling across time, Lee-Jones's theatrical coup can really only be pulled off once without becoming a new convention. However, equipped with the tools of fragmentation, duplication, competition and iteration, biodrama has the potential to further reinvent itself as a live, flexible artform; something more malleable than the stone and metal statues that stand, stiff in their legends, occupying public spaces. One of the ways in which this is happening is in history plays that are not primarily biodramas, but which contain some biographical elements. For example, *The Seven Acts of Mercy* by Anders Lustgarten (2016), discussed in Chapter 4, is a biodrama about Caravaggio interwoven with a story of estranged family in modern-day Merseyside. Similarly, Winsome Pinnock's *Rockets and Blue Lights* (2020), with its multiple metatheatrical layers revealing untold stories of freed Black Britons being re-enslaved in the 1840s, includes the painter J. M. W. Turner as one of its characters, both as a historical figure and as a character in a film-within-the-play. Before turning to these hybrid plays with multiple timelines, Chapter 3 first considers the fictional family as a focus of historical drama, enabling the history play's temporal reach to extend beyond the single lifespan of the biodrama.

3

The Intergenerational History Play

Introduction

This chapter analyses and compares four plays that are each set across multiple decades of the twentieth and twenty-first centuries: *Harvest* by Richard Bean (2005), *An Adventure* by Vinay Patel (2018), *Wife* by Samuel Adamson (2019) and *The House of Shades* by Beth Steel (2022). As I explained in the Introduction and Chapter 1, many contemporary history plays have a liquid relationship with time, and habitually make leaps between different periods. This chapter focuses on a type of theatre that traces the fortunes of one family group across successive generations: the intergenerational history play. This family group may be genetically related, or in some cases 'chosen' family. As I will demonstrate, this mode of historical playwriting has most often been used in English theatre to trace a pattern of national decline, where the fictional members of the family stand in for the nation. What is remarkable about this configuration, I argue, is the longevity of the particular playwriting formula, which can be traced back at least as far as Noël Coward's *Cavalcade* in 1931. Consequently, I will propose, it is a dramaturgy that is often constrained by a conservative, nostalgic outlook in its choices of period, and in the connections that it makes between past and present.

The four contemporary plays examined in this chapter each attempt to escape this structure of feeling using different dramaturgical strategies. *Harvest*, the earliest contemporary history play that this book considers, focuses on a farming family and uses grotesque comedy to capture a mood of resentment and despair at the beginning of the twenty-first century. Despite its surface differences, I argue that *Harvest* has more in common with Coward, and with the late Victorian dramaturgy of Shaw, than it might appear. *An Adventure* has been chosen for its success in subverting the convention of the intergenerational drama as national narrative, and in finding a more liquid dramaturgical form to reflect this. *Wife* is an example of escaping the strictures of the intergenerational history play by queering time and heteronormative family structures, and by having each historical encounter take place against the backdrop of a different imaginary production of Henrik Ibsen's *A Doll's House*. Lastly, in *The House of Shades* the 'hauntological melancholia' of the twenty-first century is made manifest by a family history saturated with ghosts, that bend our understanding of social reality.

In my first book, *Heritage, Nostalgia and Modern British Theatre*, I wrote of a cultural change in the UK that got underway in the 1970s, as the derisive attitude towards the long nineteenth century that had been prominent in the counterculture of the 1960s gave way to an era that was 'more sincerely interested' in the Victorians and Edwardians.[1] In a decade of political shocks and social unrest, amid the identity crises brought on by post-imperial decline, 1970s theatre and television audiences looked to stories that evoked the textures of everyday life in the 'knowable communities' of the past, be it the street life of the Victorian terrace or the fields of rural England. I argued that these dramas were 'part of an important coming-to-terms with modernity'.[2] In the twenty-first century, an age of accelerated democratic, economic, technological and environmental instability, this impulse seems as strong as ever in English theatres, as contemporary history plays attempt to show, or to ask, 'how did we get here?'.

As I have noted elsewhere,[3] it has become commonplace to see the English nation as a family, following George Orwell's formulation in 'The Lion and the Unicorn': 'a rather stuffy, Victorian family … with all

---

[1]　Poore, *Heritage*, 45.
[2]　Poore, *Heritage*, 43.
[3]　Poore, *Heritage*, 16.

its cupboards bursting with skeletons ... there is a deep conspiracy of silence about the source of the family income ... Still, it is a family ... A family with the wrong members in control'.[4] Orwell's description here expresses its ideas through theatrical modes. The stuffy Victorian family with the wrong members in control recalls the tyrannical 'heavy fathers' of Victorian melodrama. Cupboards bursting with skeletons suggest the Ibsenite family drama, or the Wildean society comedy, which hinge on the keeping or disclosure of family secrets. And the deep conspiracy of silence about the family income – as well as being a clear reference to Empire – sounds a lot like the plot of an early Bernard Shaw comedy (*Widowers' Houses* (1892) *or Mrs Warren's Profession* (1893)) or like *The Voysey Inheritance* (1905) by Shaw's associate Granville Barker. Shaw's later 'tragicomedy' *Heartbreak House* (1916) rests on the complex metaphor of England as a house as well as a ship.[5] Jerome de Groot also notices this strategic conflation in historical drama between England, the family and the family home: 'The house, which in the costume drama is representative of stability, and Englishness that abides [is] a structure articulating a particular identity'.[6] We might think here of the London Weekend Television series, *Upstairs, Downstairs*, which ran from 1971 to 1975, and which covered social and political changes from 1903 to 1930 as they affected the Bellamy family, and of Julian Fellowes's series *Downton Abbey* (2010–15) which was an international success for ITV, and which depicted the Crawley family's Yorkshire estate. The series covered the historical period from 1912 to 1926; two spin-off films, *Downton Abbey* (2019) and *Downton Abbey: A New Era* (2022) took the story up to 1928. *Upstairs, Downstairs* was later revived by the BBC (2010–12) as a rival to *Downton Abbey*.[7]

---

[4] George Orwell, 'The Lion and the Unicorn', in *The Penguin Essays of George Orwell* (Harmondsworth: Penguin, 1984 [1941]), 6.

[5] Niall W. Slater, '*Nostoi* and Nostalgia in *Heartbreak House*', SHAW: *The Journal of Bernard Shaw Studies* 37, no. 1 (2017): 12–14. Available online muse.jhu.edu/article/661062.

[6] De Groot, *Remaking History*, 67.

[7] *The Forsyte Saga*, which was first broadcast on BBC television between 1967 and 1969, was another series covering the early years of the twentieth century (1906–21), based on the books by John Galsworthy. It, too, was revived for twenty-first century audiences by ITV in 2002–3.

Both of these TV series illustrate the popular conceit of making a single family, in a single house (or stately home) emblematic of the nation. The need to look back, now usually from a distance of almost exactly a century, on a version of the *roman national*[8] – a foundational myth that the nation tells itself about itself – continued unabated into the 2010s and 2020s.[9] Most of the dramatic focus is on the early and middle years of the last century, and even at this chronological remove, the shock of the transition from the 'long, hot Edwardian summer' to the horrors of the trenches and then the dissipation of the Roaring Twenties is a trope that never seems to get old. Of course, the choice of family in these stories – always White, usually upper or upper-middle class on TV; usually White, usually working class, on stage – says a great deal about how 'England' and English identity is conceived and perpetuated, about who is felt to 'belong' and who is assumed to be an outsider or a threat. Patrick Wright, writing in 1985, ruminated on 'the vague idea of "Deep England"', in which 'a sense of external threat has played a crucial part'.[10] The 'house and family' metaphor of Englishness plays heavily on ideas of an inherited, inalienable 'birthright' which the social and political changes of modernity are always threatening to limit or destroy.

The Intergenerational History Play in the Twentieth Century

In order to better understand the intergenerational history play as a conservative, nostalgic form, it is useful to consider how playwrights have used the 'nation as family' trope in earlier times. The idea of history as a 'parade' of monarchs, battles and events can be linked

---

[8] For Andress, the *roman national* is a more emphatic version of the French term *récit national* (Andress, *Cultural Dementia*, 1497).

[9] See Poore, *Heritage*, 41–5 for examples of a similar pattern in the 1970s.

[10] Patrick Wright, *On Living in an Old Country* (Oxford: Oxford University Press, 2009 [1985]), 81.

to the pageants of medieval Europe, which performed the history of the world as they understood it, from Genesis to Apocalypse. This in turn evokes Wickstrom's idea of 'processional history', as discussed in the Introduction, an 'unalterable flow' that 'motors us along the path of serial succession.'[11] Equally, the 'chronicle play' is understood as a type of history play popular in the 1590s, based on the revised 1587 edition of Raphael Holinshed's *Chronicles*. Among this group are usually included Marlowe's *Edward II* (1592) and the three parts of Shakespeare's *Henry VI* (c. 1590–2).[12] Here, the historical content is treated as another fixed framework of succession, and scenes from the lives of these historical figures were acts of both narration and nation-building. Certainly, nineteenth-century patriotic and imperial drama also used pageantry to reinforce ideas of national unity and racial hierarchy (as parodied, for example, in Gilbert and Sullivan's 'For He Is an Englishman' from *HMS Pinafore*). But Noël Coward's *Cavalcade* was one of the first theatrical productions to historicize itself so thoroughly, setting out the story of a well-to-do family, the Marryots of Mayfair, as they navigate the first three decades of the twentieth century, and dating each incident precisely. The production was an enormous commercial success. Despite costing 'an almost unprecedented thirty thousand pre-war pounds' to produce, it ran at Drury Lane for over a year and made 'well over three hundred thousand pounds' at the box office.[13]

The Marryots live through the Boer War, Queen Victoria's death, the coming of the aeroplane, the sinking of the *Titanic*, the First World War and the accelerating pace of life in the 1920s. The play concludes with the Marryots, elderly now, toasting the arrival of 1930 with their friend Margaret: 'Now, then, let's couple the Future of England to the past of

[11] Wickstrom, *Fiery Temporalities*, 19.
[12] Chris Baldick, 'chronicle play', in *The Oxford Dictionary of Literary Terms* (Oxford: Oxford University Press, 2015). Available online: https://www-oxfordreference-com.libproxy.york.ac.uk/view/10.1093/acref/9780198715443.001.0001/acref-9780198715443-e-201.
[13] Sheridan Morley, 'Introduction', in *Noël Coward: Collected Plays Three* (London: Methuen Drama, 1994), xii. It is perhaps fitting that, according to Morley, the writers of *Upstairs, Downstairs* named the main characters after their equivalents in Coward's *Cavalcade* (Morley, 'Introduction', xii).

England … Let's drink to our sons who made part of the pattern and our hearts that died with them … and let's drink to the hope that one day this country of ours, which we love so much, will find dignity and greatness and peace again.'[14] Coward's curtain speech on the first night complemented this sentiment: 'I hope this play has made you feel that, in spite of the troublous times we are living in, it is still pretty exciting to be English.'[15] Extravaganzas like *Cavalcade*, with their large-scale production numbers, are clearly not 'historical realism' in the sense intended by Berninger (see Chapter 1), but they do use real historical events as their framework: they rely on a stable, narrativized sense of 'the real' even as they portray the modern world as a nightmarish chaos and embrace a spiritualized conception of national identity.

Coward navigated another journey through recent history with the much more Naturalistic family drama *This Happy Breed*, which premiered in 1942. It traces the lives of a working-class London family, the Gibbons, from 1919 to 1939; Frank Gibbons and Bob Mitchell knew each other from their wartime service, and the Mitchells and the Gibbons find themselves as next-door neighbours after demobilization. We see the children of the two families grow up and develop ambitions and romantic attachments; at one point the youngest Gibbons child, Reg, falls in with a young communist, Sam Leadbitter. When Reg is involved in street disturbances during the 1926 General Strike, Frank insists, 'We don't like doing things quickly in this country … We're used to planting things and watching them grow',[16] and later explains sternly that after the war, 'The country suddenly got tired … But the old lady's got stamina … and it's up to us ordinary people to keep things steady.'[17] Both Sam and Reg are shown to grow out of their youthful convictions

---

[14] Coward, *Plays Three*, 155. This is said at a time when the British Empire – the largest that the world has known – was near its zenith, and the only wars that were being fought were against the liberation movements of Indigenous populations. It remains unclear what kind of 'greatness' would satisfy Jane in this moment, determined as she is to see England as some oppressed or occupied nation.

[15] Quoted in Oliver Soden, *Masquerade: The Lives of Noël Coward* (London: Weidenfeld and Nicolson, 2023), 249.

[16] Noël Coward, *This Happy Breed*, in *Noël Coward: Collected Plays Four* (London: Methuen Drama, 1999), 280.

[17] Ibid., 298.

to become contented workers and 'family men'. J. B. Priestley's *Time and the Conways* (1937), although usually considered a 'time play' rather than a history play, uses a similar timespan to follow the decline of a middle-class, land-owning family from 1919 to 1937. Rather than follow a linear timeline, it begins on the twenty-first birthday of Kay Conway in 1919, with the second act leaping forwards to 1937 to view the family's disappointments and impoverishment (both economic and emotional), and the third act returning us to 1919 in the knowledge that Kay will die young and that the Conways will never be quite the same. Like *This Happy Breed*, the play features a young left-wing radical, Madge, who in this case becomes a schoolteacher and reminisces bitterly in 1937 about 'When I still thought that we could suddenly make everything better for everybody. Socialism! Peace! Universal Brotherhood! All that.'[18] *Time and the Conways* concludes with the motifs of time travel, premonitions and alternative timelines, in conversations between Kay and her 'queer' intellectual brother, Alan.[19] Nevertheless, the play also uses history as a framework, with the hopefulness of the post-Armistice period and the gloom and cynicism of the late 1930s in England mirroring the family narrative.

If Coward and Priestley in these examples presented the passage of time in the intergenerational history play as an opportunity for bittersweet reflection and yearning for what might have been, Arnold Wesker added more overt political content to the pattern. Wesker's trilogy of plays, staged between 1958 and 1960, concerns a Jewish family from the East End of London, the Kahns, who are committed to communism. The first of what is known as 'the Wesker Trilogy', *Chicken Soup with Barley* (1958), spans the years 1936 to 1956. The second play, *Roots*, is set in 1959, the year that it was staged; the third, *I'm Talking About Jerusalem* (1960) has two acts which unfold over thirteen years, from 1946 to 1959. The trilogy thus encompasses two intergenerational history plays, and a middle play that takes place in real-time in the

---

18 J. B. Priestley, *Time and the Conways, and Other Plays* (London: Penguin, 1969 [1937]), 173–4.
19 Ibid., 159, 194–7.

historical present. *Chicken Soup with Barley*, therefore, has the most expansive historical canvas; the Kahns, powered by matriarch Sarah, are shown in Act 1 taking part in the Battle of Cable Street, when Oswald Mosley's Blackshirts attempted a provocative march through Jewish neighbourhoods, protected by mounted police, but were forced to turn back by local residents and activists taking to the streets. In Act 2, set just after the Second World War, Sarah's feckless husband Harry's health fails, and in Act 3, with Soviet tanks arriving to suppress the Hungarian Uprising of 1956, Sarah and Harry's son Ronnie argues with Sarah, who clings to her faith in communism despite the brutal, repressive behaviour of the USSR.

While *Cavalcade* and *This Happy Breed* might seem polar opposites to *Chicken Soup with Barley*, it is really only the royalty – and flag-worship – that has changed; the same note of melancholy and loss, in the face of the unmooring progress of modernity, is present to different degrees. At the end of *Chicken Soup*, Ronnie asks, 'What's happened to us? Were we cheated or did we cheat ourselves?', but as Katharine Worth remarks, '[t]he question is put by Ronnie but it could have been asked by almost any character in the melancholy, time-haunted drama of the English realists'.[20] However, it can equally be said that the loss of faith in the socialist future is brought about in Wesker by historical events, such as the suppression of the Hungarian Uprising, or the revelations about the Communists' treatment of Jewish volunteers in the Spanish Civil War. The jingoism of Coward's twentieth-century histories, conversely, is much more the *roman national*, a belief in a mystical idea of nation that cannot be punctured by actual events.[21]

---

[20] Katharine Worth, *Revolutions in Modern English Drama* (London: Bell, 1973), 34.

[21] At the end of *Cavalcade*, the scene suddenly cuts to darkness and silence, 'and away at the back glows a Union Jack' as the entire company sings 'God Save the King' and 'the Union Jack flies over their heads' (Coward, *Plays Three*, 157). Here, the Union Jack – which is associated exclusively with England in the play – acquires a mystical, quasi-religious ability to calm and unite, the timeless antidote to the chaos and profligacy of modernity. National identity, that is, a Britishness that does not acknowledge Scotland, Northern Ireland or Wales, still less the Empire on which its prosperity rests, is asserted with an apparently desperate intensity and earnestness.

Despite its familiarity from Priestley and Coward's commercial successes, Wesker notes that *Chicken Soup* was regarded by the Royal Court as a challenging play to stage because of its time scheme: 'such a difficult play spanning twenty years of contemporary history'.[22] However, this two-decade vantage point was to become the standard in epic political dramas of the decades that followed. David Hare used the time span of 1943–62 in *Plenty* (1978) and Peter Flannery's *Our Friends in the North* (1982) used the slightly shorter period from the election of Harold Wilson in 1964 to that of Margaret Thatcher in 1979. By contrast, as this chapter will explore, intergenerational history plays of the twenty-first century often use a much longer historical sweep. David Greig's *Victoria*, set in rural Scotland but commissioned by the RSC and staged at the Barbican in 2000, covers three generations and sixty years, beginning with friends talking about joining the International Brigades in the Spanish Civil War. *Harvest*, *The House of Shades*, *An Adventure* and *Wife* – along with *Oil* by Ella Hickson (2016), mentioned in the Introduction – all cover between sixty and 160 years of historical change and use various strategies to manage their cast of characters and their manipulation of time. Sometimes characters are 'Orlandified' – given fantastically long lifespans, as discussed in Chapter 1 – sometimes the drama spans three generations in linear time, and sometimes the protagonists interact with ghosts or transhistorical figures.

Intergenerational Plays Today

The four examples from the present century that are the focus of this chapter are not the only instances of family history plays that are centred on a particular house and that examine social progress and intergenerational tensions. The adaptation of Andrea Levy's novel *Small Island* for the National Theatre in London in 2019, for example, functions as an expanded retelling of the mid-century years, centred

---

[22] Wesker, 'Introduction', in *Plays 1*, xv.

on the national-origin myth of the Second World War,[23] and this time belatedly including the wartime contributions of soldiers – and the peacetime contributions of workers – from the British Empire. Archie Maddocks's *A Place for We* (2021), which premiered at Park Theatre, London, in a co-production with Talawa Theatre, updates and develops this narrative strand on immigration from the Caribbean, being set in 'one building in Brixton, beginning in 1971 and spanning up until 2021'.[24] Alexandra Wood's *The Tyler Sisters* (2019) at Hampstead Theatre has one scene set in every year between 1990 and 2030. The production's set and period details were kept to a minimum, a 1990s television mounted in the corner counting off the years, and the political changes of that recent past, and putative future, kept deliberately hazy. Oladipo Agboluaje's *Here's What She Said to Me* was produced at Sheffield Theatres in 2020, and then toured England in 2022; it is the story of 'three generations of proud African women connecting with each other across two continents, across time and space' between the late 1960s and the present day.[25] As this description suggests, the Utopia Theatre production was notably more fluid than the four plays examined in the latter part of this chapter, but social and political context was more lightly sketched in. Alana Valentine's *The Sugar House* is set in the Pyrmont district of Sydney, Australia and was produced at Finborough Theatre in 2021; events take place between the 1950s and the present, and it likewise focuses on 'three generations of remarkable women' and processes of social change and gentrification.[26] Tena Štivičić's *3 Winters*, at the National Theatre in London in 2014, is an intergenerational history play set in Zagreb, Croatia, with scenes taking pace in 1945, 1990 and

[23] See Paul Gilroy, *After Empire: Melancholia or Convivial Culture?* (Abingdon: Routledge, 2004), 127.

[24] Archie Maddocks, *A Place for We* (London: Samuel French, 2021), no pagination.

[25] *Here's What She Said to Me* Utopia Theatre (marketing pack). Available online: https://www.utopiatheatre.co.uk/wp-content/uploads/2022/08/HWSSTM-Marketing-Pack.pdf (accessed 22 December 2022).

[26] 'The Sugar House by Alana Valentine', Finborough Theatre. Available online: https://finboroughtheatre.co.uk/production/the-sugar-house/ (accessed 30 October 2021). The 'sugar house' of the title is the refinery where Narelle's father had worked, which is now being converted into expensive apartments.

2011. Tom Stoppard's *Leopoldstadt* (2020) clearly also belongs to this pattern of playwriting; in addition, it is a diasporic story of migration to Britain and the United States. The family drama begins in 1899 and ends in 1955 in Vienna, taking in the collapse of the Austro-Hungarian Empire, the *Anschluss* and the Holocaust, positioning its scenes (1899, 1900, 1924, 1938, 1955) around, but not directly in, the specific horrors of the war years. *Standing at the Sky's Edge*, a collaboration between Chris Bush and composer and lyricist Richard Hawley, was first performed at the Sheffield Crucible in 2019, and has since been revived at Sheffield and transferred to London's National Theatre.[27] It used the three-generation storyline formula (one beginning in 1960, one in 1989 and one in 2015) to tell the story of Sheffield's Park Hill estate, and, by extension, 'the story of post-war Britain in microcosm', according to Bush.[28] The action centres on one flat and characters' lives overlap, both in the narrative – for example, when steelworker's son Jimmy from the first timeline and Liberian refugee Joy from the second timeline, fall in love – and in the staging, as simultaneous scenes take place in different periods.

As can be seen from the correspondences noted above, there is scope for many more comparisons between intergenerational plays on the basis of historical span, the perspectives of women's experience over the generations, or migration narratives. Notably, theatre from the United States seems to have few of these family-as-nation plays, with Norris's *Clybourne Park* – discussed in Chapter 4 – one of the only recent examples, and one that explicitly acknowledges that experiences of living in the USA since the 1950s have been radically different for African American citizens compared to White ones. What I have sought to do in with the examples that follow is to draw explicitly on that tradition of Coward, Priestley and Wesker, to see how ideas of England

---

[27] At the time of writing, *Standing at the Sky's Edge* is also due to transfer to the West End, underlining the mainstream appeal of this form of intergenerational drama. The focus on high-rise post-war housing also harks back to Flannery's *Our Friends in the North*, mentioned above.

[28] Chris Bush, 'Introduction', in *Standing at the Sky's Edge* by Chris Bush and Richard Hawley (London: Nick Hern, 2022), 7.

as 'home' have been politicized in different ways, and to what degree the dramaturgies of the family history play have been transformed in the twenty-first century.

Harvest

Richard Bean's *Harvest* opened to critical acclaim at the Royal Court in 2005, winning the Critics' Choice Award for Best New Play. Set at Kilham Wold Farm near Driffield in East Yorkshire, it traces the history of the Harrisons, a farming family and landowners since the late nineteenth century, as they face the succession of wars, recessions and economic reforms that have impacted on agriculture in the twentieth century. It begins as a narrative of the First World War: two teenage brothers, William and Albert, both want to volunteer to fight. While Albert stays to look after the farm, William enlists and loses both legs when his own army's tank runs over them. He returns to the farm to live with Albert, who has married his teenage sweetheart, Maudie. Like Ella Hickson's *Oil* a decade later, *Harvest* uses a scene featuring the plucking of a chicken to bring us into the bloody, matter-of-fact world of the farm, where animal carcasses are prepared by hand.[29] Also like *Oil* – though here not in an overtly fantastic way – *Harvest* gives its central character William a very long lifespan, in this case 109 years, so that the changes wrought by the century can be played out in a single person's experience. In the play's final scene, two intruders, Danny and Blue, find William's letter from the Queen congratulating him on his 100th birthday and assume that he is dead, as does the audience until he appears dramatically in his electric wheelchair, holding a shotgun.

In a sense, then, *Harvest* is a modern inheritor of the Wesker trilogy's structures, combining and elongating the intergenerational patterning of *Chicken Soup* with the decline of rural life and loss of hope presented in the trilogy's third play, *I'm Talking About Jerusalem*. In another sense, however, the longevity of William, and Laura – his niece who

[29] Bean, *Harvest*, 24–5.

came to work on the farm during the Second World War – means that
the play is not really about multiple generations of a family through
time, but the problem of *not* producing a new generation to inherit
the farm. The backstory is that William and Albert's grandfather won
the land in a bet with the local squire.[30] After the First World War,
Albert and Maudie are unable to conceive: 'Fastest way of losing this
land is having no-one to work it', says Albert.[31] Laura and a local Nazi
prisoner-of-war, Stefan, move in and have a son, Alan, but he has no
interest in the farm and moves abroad; the play also mentions four
offstage daughters, each of whom has apparently 'upped and offed to
university and become so bloody full of themselves that I never see
them', according to Laura.[32] For a while in the 1970s and 1980s, a live-
in 'pig man' called Titch becomes like a surrogate son to Stefan and
Laura, but he (rather incongruously) hangs himself between the 1995
and 2005 scenes, having threatened to do so previously after taking
umbrage at the vet's report on the pigs.[33] In the last Act, the burglar
Blue is cornered by William and Laura and made to promise, at
gunpoint, that he will be their new pig man, the implication being that
this is a job that no one in the twenty-first century would do, especially
'with a song in yer heart', unless they had a shotgun trained on them.[34]
In common with *Oil*, the final scene is played for laughs, focusing on
bodily infirmity, sexual violence and cartoonish characters, such as the
insufferable solicitor Lewis, a vision of Wesker's Ronnie Kahn as the
middle-aged bore he may have turned into.

Critics at the time noted *Harvest*'s 'epic' aspirations, with the word
used in seven of the reviews collected in *Theatre Record*. John Nathan
succinctly summarizes the appeal and promise of this kind of history

---

[30] Ibid., 49–51.
[31] Ibid., 48.
[32] Ibid., 90.
[33] Ibid., 98. We are left to assume that Titch perhaps 'cried wolf' once too often and
accidentally hung himself, but the effect is rather jarring given his cheery refusal to hold
onto any offence or bad opinion for more than a few seconds. As with other elements
of the play's construction, we might suspect that Titch has to be 'killed off', because
otherwise the crisis of family renewal in the final scene would not be sufficiently acute.
[34] Ibid., 117.

play: 'Bean's considerable achievement is in giving each of his play's seven periods the sense of a distinct era. Each jump in time sees a new threat to the farm and a new source of salvation ... The play's poignancy lies in applying the time-lapse techniques we are used to seeing in natural history programmes to human lives.'[35] Nevertheless, the epic elements of the play raise several problems of plausibility, even if we accept its farcical, Rabelaisian representation of history. The prehistory of Grandad Harrison winning a bet offers a handy explanation for two working-class brothers having their own farm in 1914, although (as Benedict Nightingale notes in his review),[36] the blurb on the published play script provides details of this event that the play itself never does, suggesting that, as Sheridan Morley observes, Bean 'has more material than he can handle'.[37] Michael Coveney, too, points to some of the play's dramaturgical shortcomings when he opines that 'Bean doesn't really do texture, he assembles a play by accumulation.'[38] The play might have demonstrated, through its dramaturgy, that the ruling class will always recoup their losses in the long run, and that the Harrisons' ownership of the farm was a historical blip sustained by the twentieth century's limited political experiments with social democracy. However, *Harvest* is more specifically political than historical, for all its leaping between the decades. As Nicholas de Jongh argues, *Harvest* begins as 'a promising social-realist drama ... The Harrisons are shown struggling to survive in the twentieth century, to resist the intrusive forces of government

[35] John Nathan, review of *Harvest* by Richard Bean, directed by Wilson Milam, Royal Court Theatre, London, *Jewish Chronicle*, 16 September 2005, reproduced in *Theatre Record* 25, no. 9 (2005): 1127.

[36] Benedict Nightingale, review of *Harvest* by Richard Bean, directed by Wilson Milam, Royal Court Theatre, London, *The Times*, 10 September 2005, reproduced in *Theatre Record* 25, no. 9 (2005): 1123.

[37] Sheridan Morley, review of *Harvest* by Richard Bean, directed by Wilson Milam, Royal Court Theatre, London, *Daily Express*, 9 September 2005, reproduced in *Theatre Record* 25, no. 9 (2005): 1126.

[38] Michael Coveney, review of *Harvest* by Richard Bean, directed by Wilson Milam, Royal Court Theatre, London, *The Independent*, 12 September 2005, reproduced in *Theatre Record* 25, no. 9 (2005): 1125.

and the menace of the squirearchy.'[39] Yet these 'promising themes' are abandoned by 1958, at which point Bean 'has crashed his play in the realms of farcical comedy and family melodrama'; the subsequent historical-dramatic conflicts 'all give way to the pigfarming issue'.[40]

Accordingly, political choices only come sharply into focus in the 1995 scene, titled 'Suffragette'. European Union animal welfare regulations, the power of the supermarkets, and the resultant unprofitability of livestock farming (as compared to the EU subsidies given to arable farmers) become the subject of discussion with the certifying vet, in a way that they weren't before. It is unfair to hold the history plays of the past responsible for the future history that they did not foresee; however, the place where *Harvest* comes to rest is very similar to the campaigning positions of Leave EU, Vote Leave and UKIP during the Referendum on European Union membership that took place a decade later. There is the same call to land and identity, to 'real people', the 'somewheres', as David Goodhart put it.[41] Although they do not express these sentiments, Laura and William are claimed by the play's framing as the kind of people who (in the language of the Brexit campaigns) 'want their country back'; EU farming policy is, in the play's story arc, apparently doing to them what Hitler and Kaiser together could not. Professionals' knowledge comes in for scathing mockery, particularly in the form of the insufferable, patronizing solicitor Lewis; this is a farm that has, in the words of Vote Leave campaigner Michael Gove, 'had enough of experts'. The play's reactionary tendency – simultaneously authoritarian and dismissive of laws and regulations – finds its ultimate expression in the treatment of Blue and Danny, two thugs from Hull. They break into the farmhouse, defecate in the family safe and conspire to rape Laura. The dramatic release when William '*shoots DANNY at very close range*', killing him, is an unsettling mix of comedy and the

---

[39] Nicholas de Jongh, review of *Harvest* by Richard Bean, directed by Wilson Milam, Royal Court Theatre, London, *Evening Standard*, 9 September 2005, reproduced in *Theatre Record* 25, no. 9 (2005): 1123.

[40] De Jongh, *Theatre Record*, 1123.

[41] See David Goodhart, *The Road to Somewhere: The New Tribes Shaping British Politics* (London: Penguin, 2017).

catharsis of vigilantism.[42] In 2005, when the play was staged, memories of the Tony Martin murder trial were still fresh.[43] In 1999 two burglars broke into a derelict farmhouse on Martin's land in Norfolk, as Blue and Danny do in the play; Martin shot and killed one, a 16-year-old boy, and wounded the other, a 29-year-old man. Support for authoritarian measures like the return of capital punishment were found to be linked to support for Brexit.[44] Martin claimed of the incident, 'When I walked down that staircase that fateful night I took back control of my home';[45] 'Take Back Control' was also the Vote Leave slogan in the EU Referendum campaign.[46]

It may sound paradoxical to criticize *Harvest* for its prescience about an 'ordinary, decent people' narrative that took another eleven years to erupt at the centre of British political life. But my reservations about the play are that it wants to have its cake and eat it, as the famous Johnsonite Brexit slogan had it.[47] It wants to use the gravitas of historical events to lend the play a tragic inevitability, even as it makes comic capital out of each one. A processional history made up of overdetermined moments – the long hot summer of 1914, war brewing in the 1930s, Britain's 'finest hour' and so on – is used to justify a specific, comic rage directed at criminals and the EU. Indeed, the assertion that the EU *are* criminals does not seem too far-fetched a conclusion to draw from *Harvest*. The Harrisons have been farming pigs rather than crops for half of the last

---

[42] Bean, *Harvest*, 113.

[43] Mark Shields, 'Tony Martin: Man Who Shot Burglars Knows He Still Divides Opinion', BBC. Available online: https://www.bbc.co.uk/news/uk-england-norfolk-49355814 (accessed 28 June 2022).

[44] See, for example, Eric Kaufmann, 'It's NOT the economy, Stupid: Brexit as a Story of Personal Values' (blog), *The London School of Economics and Political Science*, 7 July 2016. Available online: https://blogs.lse.ac.uk/politicsandpolicy/personal-values-brexit-vote/ (accessed 22 May 2022).

[45] Shields, 'Tony Martin.'

[46] 'Why Vote Leave', voteleavetakecontrol.org. Available online: http://www.voteleavetakecontrol.org/why_vote_leave.html (accessed 28 June 2022). The Martin case goes unmentioned in the reviews of *Harvest*, but the correspondences were sufficiently strong for me to make a note of it when I saw the play's Royal Court premiere as a postgraduate student.

[47] See Paul Dallison, 'A Brief History of Having Cake and Eating It', *Politico*, 31 August 2017. Available online: https://www.politico.eu/article/a-brief-history-of-having-cake-and-eating-it/ (accessed 28 June 2022).

century, and so the play's title is something of a misnomer. Possibly it was retained because it contains the implicit threat regarding history: as ye sow, so shall ye reap.

In terms of its dramaturgy, then, *Harvest* gestures towards the Brechtian epic, with leaps in time illustrating historical processes and their impacts on working people. However, it lands more in the realm of the Shavian, poking fun at social norms and making farcical comedy out of weighty subjects. The key difference is the kind of humour deployed: in *Harvest* it is an anarchic, alternative-comedy enjoyment of excess and bad taste rather than the subverting of theatrical genres that we find in Shaw's plays. It is Shavian, too, in terms of its 'solid modernity': *Harvest* ultimately never becomes liquid, in Grochala's terms, distorting temporal realist conventions. Rather, its attempt to depict historical forces operating on an English farming family is undercut by the atypicality of the absurd twists of fate that are heaped on them: teenagers who stand to inherit a farm because of a bizarre bet about a dog in 1875; a pig man who enjoys pretending to hang himself; four daughters when Stefan and Laura hope for a son to continue the pig farm; the only son who then marries a vegan. In their social and economic environment, *Harvest*'s characters are a long way from Coward's Marryots of Mayfair, but the play's perspective is, if anything, more nihilistic than the 'Twentieth Century Blues' that *Cavalcade*'s signature song evokes. The tone is radically different, but the dramaturgy of attrition – of sorrows coming in battalions, as history happens *to* the family – is remarkably similar.

An Adventure

My second case study in this chapter is Vinay Patel's *An Adventure*, which premiered at the Bush Theatre, London, in 2018. The action takes place between 1954 and 2018, in India, Kenya and England. It begins when the teenage Jyoti is interviewing potential husbands; after an unpromising start to his first meeting with her, Jyoti decides to marry Rasik. As she later recalls, 'I thought you were a joke, but a slightly better joke than the others.'[48] Rasik is poor, but he has a plan to work in Kenya, where he was born; he buys land, and a local farmer, David, cultivates it. After a year, Jyoti joins him and they have a daughter, Sonal, but as the anti-colonial struggle and the government's draconian response to it intensifies, Rasik sells their land and they prepare to move to London. David, who is involved with the Mau Mau rebel forces – a fact that Jyoti and Rasik were both aware of – calls on them on the run from the police. He asks them to hide him, but they are scared of the consequences if they are caught and unable to leave (and worried, also, about how Asian people will be treated if the uprising succeeds).[49] Although we sense a terrible fate awaits him as he slips away, following Jyoti's advice to take the back alley, the stage directions tell us that '*She looks at him with infinite care.*'[50] In London, they have another daughter, Roshni, and Rasik trains to be a surveyor while Jyoti becomes passionately involved with trade union activism during the late 1960s and 1970s. The couple are travelling in different directions, and they disagree over Sonal's plans to go to university; in a betrayal of Jyoti's politics and her independence, Rasik crosses his office's picket line, is rewarded with promotion and a bonus by his employers, and immediately puts down a deposit on a house that they had always admired. From this point on, it seems Jyoti has little choice but to play the part of a suburban housewife.

The play leaps forward to 2018: Joyti is in her late seventies, Rasik is now in his mid-eighties, with a catheter bag and a wheelchair named Steve. They return to India for Jyoti's sister Shantiben's funeral, and Jyoti is upbraided by her niece, Joy, for the infrequency of their visits. They no longer need their relatives' 'charity' of old clothes: 'Because India is the future ... they used to say Ahmedabad was "The Manchester of

---

[48] Vinay Patel, *An Adventure* (London: Methuen Drama, 2018), 120.

[49] Conversations in this part of the play highlight the precarious position of Asian people in Kenya at this point. David insists to Jyoti, 'We're on the same side here', but later mentions to Rasik that he sees Asians as complicit in colonialism: 'The British are trying to crush the last of us. And they're using your people to do it'; to David, Rasik is not 'a Kenyan' (Patel, *An Adventure*, 44, 52, 54).

[50] Patel, *An Adventure*, 59.

the East" … And now we're Manchester, you know? Just Manchester. No need for hand-outs, no need for charity'.[51] Jyoti arranges for them to visit Nairobi on the way home to England as a surprise, but she is berated by David; their refusal to shelter him led to his arrest and torture by the colonial soldiers. The final scene takes place at Danson Park Watersports Centre in a comic replay of Act 1 Scene 2, which took place on Dandi Beach in India when they were young and full of hope. Jyoti in 2018 reflects on where their 'adventure' has brought her: 'I got trapped in your story and you built your life on top of mine'.[52] 'What a fucking mess!' she cries, throwing the coin she gave to David 'for luck' into the water.[53] Rasik insists on being pushed into the water, to give Jyoti the choice of whether she wants him: 'The only adventure left'.[54] As he emerges, eventually, 'renewed, replenished', they are joined by the two young versions of themselves.[55]

As the above synopsis implies, *An Adventure* combines a familiar story of political change in the 1970s and 1980s that creates tensions within families, with a migration story that touches on the shameful behaviour of the British in Kenya before decolonization. In some ways it might be compared to Flannery's *Our Friends in the North* (1982). That play told the story of the betrayal of working class hopes in the northeast of England after the Second World War, but featured a parallel plot about the decolonization of Rhodesia (now Zimbabwe).[56] However, in Patel's play it is a single story illustrating the impact of decolonization on the UK, and more significantly here, on Rasik and Jyoti, who have left post-Partition India only to witness an anti-colonial struggle in Kenya, and to become part of the class and race friction of 1970s England. As the title suggests, *An Adventure* is epic both in time

---

[51] Ibid., 99–100.
[52] Ibid., 117.
[53] Ibid., 118.
[54] Ibid., 119.
[55] Ibid., 124.
[56] When the play was adapted for BBC television to great acclaim in 1996, this subplot was removed.

and place, making most other family dramas look limited in scope.[57] Where, for the Harrisons of *Harvest*, there is no doubt where 'home' really is, for the Karia family it is at least three times more complicated. As a teenager, Sonal imagines her 'home home' is not London, not Ahmedabad, but Nairobi;[58] her mother tells her: 'Sonal, do you know what "home" really is? It's not a place, it isn't a noun. It's a verb. Home is where you fight to be. And that's hard wherever you go.'[59] Moreover, *An Adventure*'s framing of post-war life is very different from that of the Kahns in the Wesker trilogy, in that the experience of the war against fascism is further complicated for Africans who fought as imperial subjects. As David recalls of his war service in Ethiopia, 'I put my rifle to a face not all that different to mine ... it felt like I'd murdered my own history for a future I would never, ever be a part of.'[60]

Dramaturgically, the play becomes more 'liquid' towards the middle; as Sonal is born, Rasik keeps turning back to the audience to narrate a letter that he is composing to Joyti's sister Shantiben; the stage directions say '*The world goes soft.*'[61] A moment after they hold her for the first time, there's a family photograph taken by David, and then a noisy crowd gathers outside, signifying the Mau Mau rebellion.[62] Family life and political life speed toward one another. As the notes at the start of the play state: 'The first act should be a rush/ The second act should be a quiver./The third act should take its time.'[63] The same note also cautions, 'None of it should feel like history', and this is achieved in part through the technique discussed in Chapter 1, of using today's language

---

[57] For example, *Harvest* was perhaps always going to be a play about rural White people, but in the early years of the twentieth century, imperialism is presented, through the preposterous figure of Lord Agar, as merely adventuring, posturing and silly dressing up.

[58] Patel, *An Adventure*, 82.

[59] Ibid., 83.

[60] Ibid., 45. In the Bush Theatre production, the actor playing David, Martins Imhangbe, moved earth around the farm with a broom as he delivered this monologue, creating circle patterns, emphatically pushing the earth away and then smoothing it over, providing a physical parallel to the feelings of vengefulness, disillusionment and disavowal that are expressed verbally.

[61] Patel, *An Adventure*, 48.

[62] Ibid., 49.

[63] Ibid., 4.

to make the characters' dilemmas feel contemporary: 'The dialogue is written mainly to reflect modern colloquial English.'[64] This is noticeable from the opening scene, with a Jyoti who very much appears to be in control, swearing and mocking and directing the interview, and despite the 1950s setting, seemingly using very 'online dating' techniques to sort and rank her possible suitors and their photographs: her first remark to Rasik is that, in effect, he doesn't look like his profile picture.[65] *An Adventure* makes use of multi-rolling to bring characters visibly into contact with their older and younger selves. While Rasik is watching a newsreel about the Mau Mau, a mysterious man enters the cinema; he is revealed to be the older Rasik (Selva Rasalingam), replacing the younger actor who had been playing him (Subham Saraf). This transition is repeated with Joyti in the next act, but takes much longer to happen, her 'older' version (Nila Aalia) only replacing her younger self (Anjana Vasan) on her third appearance, as she sees the recording of her contribution to a documentary that we saw her filming at the start of the act.[66] It is as if Jyoti only becomes 'older' after Rasik has killed her political aspirations. The dramaturgy is unusual, too, in that Jyoti and Rasik are always central to the narrative; the focus does not switch to the younger generation as it does in the other intergenerational dramas discussed here.[67] The play features other uncanny effects: watching the newsreel, the footage momentarily morphs to show David among the captured fighters (before it actually happens in the story). When Jyoti and Rasik meet David again in Nairobi, he 'may well look exactly the same' and 'moves with the energy of a man a third

---

[64] Ibid., 4.

[65] Ibid., 5.

[66] Ibid., 76, 87, 95.

[67] Partly, the play's acknowledgements make clear, this is in tribute to the playwright's grandparents 'for being brave enough to strike out across the seas' (Patel, *An Adventure*, 3); it is *their* story that is the adventure, not so much their children's. As Sonal complains when Jyoti is set against her going to Newcastle University: 'This isn't fair. You guys moved all over, but you won't even let me go a couple of hundred miles!' (Patel, *An Adventure*, 81). Or, as Patel puts it self-deprecatingly, it is a story of 'a generation that crossed three continents before they were thirty ... All so that their kids might become accountants' (Patel, *An Adventure*, 4).

of his age,'[68] stage directions that reflected the appearance of David in the Bush production. Patel emphasizes that this is 'A play of myth, of feeling, more than fact'.[69]

In *An Adventure*, conflict comes both from first-hand involvement in the world and from within. It is the most profoundly ambivalent of the plays analysed in this chapter. Although it follows the 'hero's journey' model to a remarkable degree compared to the others, it imbues it with a very different structure of feeling from conventional stories in this mould. There is melancholy and loss, but the family history is not configured as a national narrative, and the play undercuts the possibility of a sentimentalized nostalgia at every turn. In effect – as the title indicates – it asks what kind of odyssey, and what kind of return journey, is open to those whose feeling of 'home' is complicated by migration.

Wife

Samuel Adamson's play *Wife*, which premiered at the Kiln Theatre in 2019, uses some of the same tropes as *The Pride*, discussed in the next chapter, to convey the changes in how gay and lesbian people have lived in the last half-century. *Wife* is structured around conversations that take place after different productions of *A Doll's House* in 1959, 1988, 2019 and 2042. As *The Pride* would lead us to expect, the late 1950s are closeted, repressive and suspicious; Daisy takes her sneering, dismissive husband Robert backstage after a production of Ibsen's play to meet lead actor Suzannah Heywood, with whom she is having a secret affair; when the two women are finally alone and Daisy reveals that she is pregnant, Suzannah breaks it off.

---

[68] Patel, *An Adventure*, 108.
[69] Ibid., 4. In an interview, Patel added that the casting decision to have Martins Imhangbe play both the younger and the older David, 'it made sense to lean into this feeling of the act being on the precipice of this world and the next' (Tom Ue, 'Going on *An Adventure* with Vinay Patel', *New Writing* 17, no. 2 (2020): 5. doi:10.1080/14790726.2019.1586956).

Act 2, in 1988, takes place in the Frog and Trumpet pub adjacent to the theatre; a gay couple, Ivar and Eric, have just seen a radical Norwegian revival of *A Doll's House*. Ivar is flamboyant and outspoken where Eric is cautious and self-conscious; 1988 was, of course, the height of Thatcherism, and Section 28 is given a mention,[70] while both men are ejected by the homophobic landlord.[71] Ivar, we discover, is the son of Daisy and Robert from the first Act: Daisy is now on her own and an alcoholic, while Eric is her carer. In Act 3, set in 2019, Ivar is wealthy and middle-aged, and married to Cas, a cartoonish, narcissistic actor many years his junior whose career he finances. Unlike in *The Pride*, same-sex marriage is now legally recognized, having been introduced by the Coalition Government of 2010–15. In common with Campbell's play, the freedoms of gay life in London are shown to have created their own problems. Where in *The Pride* this reversal from the closeted 1950s is represented in tragic mode, here the treatment is more tragi-comic. Clare in 2019 is the daughter of Eric, who has died recently, shot at a Pride rally in Australia; Clare and her fiancé Finn feign interest in investing in Cas's 'gender-fucked' rewrite of *A Doll's House* so that Clare can ask Ivar what Eric had been like as a young man.[72]

Finally, in the last Act, which takes place in 2042, a second Daisy – this time the daughter of Clare and Finn – seeks out another actor called Suzannah backstage at the same theatre, to ask her about the tambourine that has been passed down through her family and that has names, messages and drawings from the actresses who have played Nora through the ages inscribed on it. The theatre, as an art form, is in a bad way in 2042; this theatre building is to be demolished, and acting on stage is seen as a comedown.[73] Suzannah recoils from the possibility that she might have inspired Daisy to be an actor. They imagine the lesbian life that the 1950s Daisy and Suzannah, whose inscriptions both appear on the tambourine, might have led – not the actual life of misery

---

[70] Samuel Adamson, *Wife* (London: Faber and Faber, 2019), 48.
[71] Ibid., 52.
[72] Ibid., 62.
[73] Ibid., 91–3.

and regret that the events of *Wife* point to – and the play ends with the 1950s garden party where Suzannah and Daisy first met. Rather like Harold Pinter's *Betrayal* (1978) the chronologically earliest scene is presented last so that we can recognize, with hindsight, the full force of that moment of realization and possibility.

Wife, then, deploys a version of what Steve Waters calls the 'Post-Brechtian Act' where 'the act structure works like a tear in the fabric of the play; its breaks are not disguised, they are emphatically visible'.[74] Hence, in the transitions between periods, for a few seconds they push up against one another, and onstage figures seemingly belong to neither one era nor the other. The stage directions say things like: '*The machinery of* Wife *is exposed: Stage Managers enter*',[75] or '*The machinery of* Wife *is exposed. Finn picks up the tambourine and looks at it. He is lost to the transition*',[76] or '*Wife's machinery is revealed: everything is removed*.'[77] This is an encapsulation of the contingent quality of history on stage that I discussed in Chapter 1; it was also genuinely exciting and disorientating to witness in the original Kiln production, directed by Indhu Rubasingham, where the rupturing of time and the bursting-through of Noras for each new age produced a series of jarring and cacophonous affects before we, as an audience, were able to find our feet in the next era. In addition, Suzannah is played by the same actor in each sequence, whether a traditional period-dress Nora in the 1950s, a punkish, cocaine-snorting, tax-evading Norwegian Nora in the 1980s or one who's been relegated to the role of 'her motherfucking husband' in Cas's version in the play's present day.[78] There are also moments of physical action that reproduce themselves across the decades; one hand being placed over another in precisely the same way: Peter and Nora, Eric and Suzannah, Ivar and Clare. There is the tambourine, as mentioned, and the ghost of Robert, who appears in Act 4, wandering

[74] Waters, *The Secret Life of Plays* (London: Nick Hern, 2010), 47–8.
[75] Adamson, *Wife*, 35.
[76] Ibid., 87.
[77] Ibid., 98.
[78] Ibid., 62.

the theatre looking for (the first) Daisy. Marjorie, Suzannah's dresser, is mentioned as an offstage character throughout the play but finally appears in 2042, and 'Everything about her is 1950s', as if she, too, haunts this theatre on the edge of demolition.[79] In summary, *Wife* is stuffed with dramaturgical devices to make us look at queer history, and the queerness of theatre, anew.

The counterpoint to this view is that too much is going on, and that *Wife* is forced into too many contrivances in order to make every generation's characters intersect and interact with those of the last and the next.[80] For example, in plot terms, Suzannah *has* to wander into the bar where Finn and Clare are waiting for Ivar – and to have every word of her phone conversation overheard by Clare – in order for her to report Cas's rumoured cheating to Ivar, having only just met him. And are we to believe that Ivar has a moment of realization, when confronted with the tambourine, and a determination not to turn into his mother, that makes him realize there and then that he *has* to divorce Cas?[81] On seeing the original production, I was disappointed that what might have been a history play about changing social attitudes, set around *A Doll's House*, also had to be a family drama, as though the only way to make us care about characters in the theatre – still – is to assert a genetic relationship. Yet, on reflection, perhaps the family plot isn't an old-fashioned contrivance to link disparate times; maybe, instead, it's a way to connect two hereditary lines, the 'straight' and

---

[79] Ibid., 92.

[80] In generally positive and admiring reviews, this was an occasional canard among critics; Letts in *The Sunday Times* and Treneman in *The Times* both opined that a chart or family tree would have been useful (Quentin Letts, review of *Wife* by Samuel Adamson, directed by Indhu Rubasingham, Kiln Theatre, London, in *The Sunday Times*, 9 June 2019, reproduced in *Theatre Record* 39, no. 11 (2019). Available online: https://www-theatrerecord-com.libproxy.york.ac.uk/magazine/issue/1866 (accessed 30 April 2023); Ann Treneman, review of *Wife* by Samuel Adamson, *Theatre Record*.) Notably, very few of the critics assumed that Adamson did not know what he was doing with the play; only Tom Wicker in *Time Out* argues that the play 'sometimes stumbles in trying to do too much' (Tom Wicker, review of *Wife*, *Theatre Record*). This is in marked contrast to the reception of Hickson's *Oil*, as I discuss elsewhere (Benjamin Poore, '"You Can't Be Here": The Playwriting Dialectic in Ella Hickson's *Oil*', *Modern Drama* 63, no. 1 (2020): 21–38. doi:10.3138/MD.1054R).

[81] Adamson, *Wife*, 86.

the 'queer'. Daisy and Robert, Eric and Lydia, Clare and Finn, weren't right for each other, but they produced an Ivar and a second Daisy. The reproductive history allows us to connect the generational dots that might otherwise be lost, to lives in the closet, or silenced by Section 28, or cut short by AIDS. The truth-teller and sometime *deus ex machina* Suzannah is lesbian throughout, different yet the same in each era. And, it might be countered, the plotting of Ivar and Cas's break-up is *meant* to be rather ramshackle, because the play doesn't follow the same generic conventions in each Act; it's a poignant historical drama (or melodrama, even) at the beginning and the end, with two escalating Acts of satirical and farcical comedy in the middle.[82]

The rigid familial plotting of *Wife* means that the play never quite becomes 'liquid' in Grochala's sense, because its presentation of the 'lived experience of social reality in twenty-first century Britain' is not communicated as 'fundamentally different' to the 1950s or the 2040s.[83] The 'exposed machinery' between acts is perhaps more decorative than generative, because timelines remain stable and explicable through the familial logic of an Ibsenite 'solid modernity'.[84] However, what's remarkable about *Wife* compared to the other intergenerational dramas under scrutiny here is that there are no domestic scenes; the 'house' is a theatre and its environs; its backstage spaces and the places its people spill out into. And, given its Norwegian point of departure, it seems fitting that there is no attempt to make the theatre into England and England into theatre as *Cavalcade* does. It's about queer history and theatre history, and how they've intersected, and the love stories

---

[82] Notably, *Wife* was one several new plays in the late 2010s and early 2020s that reassessed the historical concerns of *A Doll's House*. The same year as *Wife* premiered, Tanika Gupta reimagined Ibsen's play in 1879 India, while in 2017 Lucas Hnath's *A Doll's House Part Two* – set fifteen years after Nora left – opened on Broadway and was produced at the Donmar Warehouse in London in the summer of 2022. Most strikingly in connection with *Wife*, Stef Smith's *Nora*, a 'radical new version' of *A Doll's House*, opened at Tramway, Glasgow, in March 2019. It reimagines Nora Helmer's story taking place in 1918, 1968 and 2018, with the actors playing the three Noras remaining onstage throughout and their experiences and narration overlapping.

[83] Grochala, *The Contemporary Political Play*, 77.

[84] Ibid., 77.

that we never hear about, and the love stories that we have to make up because they're only hints on a tambourine.

The House of Shades

My final case study, Beth Steel's family saga *The House of Shades*, takes us full circle, to the single-location, working-class environment of *This Happy Breed* and *Chicken Soup*, and also returns us to the latter's narrative trajectory of decline, depicting the lost causes of the Left. *The House of Shades* premiered at the Almeida Theatre, London, in 2022. There are few direct references, but we infer that the setting is the East Midlands, in a small town with a bicycle factory, presumably modelled on the Raleigh factory in Nottinghamshire. A harrowing journey from the mid-1960s to the end of the 2010s – post-Brexit, pre-Covid – the play has five acts, and each act brings a death in the Webster family. As the play opens, a neighbour talks to the audience as she washes the corpse of Harry Webster, Edith's husband and Constance's father, a violent, abusive man. At the end of the act, Laura, Constance and Alistair's pregnant daughter, 'appears in a white nightie, bleeding between her legs, and collapses'; we later discover that her mother performed a home abortion on her, and Laura died as a result.[85] Act 2 begins with the christening party for Natalie, the daughter of Agnes and her husband Eddie, and granddaughter of Constance, and ends with the house on fire and Edith's death. Alistair dies in Act 3, Constance in Act 4, and Jack, their son and Agnes's twin, in Act 5. Jack had embraced Thatcherism, married a fellow Tory, Helen, and was no longer on speaking terms with his 'Old Labour' father and sister; in his later years he had built up his own bike shop into a profitable business and was opening a new factory on the night he died.

This synopsis of *The House of Shades* hardly does it justice, however. Thus far I have only described the play's outer, material world. There is another world always present among the Websters, that of ghosts, visions

---

[85] Beth Steel, *The House of Shades* (London: Faber, 2022), 28.

and shades; Laura haunts the rest of the play, particularly her mother; her hoop rolls unaccountably into the room,[86] doors open and close, footsteps are heard running up the stairs; by 1996, the stage directions tell us '*Laura, in her clean white nightie, is now a settled presence in the house.*'[87] She '*hides/submerges herself into the architecture of the house*'; as Constance lies dying in hospital, Laura '*creeps from under the bed*'.[88] Yet *The House of Shades* is far from a Gothic thriller, and the dead and the imaginary make themselves known in a multitude of ways. Alistair is guided to his death by a very matter-of-fact, conversational apparition of Nye Bevan.[89] In the next scene, Jack talks to Alistair's corpse, and he answers back. As he remarks, 'Death silences no one, least of all the dead.'[90] Constance is escorted away by a figure called The Entertainer, dressed as if from the 1950s, representing the life of showbusiness glamour she might have had.[91] At the same time, due to careful multi-rolling specified in the stage directions, Constance as she was in Act 1 is able to talk to Dying Constance, and the twins Jack and Agnes are shadowed – sometimes seen, sometimes unseen – by their teenage selves.[92] The way that each character is led to their death in their own way, with death as a slow procession, is calculated to wrongfoot and unsettle: '*Edith, unbeknown to those present, steps out of the coffin and heads for the wall. Before passing through it, sensing something, she stops. Slowly she turns around and sees us all there watching …*'[93] The dramaturgical presence of the dead – the mundane, familiar dead, rather than Gothic spectres – enables Steel to plant significant pieces of backstory in the play's later stages: Alistair tells Jack what Constance was like when they first met, after he has died;[94] the horrific abortion scene and its aftermath

[86] Ibid., 51.
[87] Ibid., 55.
[88] Ibid., 76.
[89] Ibid., 62–7.
[90] Ibid., 70.
[91] Ibid., 93–4.
[92] Ibid., 71–80.
[93] Ibid., 53.
[94] Ibid., 69.

is only re-enacted as Constance lies dying;[95] hints of incest arrive very late.[96] Some may find this to be over-egging the family narrative, but I see it as a way of avoiding the front-loading that can happen in family sagas, with the later acts losing momentum – especially if they set out to trace a history of decline. The final scenes are anything but predictable, and we are spared the big family argument about politics (Sarah and Ronnie in *Chicken Soup*; Marlene and Joyce in *Top Girls*) that can feel like the inevitable destination of social realist drama; there is no need for such an argument because the characters have been having them all the way through.

The House of Shades might, on first impressions, appear to conform to the convention that I have identified elsewhere as 'supernatural realism': a realist play with supernatural elements that, paradoxically, act as guarantors of the grounded historical credibility of the drama: only by showing what is 'not real' can you circumscribe the representation of 'the real'.[97] However, as noted above, *The House of Shades* does not make hard and fast distinctions between the world of the living and that of the dead, and is consequently much more than a straightforward 'ghost play' with a haunting that needs to be explained and laid to rest. In a sense, then, it is the opposite of my earlier formulation; it presents 'shades' that are not, in the world of the play, ghosts, not other worldly, but part of that world. We might even call it 'realist supernaturalism'.

The play's epigraphs provide some clues as to how to interpret this move politically. Act 1's epigraph is from Mark Fisher: 'You don't have to believe in the supernatural to recognise that the family is a haunted structure.'[98] If we follow Fisher's thinking on the cultural stasis of the twenty-first century, we might find statements like this one in the essay 'Lost Futures', seeking to identify a 'hauntological melancholia': 'In 1981, the 1960s seemed much further away than they do today. Since then, cultural time has folded back on itself, and the impression of

[95] Ibid., 80–1.
[96] Ibid., 92, 105.
[97] Poore, *Heritage*, 149–52.
[98] Quoted in Steel, *Shades*, 3.

linear development has given way to a strange simultaneity.'[99] In this respect, Steel's play 'folds back on itself'; this 'strange simultaneity' is at the heart of *The House of Shades*, pushing against the linear time of 1965–1979–1985–1996–2019. The leaps in time can thus be read as disrupting the means by which 'Capitalism seamlessly occupies the horizons of the thinkable.'[100] We see the 'slow cancellation of the future' (discussed in the Introduction) play out on a personal level: in Constance's disappointed hopes of a glittering career; in her own 'cancellation' of Laura's future; in Alistair's mortifying 'big moment' at the trade union meeting, cruelly recounted by Constance, and so on.[101] On a political level, it is also present in Alistair's conversation with Nye Bevan, at the midpoint of the play:

> **Alistair** Christ, we didn't just believe it was possible.
> **Bevan** The eradication of poverty.
> **Alistair** We believed it was inevitable!
> **Bevan** The change of society as we knew it.
> **Alistair** Instead people have been changed to get used to the society that we have.
> **Bevan** With all its unnecessary cruelties.
> **Alistair** And I no longer believe it will ever be different.[102]

However well worked this formulation is, I want to sound a note of caution, as we seem to have been hearing this same story for sixty years. Sarah Kahn's repeated injunction at the end of *Chicken Soup with Barley* – 'Ronnie, if you don't care you'll die' – echoes through the decades in these plays.[103] As the critic Tom Nichols argues, citing the popular music of the 1970s from Billy Joel and Bruce Springsteen to the Kinks and the Jam,

> Whether economic times are good or bad, this lament for the old days of factories and mills – jobs that were long gone before some voters

[99] Fisher, 'Lost Futures', 9.
[100] Fisher, *Capitalist Realism*, 8.
[101] Steel, *Shades*, 47–8.
[102] Ibid., 56.
[103] Arnold Wesker, *Plays One: The Wesker Trilogy* (London: Methuen, 2001), 79.

were old enough to cast a ballot or even born yet – never changes …
if we are to take seriously the idea that liberal democracy has failed in
this generation, then we must at least recognize that for half a century,
every generation of liberal democratic citizens has apparently felt the
same way … this might say more about irrational nostalgia than about
living conditions.[104]

I think Nichols seriously underestimates the lived experience of being
surrounded by post-industrial dereliction, and I would suggest that
he rather too easily dismisses the post-war years of growing economic
equality as 'a completely unnatural situation' that could not be repeated
in the US, or elsewhere.[105] Nevertheless, his point about the resilience
of this second-order nostalgia, for an idea of an industrial age of several
generations ago, is well made. It is notable that in their identification of
historical turning points, when hope was lost and disillusionment set
in, these family dramas habitually reach for the 1980s and Thatcherism.
This means their pivotal characters – those who were actually of working
age in the 1980s – are now mostly elderly. In *The Seven Acts of Mercy*,
discussed in Chapter 4, it's the grandfather who actually remembers
1980s militancy. In *An Adventure*, Jyoti and Rasik are looking back on
the union activism of the 1970s from old age. In *Wife*, Ivar goes from
being a young radical in the 1980s to a quiescent figure in his late fifties
in 2019; in *The House of Shades*, Thatcherism divides Jack and Agnes,
and neither live to the play's end.

Conclusion

Together, the 'family sagas' analysed in this chapter take the politically
conservative form deployed by Coward and rework it to include
alternative perspectives on class, race, decolonization, sexuality
and national identity. This chapter has examined plays that take the

[104] Tom Nichols, *Our Own Worst Enemy: The Assault on Democracy from Within* (New York: Oxford University Press, 2021), 146, 148.
[105] Ibid., 150.

conventional idea of England as a family, a house and a home, and ask what happens when the home is beset by perceived intruders (*Harvest*); when a house doesn't stand in for home (*An Adventure*); or when the 'house' is a theatre, and home the world of *the* theatre (*Wife*). Lastly, *House of Shades* asks what happens when the family home is pulled down, as at the end of Act 4, 'demolished before us' with Constance's death, to be replaced by an unrecognizable post-Brexit country – a house without a home – where babies are born to migrant workers in factory toilets.[106] Content changes markedly in these contemporary iterations of *This Happy Breed*, but form less so; dramaturgically, these contemporary history plays hint at different kinds of liquidity, a collapsing of time and space, or a radical subjectivity, but in order to convey their family histories they cannot do away with chronology and causal, linear narratives.

However, most still locate a decisive rupture in British society as taking place in the 1980s as a result of Thatcherism. It has become the conventional focal point for narratives of disillusionment, melancholy and decline, taking over from the loss-of-innocence moments of the First World War, the Spanish Civil War or the post-war consensus that earlier plays had used to shape similar emotional trajectories. Yet Thatcherism as a historical centre point becomes increasingly untenable for plays set in the present, as those affected at first hand become older pensioners. The representation of the last forty years-plus as being 'more of the same', only getting progressively harder and worse, may chime with the recurring notion of the slow cancellation of the future, and the bitter disappointments of New Labour's shift to the right in the 1990s and 2000s. Yet it leaves some profound contemporary problems with historical roots untouched. For example, the intergenerational history play, while preoccupied with ideas of house and home, has not yet found a way to capture the vicious impacts of the move from a

---

[106] Steel, *Shades*, 109.

production-based to an asset-based economy,[107] where large divisions open up between and within classes because of the gulf between property owners and renters. This social chasm is closely interwoven with other changes that have accelerated in the last thirty years, like the growth in personal debt,[108] and the unacknowledged impact of inherited wealth on younger generations' life chances.[109] The rising costs of social care for elderly people, and of childcare when both parents need to work to meet housing costs, are also underexamined using the intergenerational history play model.

Meanwhile, in Peter Morgan's Netflix series *The Crown* (2016–23), the upwardly mobile, nostalgic fantasies of *Upstairs, Downstairs* and *Downton Abbey* reach their logical conclusion with a six-season retelling of the last seven decades of UK and world history. The family through whose eyes we see these events is, of course, that of Queen Elizabeth II, their lives of immense privilege rehabilitated, via the magic of period drama, into the struggles of everyday people. The family home becomes the country itself, as after each row the royals storm off to their palaces and country estates rather than their bedrooms. In the present cultural climate, government ministers become exercised over whether viewers might mistake *The Crown* for 'real' history, but few comment on how it naturalizes hereditary wealth and deference.[110] In response to

---

[107] William Davies refers to this movement as 'the disenchantment of politics by economics' (Davies, *Not Normal*, 13). See also Michael McKinnie's *Theatre in Market Economies* for a summary of these economic changes which chimes with Davies's assessment (Michael McKinnie, *Theatre in Market Economies* (Cambridge: Cambridge University Press, 2021), 4, 16).

[108] Davies, *Not Normal*, 17, 39.

[109] See, for example, Gaby Hinsliff, 'Why Inheritance is the Dirty Secret of the Middle Classes', *Guardian*, 3 December 2022. Available online: https://www.theguardian.com/money/2022/dec/03/why-inheritance-is-the-dirty-secret-of-the-middle-classes-harder-to-talk-about-than-sex?CMP=Share_AndroidApp_Other (accessed 5 December 2022).

[110] See Hayley Maitland for an irreverent summary of the controversies over 'accuracy' (Hayley Maitland, 'The Crown Isn't the Problem', *Vogue*, 22 October 2022. Available online: https://www.vogue.co.uk/arts-and-lifestyle/article/the-crown-disclaimer (accessed 22 December 2022). At the time of writing, a Google search for 'What *The Crown* Got Wrong' returns 256,000 hits. For a detailed consideration of the series' assumptions and strange tonal shifts, see McHenry and VanArendonk (Jackson McHenry and Kathryn VanArendonk, 'Does *The Crown* Like the Royals or Not?' *Vulture*, 10 November 2022. Available online: https://www.vulture.com/article/the-crown-season-5-charles-diana-royal-sympathy.html (accessed 22 December 2022).

these televised lullabies of duty and continuity, contemporary English history plays have not yet exploited their full dramaturgical potential: to resist the familiar comforts of deference, despair and melancholia; to represent social reality in the twenty-first century; and in so doing to shake the political foundations of family, nation, house and home.

4

Polychronic History Plays

Introduction

All history plays manipulate time, but some do it more overtly than others. When a stage drama mixes contemporary and historical scenes, a relationship between past and present is strongly implied. This might be a material, cause-and-effect connection, or a more poetic, metaphorical correspondence. This chapter groups together these plays of multiple timelines as *polychronic history plays*. By 'polychronic' I mean any history play that takes place in two or more distinct periods of time, extending beyond a single human lifespan. In a polychronic history play, the audience sees stories in different time periods developing in parallel. I find this a useful way to discuss the temporality of history plays because it separates out the manipulation of historical time from other dramaturgical features, providing an alternative means of grouping and registering what history plays do when they invoke the past. The most common type of polychronic history play is a *dual timeline* play – that is, with two different historical settings, which may be brought together at the end of the play, or which may simply be juxtaposed, inviting the audience to consider the connection. Steve Waters calls one version of this type of play the 'Post-Brechtian Act', which may consist of 'two self-contained acts, even plays, forced into violent counterpoint', like Caryl Churchill's *Cloud Nine* (1979) 'with its split between imperial Africa and late-1970s Britain'.[1] My key examples in this chapter are *The Pride* (2008/13) by Alexi Kaye Campbell, *The*

[1] Waters, *Secret Life of Plays*, 48.

Seven Acts of Mercy (2016) by Anders Lustgarten, *Clybourne Park* (2012) by Bruce Norris, *Love and Other Acts of Violence* (2021) by Cordelia Lynn, *A Museum in Baghdad* (2019) by Hannah Khalil and *Rockets and Blue Lights* (2020) by Winsome Pinnock. Considered in this order, they range from simple dual timeline structures to still more ambitious and dizzying temporalities. Moreover, because a dual timeline play is always being experienced in the theatre at a different point in history to its setting – even when that setting is framed as contemporary – plays with two or more timelines, in effect, are always about the interplay between at least three historical periods. As I will demonstrate, polychronic timelines are increasingly being used in contemporary history plays as a springboard into more complex and hybridized encounters with possible pasts.

In my first monograph, *Heritage, Nostalgia and Modern British Theatre*, I brought together, in the final chapter 'Staging Hauntings', a series of British plays of the 1990s and 2000s in which 'the first act has a Victorian setting and the second a contemporary setting'.[2] Given what appears to be this doubled, balanced structure, it is useful at this point to think of them as 'dual timeline' history plays. However, rather than utilizing the *Cloud Nine* model of two periods in juxtaposition, many of these plays actually 'alternate between contemporary and Victorian events' and may feature 'parallel scenes where characters from both time periods share the stage space' unbeknownst to one another.[3] In that first book, I read these dramas primarily as ghost plays, with the past being shown to haunt the present, and vice versa. Mark Berninger has also written of this type of history play as a detective story, 'centred around the discovery of a dead body', citing as examples Shelagh Stephenson's *An Experiment with an Air Pump* (1998) or Théâtre de Complicité's *Mnemonic* (1999). For Berninger, the corpse is 'not only the most telling trace of past life but also demands an explanation, it demands to be brought back to life, to have its story told. This becomes the starting point for history's process of construction, as alternative

---

[2] Poore, *Heritage*, 146.
[3] Ibid., 146, 148.

stories of the past can also be constructed around the "evidence" of the dead body.[4] Viewed this way, the dual timeline history play that features a discovered corpse works as a form of oppositional history, an attempt to recoup the voices of the lost, the marginalized and the silenced. In the present study, I want to look again at what these plays are doing, this time from the perspectives of temporality, narrative and historiography.

Dual Timeline Temporality

We can start by considering what it is that audiences are invited to do, cognitively and aesthetically, in attending a dual timeline history play. Moving the setting between two different historical periods is a self-consciously 'writerly' move on the part of the playwright; it draws attention to the constructed quality of the play and to the presence of the creative team in making and executing that choice. As Waters notes, when 'coherence of form and tone within a play is repudiated' then it 'compel[s] the audience to engage in what Raymond Williams called "complex seeing"'.[5] In his example of the play with two acts set in different eras, the 'act structure works like a tear in the very canvas of the play; its breaks are not disguised, they are emphatically visible'.[6] Cordelia Lynn's *Love and Other Acts of Violence*, discussed later in this chapter, stages precisely this kind of rupture, making it all the more emphatic by having it take place around twenty minutes before the end of the production's running time. Breaking the conventions of single-timeline history plays not only draws attention to the creative presence of the playwright in shaping the narrative; it also reminds audiences of the acts of selection that have taken place in presenting this story (or this pair of stories). This might encourage spectators to view the action somewhat differently: if we are encountering characters who are being

---

[4]   Berninger, 'Variations', 56.
[5]   Waters, *Secret Life*, 47.
[6]   Ibid., 47.

identified with a chosen period, in what ways are they intended as 'typical' of that era, or indeed as being 'motivated by external events rather than by individual temperament', as Peacock says of Brenton and Hare's historical characters in the 1970s and 1980s?[7] The 'writerly' introduction of a second historical era also invites the audience to consider whether there is a causal relationship between the earlier and the later era and its dramatic action. As David Edgar remarks in *How Plays Work*, 'Plays which put together two or three apparently unrelated narratives and invite the audience to connect them … imply or even insist that making cause-and-effect connections is harder than it used to be, but they also assert the overwhelming human urge to do so.'[8]

In a history play, causality is not only a question of character interaction and conflict, but of historical change. As causality is a subject of relevance to historians as well as dramatists, in this section I want to select some aspects of Mark Hewitson's consideration of causality and narrative, in his book *History and Causality* (2014), and apply them to theatre and playwriting. I propose that by invoking historical settings and events, playwrights are involved in a historiographical process, even – perhaps especially – when their historical narratives are counterfactual or consciously anachronistic. As Chapter 1 established via a discussion of Hayden White's work, historical writing and fiction have a series of genres, modes and tropes in common; in the words of Alun Munslow, 'history and fiction, as well as writing and reception, are imaginatively organized', meaning that 'both sets of activities are fictive because both are authored'.[9] Munslow reminds us that this choice of genre, and the selection of detail to fit it, implies an explanation for the historical phenomena that are being narrated: 'So, if a history is emplotted as a tragedy it is "explained" as a tragedy.'[10] In a later section of the book,

[7] Peacock, *Radical Stages*, 170. Peacock also discusses the selection of the 'typical' in the presentation of character in David Edgar's 'factional' group biography history plays, *Maydays* (1983) and *Destiny* (1976) (Peacock, *Radical Stages*, 171).

[8] David Edgar, *How Plays Work* (London: Nick Hern, 2009), 115.

[9] Munslow, quoted in Mark Hewitson, *History and Causality* (Basingstoke: Palgrave Macmillan, 2014), 118.

[10] Munslow, quoted in Hewitson, *History and Causality*, 119.

Hewitson demonstrates, via an example of a list of causes of the First World War, that all explanations rely on the prior selection of events that suggest an explanation that the historian has in mind.[11] So, while ideas of historical cause-and-effect may look objective and rigorous, they can be just as prone to the processes of selectivity – and just as reliant on the imagination – as creative writing about the past. Of course, playwriting has its differences from historiographic prose. As Waters was quoted as saying earlier in this chapter, most contemporary plays do not explicitly argue for the connection between one era and another but place the two eras and sets of dramatic actions in juxtaposition with each other. Nor do most contemporary history plays use a 'narrator' or 'playwright' to argue for a relationship between the play's temporal elements, and where they do – as in Lucy Kirkwood's *Rapture*, discussed in the Coda – we are rightly suspicious of such figures. So, as Paul Ricoeur states in *Time and Narrative*, 'poets' (and by extension playwrights) usually create 'plots that are held together by causal skeletons' but that 'are not the subject of a process of argumentation'.[12] We might think of this juxtaposition in terms of Ricoeur's classification of historical explanations within narrative, where he identifies 'analogical or metaphorical categories' like 'baroque', which can be 'taken out of context and transposed on the basis of a reasoned comparison to periods other than the baroque, strictly speaking'.[13] In a dual timeline history play, one historical period is 'taken out of context' and is transposed with another period, for which it becomes a metaphor.

The Puzzle and the Hinge

From a historiographical perspective, then, it may be more productive to think of dual timeline plays as modelled on the idea of the puzzle,

---

[11] Hewitson, *History and Causality*, 133–5.
[12] Ricoeur, quoted in Hewitson, *History and Causality*, 126.
[13] Ibid., 122.

as discussed by Hewitson via the work of philosopher David Carr.[14] This puzzle is constructed by the playwright, certainly, but then to an extent, the historian constructs their own object of study by selecting events and extrapolating explanations from them (Hewitson quotes the philosopher Paul Roth, who observes that events are 'not known to be of nature's making rather than of ours').[15] 'Puzzle' works better as an analogy, I think, than 'detective story', as suggested by Berninger, for the audience's interpretative process of linking these historical eras together, since the deductive reasoning of detection is impossible to apply to history (there are no 'universal laws'). The audience's interpretative process is also highly contingent in the history play, since we cannot fully know the 'laws' of the world(s) of the play, and the play's dramaturgy, until we have experienced the whole performance, or read the whole play text. *Love and Other Acts of Violence* and even Bernard Shaw's *Saint Joan* (1922) come to mind as examples of history plays that reveal their temporal 'laws' very late in the running time. In the latter, the Epilogue takes place twenty-five years after Joan's execution; the principal characters reassemble in King Charles VII of France's dream to discuss Joan's posthumous exoneration at a subsequent trial, and a Gentleman arrives from the Vatican in the year 1920 to announce that Joan has been made a Catholic saint. Charles returns to sleep, but Joan and a soldier from hell continue their conversation, independent of the dream that had summoned them.[16]

Before turning to analysis of the plays, it is useful to turn back to fictional narrative and temporality to better understand the puzzle that an audience may be confronted with in dual timeline plays. In narratological terms, all polychronic history plays proceed by the strategic use of analepsis (flashback) and prolepsis (flash-forward). For David Ian Rabey, 'The relationship [between theatre and time] is like a *hinge*: it lets you swing from one place to another (imaginative,

---

[14] Hewitson, *History and Causality*, 139–40.
[15] Ibid., 137.
[16] Bernard Shaw, *Saint Joan* (London: Methuen Drama, 2008), New Mermaids edition, ed. Jean Chothia, 118–36.

physicalized, past/future) in a move *in and through* the present (which is redesignated and shown as pivotal).[17] This can be theorized in terms of the schemes of theatrical temporality that Rabey collects together in his book, *Theatre, Time and Temporality*. As he notes, Keir Elam's 'four temporal levels' include 'historical time' – 'the historical context of dramatic events' – but do not include time as experienced by the audience, what Jay Gipson King classifies as 'Audience time ... time as experienced by a spectator sitting in the house.'[18] I would add that there is a further temporality that comes into play when history plays are performed, what we might call 'audience historical time': the spectators' sense of how distant or proximate they are, historically, to the events represented onstage. The particular cognitive challenge – the 'puzzle' – of a live encounter with a dual timeline play lies in this ongoing combination of movements between clock time, Elam's historical time, *audience* historical time, Gipson King's audience time, dramatic time ('the progression of the plot or dramatic action') and narrative time ('the fictional time experienced by the *characters* within the story').[19]

This contrary motion – rather like the six faces and dozens of movable blocks on a Rubik's Cube, being twisted conversely at opposite sides, and then turned around and twisted again – produces a disorientating effect with regard to the present. Narrative theory scholar Mark Currie, in his book *About Time*, proposes that 'When we read a novel we make present events that are in the past, and when we live life we often do the opposite: we live the present as if it were already in the past, as if it were the object of a future memory.'[20] This means that 'there is a hermeneutic circle between the presentification of fictional narrative and the depresentification of lived experience.'[21] Under the special conditions of theatrical performance, I suggest that

---

[17] David Ian Rabey, *Theatre, Time and Temporality: Melting Clocks and Snapped Elastics* (Bristol: Intellect, 2016), 28.
[18] Quoted in Rabey, *Theatre, Time and Temporality*, 91.
[19] Ibid., 91.
[20] Mark Currie, *About Time: Narrative, Fiction and the Philosophy of Time* (Edinburgh: Edinburgh University Press, 2010), 30.
[21] Ibid., 31.

for an audience, depresentification operates in a different way, since the movement between historical eras leads us to question *when* the present (in audience historical time) is. Because, as noted earlier, we may not finish moving between eras until the end of the performance, we don't know if we're in the middle, between past and future, or if we're at the historically latest point. As Currie puts it, what is the 'base temporality in relation to which the prolepsis [or analepsis] is anachronous'?[22] To return to Rabey's analogy of the hinge, then, the movement through time in the dual timeline history play is '*in* and *through* the present'; future events (in our present) 'hinge on' the past that we are presented with. And, if the play should travel forward into the future as well as the past – as in Ella Hickson's *Oil* or Samuel Adamson's *Wife*, discussed in Chapter 3 – then our present becomes pivotal, whether featured in the play's dramatic representation or not. A hinge can, of course, if detached from the door jamb, rotate 360 degrees, producing the effect of circular time. Dual timeline plays, then, are never really only about two historical eras, because the 'now' of audience historical time is the hinge on which the action pivots. On occasion, this audience time may be close to the present time of the play's chronology, as when Shelagh Stephenson's *An Experiment with an Air Pump* is set in 1999, which was one year into the future when it was first staged at the Manchester Royal Exchange, but was ten years in the past when it was revived at Hampstead Theatre in 2009. Or the play's present time may be close, but consciously distant, as when Winsome Pinnock sets the contemporary part of *Rockets and Blue Lights* (2020) around the bicentenary of the Abolition of the Slave Trade Act, in 2007 – long enough to feel contemporary but also historical.

Dual timeline stories have also been popular in fiction and film; we might think of *The Hours,* adapted from the 1999 novel by Michael Cunningham into a 2002 movie by Stephen Daldry, or of A. S. Byatt's 1990 novel *Possession,* adapted and directed by Neil LaBute in 2002. Such narratives, particularly where they cross over from literature to

---

[22] Ibid., 35.

cinema, invite admiration for their feats of timeline plate-spinning, but achieve a kind of closure, even if a melancholy one, in ways that are similar to the 1990s 'ghost' plays about the Victorians. By contrast, the time-bound nature of the polychronic history play holds its audiences suspended in historical time – we are 'in' history – and meaning isn't revealed until the last moment, when we know not only what the 'writerly' playwright will do to manipulate the relationship between these worlds, but also what is possible in each of the worlds of the play and what is not. We won't know this until the play has shown us all there is to show. Polychronic plays primarily offer a way of working through *feelings about history* instead of making a pseudo-objective historical argument. This, I would a propose, is all the more necessary in the present political and cultural climate, where ideas about the past are driven by emotion, however much populist and authoritarian leaders might style themselves as bluff voices of reason or 'common sense'.[23]

The Pride

My first example of how this type of history play operates in the twenty-first century is Alexi Kaye Campbell's *The Pride*. It was first staged at the Theatre Upstairs at the Royal Court in 2008, was subsequently produced Off-Broadway in 2010, and was revived by its original director, Jamie Lloyd, at Trafalgar Studios in London in 2013. The play is a four-hander set in 1958 and 2008, with scenes alternating between the two periods. In each era there is an Oliver, a Philip and a Sylvia, though not the same ones; the fourth actor plays all the other roles. They are occasionally aware of each other's presence as the scenes and eras change. As Campbell says in the Author's Note, 'The two different periods should melt into each other. They are distinct from each other in appearance but they know each other in spirit … The past is a ghost in the present just as the present is a ghost of prescience

[23] See Hannah Rose Woods, *Rule, Nostalgia: A Backwards History of Britain* (London: Penguin, 2022), 22–30.

in the past.'[24] In the 1958 timeline, Philip is married to Sylvia; she is a former actor turned illustrator for children's books, and Oliver is the children's author whose fantastical book about 'a jungle in the heart of England',[25] featuring a creature called a 'Bellyfinch',[26] is her current commission. Sylvia is very keen that Oliver and Philip should meet, and it seems important to her that they get on. Philip and Sylvia have been trying for a baby, and, we later find out, they have been told that there is no medical reason for not conceiving yet. The long opening scene is the first encounter between Philip and Oliver, where conversation is guarded, innocuous on the surface but freighted with meaning for the gay subculture of the time:

> OLIVER. I walked. I thought it would take me slightly longer.
> PHILIP. It's a lovely evening.
> OLIVER. Well, no rain in any case.
> PHILIP. All the way from Maida Vale?
> OLIVER. Yes, Maida Vale.
> PHILIP. Across the park, eh?
> OLIVER. Yes.
> PHILIP. That's a long walk.
> OLIVER. I enjoyed it.[27]

Philip seems to be somewhat mocking or dismissive of Oliver at the first meeting between the three, perhaps a little more familiar than politeness (and Oliver's working relationship to Sylvia) would warrant.[28] In time, they begin a sexual relationship, but Philip seeks to distance himself from Oliver and his feelings for him. Evidence of the affair is found by Sylvia – Oliver's favourite gold pen, left in the bedroom – but at some level it seems that Sylvia has facilitated the two men's meeting. After a violent sexual encounter between Philip and Oliver when the

---

[24] Alexi Kaye Campbell, *The Pride* (London: Nick Hern, 2013), 9.
[25] Ibid., 13.
[26] Ibid., 18.
[27] Ibid., 12.
[28] Ibid., 22.

former tries to deny his love,[29] we see the 1958 Philip presenting himself for aversion therapy, while in the last speech of the play, Sylvie announces her plan to leave Philip while he is sleeping.[30]

In the 2008 timeline, roles are reversed in some respects, as Philip (who never got further than Brighton in 1958, despite having hoped to emigrate), is a photographer who is 'always travelling';[31] Oliver is the well-travelled one in 1958. In the twenty-first-century timeline, Oliver is addicted to sex with strangers, and we first encounter him in an aborted sexual role play with a man dressed as a Nazi. Philip has recently left him because of his infidelities, and Oliver is seeking to fill the emptiness with more anonymous sex. In this timeline, Sylvia is Oliver's straight best friend and is starting a relationship with an offstage character, Mario; Oliver is sometimes demanding of her attention and time in a way that makes it difficult for her to maintain her commitments to Mario.[32] She engineers a reunion between Philip and Oliver in a park with champagne, over Pride weekend, and they reach a tentative rapprochement.

As noted above, the early scenes have a slightly edgy quality where Oliver and Philip are assessing each other, testing each other, alluding to gay subculture in coded references in a way that feels dangerous – as indeed it was in the post-war era. Philip's self-loathing and (justified) paranoia – his insistence that 'I am not like them' – is eloquently captured, and functions as a historical representation of internalized homophobia as a result of criminalization.[33] Inevitably, perhaps, the representation of a liberated gay lifestyle in the twenty-first century goes to the other extreme; by the early 2000s, even before dating and hook-up apps were widely used, sex was depicted as available everywhere, in every variety. Where Philip's pain in 1958 is his inability to accept his sexuality and all that it implies – and the actions that such acceptance

[29] Ibid., 80–1.
[30] Ibid., 117.
[31] Ibid., 41.
[32] Ibid., 66–9.
[33] Ibid., 76.

would compel him to take – Philip's pain in 2008 is a result of Oliver's neediness, his vanity, his inability to commit (until, possibly, the play's end) to monogamy. Such a contrast, intentionally or otherwise, implies a conservative liberalism where 'now it's gone too far the other way': what to do, when you have infinite options, rather than a stark, single dilemma?

In the Author's Note, Campbell explains that the world of the play should 'start to disintegrate and break up' as the story progresses, leaving behind the solid '1950s drawing-room play'.[34] Campbell expresses the hope that 'The two different periods should meld into each other. They are distinct from each other but they know each other in spirit; a young woman standing next to her elder self'.[35] Although this seems like a statement of intent for a radical theatricalization of the past, I would suggest that this is more of a signpost, a manicule to direct the audience, than a breaking with the conventions of play construction or form. An example of how this works is the stage direction in the first act: 'PHILIP *enters in his 1958 clothes; a ghost.* SYLVIA *can't see him and neither can* OLIVER, *but his presence, somehow, is felt. He emerges from the shadows.*'[36] Oliver is in conversation with Sylvia at this moment, and when this 'ghost' Philip speaks, it is only to say 'Oliver' three times as Oliver refers to 'That voice … The voice that says … You're no good', after which Philip '*stands back into the shadows*'.[37] Oliver is experiencing a moment of heightened emotion that Sylvia interprets as a danger sign ('I'll call Mario', she says, accepting Oliver's request that she stay with him that night rather than her boyfriend).[38] Neither of them can see Philip, Sylvia responds only to what Oliver is saying, and it's not clear that Oliver can hear 1958 Philip there in the room, as opposed to the voice in his head. This might seem like a rather pedantic breakdown of the moment, but what I am seeking to establish is that the 'ghost' is

---

[34] Ibid., 9.
[35] Ibid., 9.
[36] Ibid., 66.
[37] Ibid., 67–8.
[38] Ibid., 68.

only ghostlike for the audience or the reader of the play, underscoring the connections between the two periods. He does not impinge upon Oliver and Sylvia's perception of reality, on the inner 'world of the play', which remains delineated by social realism. While in scenic design terms the world may 'meld' and the distinctions between the periods 'disintegrate', it is necessary to the play's historicizing standpoint that they remain distinct. The ghosts are an affirmation of the connections and contrasts between these two timelines, rather than a puzzle that challenges that relationship.

The Seven Acts of Mercy

Anders Lustgarten's *The Seven Acts of Mercy*, first staged at the RSC in Stratford-upon-Avon, is inspired by the Baroque painter Michelangelo Merisi da Caravaggio, whose painting *The Seven Acts* [or *Works*] *of Mercy* is the altarpiece for the church of Pio Monte della Misericordia in Naples. The play can be considered, in part, as a biodrama since it imagines Caravaggio's life at the point of the painting's composition, but also uses the structure of a dual timeline play, with some scenes set in the church in Naples where Caravaggio works, in hiding after killing someone in a duel in Rome, and other scenes set in Bootle, Merseyside, in the present day. There, a retired union leader, Leon Carragher, brings up his grandson Mickey in the ways of socialism and art appreciation. Mickey '*knows far too much for his age – and far too little*'.[39] *The Seven Acts* thus also borrows from the tropes of the intergenerational history play, as discussed in Chapter 3. Leon only has months to live and is being threatened with eviction from his council flat because, according to the government's welfare reforms, it has a third bedroom and is therefore now considered 'under-occupied'.[40] Leon needs to ensure that Mickey is looked after when he dies, and, right on cue, Mickey's father Lee arrives back from Spain, having fled people to whom he owes

---

[39] Anders Lustgarten, *The Seven Acts of Mercy* (London: Methuen Drama, 2016), 10.
[40] Ibid., 29.

money. Lee is involved in removing the 'holdouts' (those who refuse to leave) from council properties that are due to be renovated as buy-to-let properties, which places him in direct conflict with his father and son.[41]

The Caravaggio sequence is refreshing in its directness and passion. The artist *'speaks with a broad Scouse accent'*,[42] and makes no secret of his contempt for the nobility and the church. His fame and talent give him licence to speak, and he tells the Marchese who was responsible for commissioning him, 'the poor have no place here. So I give 'em one. I tear the fat-faced children of bankers and kings out of their gilded frames, and in their place I put in the beggar and the tavern keeper and the whore. I give us our dignity back.'[43] Caravaggio argues about art with his model, Lavinia, who also works as a prostitute and is a talented painter in her own right; they talk about the value of art to poor people, in a way that feels relevant to a twenty-first-century audience, but unforced.[44] Their commentary helps to defuse the sense of an art history lesson that might otherwise have been suggested by the display of the painting at the ends of scenes and sequences (*'The painting flares into explosive life'*;[45] *'the glowing painting, which has the final word'*).[46] Meanwhile, in the present day, Mickey is compiling a series of photographs on his phone, a modern-day 'seven acts of mercy', and as each is enacted the relevant numbers 'illuminate' or 'burn' above the actors' heads.[47]

The play is also specific and unsparing in its depiction of poverty in England a few months after the Referendum on European Union membership and after six years of government-imposed austerity and welfare cuts. The 'spare bedroom tax', the food bank, the surreal, target-driven decisions about 'fitness to work' and the dominance of property investment over productive labour are all dealt with in ways that do not

[41] Ibid., 27.
[42] Ibid., 3.
[43] Ibid., 8.
[44] Ibid., 40.
[45] Ibid., 53.
[46] Ibid., 100.
[47] Ibid., 20, 42, 54, 66, 84, 96.

in themselves feel didactic or gratuitous. At the end, the two timelines merge, not with the discovery of a corpse or the appearance of a ghost, but with Caravaggio's exit from Naples ('Another road, another city'),[48] followed by his appearance wheeling on Leon, now at a hospice, four hundred years later. Positioned in the corner, Caravaggio is in this final scene '*The Observer, who makes the pain acknowledged and forgiven*'.[49] The idea of him appearing as a hospice porter is both absurd and moving, an affirmation of the artist's power to bear witness to pain, and our own potential to find that in their work and to feel less alone.

While it remains recognizably a dual timeline play, *The Seven Acts of Mercy* is structurally more intricate than *The Pride*, configuring as it does the three generations of the Carraghers and the familiar, familial trope of the death of socialism and of faith in the future, the 'seven acts' motif, Lavinia's ill-fated bid for freedom and Caravaggio's outlaw vision of art and society. It is a hybrid of the three types of history play analysed in this book so far, the biodrama, the intergenerational play and the dual timeline play. While this is at times an unwieldy mix, freighted with state-of-the-nation significance in its contemporary sequences, the irreverent treatment of biodrama helps to fortify the play against charges of being simply worthy or schematic.

Clybourne Park

Clybourne Park by Bruce Norris was first staged off-Broadway in 2010, and again at the Royal Court in London later that year, winning the Pulitzer Prize for Drama in 2011. *Clybourne Park* represents a more complex model than *The Pride* and *Seven Acts*, since it relies for its effects on both the conventions of the dual timeline play and also those of the adaptation of a prior canonical text. The text it adapts is Lorraine Hansberry's *A Raisin in the Sun* (1959), in which three generations of one African American family live in a small apartment in the Southside

---

[48] Ibid., 96.
[49] Ibid., 96.

of Chicago: grandmother Lena, daughter Beneatha, son Walter Lee and his wife Ruth, and their son Travis. When Walter senior, Lena's husband, dies, the insurance company pays out ten thousand dollars, of which Lena uses a portion as down payment on a house in Clybourne Park, an all-White suburb of Chicago. Mr Lindner, from the Residents' Association, attempts to dissuade the Youngers from moving in, making a counter-offer for the house on behalf of the residents to keep them out and preserve the racial homogeneity (and thus, the perceived property value) of the suburb. After Walter Lee invests both his share of the insurance money and his sister's share (which was to be used to fulfil her ambition to study in college to be a doctor) in a liquor store scheme and his friend Willy absconds with the money, Lena appears to waver, but allows Walter Lee to redeem some modicum of self-respect by turning down Lindner's offer a second time.

In fact, rather than an adaptation, *Clybourne Park* can be considered an appropriation of Hansberry's play. In Julie Sanders's definition, an appropriation 'affects a more decisive journey away from the informing source into a whole new cultural product and domain'.[50] Just as, in Sanders's example, when watching *West Side Story* it is not necessary to know Shakespeare's *Romeo and Juliet* for the musical to make sense, so *Clybourne Park* can stand alone as a contemporary, time-hopping comedy of manners, but can also be read in conversation with *A Raisin in the Sun*.[51] Norris's play makes its association with Hansberry's drama – and its invitation to compare one play with the other – overt through its title. Given how widely studied and how frequently revived the play is, the name of the Youngers' dream destination, the address where they intend to inhabit a modest three-bedroom bungalow, immediately draws attention to its appropriative strategy. (That said, the opening stage directions slightly fudge this connection by naming the location as 'in the near north-west of central Chicago',[52] rather

[50] Julie Sanders, *Adaptation and Appropriation* (Abingdon: Routledge, 2006), 26.
[51] Ibid., 27–8.
[52] Bruce Norris, *Clybourne Park* (London: Nick Hern, 2010), iv.

than the 'Southside' that is named in Hansberry's play.) Another way of looking at *Clybourne Park* is as both a prequel *and* a sequel to *A Raisin*. It is a prequel in that the first act is set in September 1959 and imagines the circumstances under which the previous occupants, Russ and Bev, may have wanted to move out quickly and sell the house for a knock-down price: namely, that their son Kenneth had experienced PTSD from his combat experience in the Korean War and had, two years earlier, committed suicide in his bedroom.

On the other hand, the play is a sequel in that the second act shows a group of modern characters – including members of the Residents' Association, a builder and the new owners of 406 Clybourne Street – meeting at the house to discuss the proposed vertical extension to the property. Lena, whose great aunt we are given to understand was the Lena from *A Raisin*, also grew up in this neighbourhood, and raises concerns on behalf of the long-time residents: 'And some of our concerns have to do with a particular period in history and the things that people experienced here in this community during that period [people who] … still managed to carve out a life for themselves and create a community despite a whole lot of obstacles?'.[53] From this, we register that after the period depicted by Hansberry's play, more Black families moved into Clybourne Park and encountered racism from the White residents. It appears that the current buyers – a White couple, Steve and Lindsey – are part of a gentrifying movement that is bringing White residents back to the area, after it had become predominantly Black in the 1970s and 1980s (as Steve clumsily tries to explain to Lena, having read a 'great article' on the subject).[54] Kathy, who apparently is assisting Lindsey and Steve with the legal and planning work on gutting and rebuilding the house, is the daughter of Karl Lindner, the Residents' Association representative whom we meet in *A Raisin* and again in the first act of *Clybourne Park*.

---

[53] Ibid., 79
[54] Ibid., 82.

Predictably perhaps, given this theatrical set-up, both acts escalate into blazing rows; in the first act, Russ is insisting on selling the house and won't intervene, despite Lindner's blandishments, to prevent the Youngers from moving in. In the second, Steve's attempt to signal his free-thinking becomes a foray into racist joke-telling in which everyone pitches in on the question of who has the right to take offence at misogynistic and/or racist jokes, as told by whom and in what context. As in Jackie Sibblies Drury's *We Are Proud to Present*, which premiered two years later, jokes function as markers of what the White characters might really be thinking and how White supremacy operates.

In addition to functioning as both prequel and sequel, *Clybourne Park* also folds the world of *A Raisin* into the conventions of the dual timeline history play, although its original setting was the year of its staging, 1959. Rather than a corpse, the key piece of evidence is a locker, stored upstairs and dragged down into the living area by the maid Francine and her husband Albert in the 1959 scene, and which is found again, buried under the now-dead crepe myrtle tree which Lena used to climb as a child. Only the builder, Dan, is interested in the letters that are stored in the locker – including Kenneth's suicide note. True to the established pattern of dual-timeline plays, Kenneth reappears as a ghost in the final sequence as Steve and Lindsey are leaving, arguing and oblivious, and as Dan begins to read the letters.

There are, perhaps, other ways of thinking about *Clybourne Park* as appropriation. White people – albeit at times awful, cringe-inducing White people – are centred in *Clybourne Park*, and the Black characters struggle to get a word in edgeways. Francine and Arnold in the first act are represented as self-possessed, dignified but wary around the privileged and volatile White family and neighbours. Lena and Kevin in the second act are much less guarded, willing to go into full argument mode with Steve; but it looks like an attempt to make both sides seem 'just as bad as each other'. There's also something of a false equivalence about the premise of the play itself, which seems to equate de facto, pre-Civil Rights Movement segregation as on a par with gentrification. Lena seems aware that the common enemy is capitalism, which uses racialization as another way to divide and rule; she begins to say that 'there are certain economic interests that are being served' by gentrifying a neighbourhood close to downtown.[55] But as noted, the argument becomes about telling offensive jokes rather than the bigger picture, implying that Black and White people alike are preoccupied with point-scoring and 'anti-PC' edginess (to use the vernacular of the 2010s). As an appropriation of Hansberry's play, *Clybourne Park* – in its focus on White pain and trauma over the Korean War – recentres Whiteness where *A Raisin* ground-breakingly centred African American experience.

We might usefully think of *Clybourne Park*'s prequel-and-sequel temporality – its deployment of both prolepsis and analepsis – in terms of Rabey's hinge, swinging between 1959 and 2009, with the actual starting point of the story gradually revealed as pivoting on events a few years earlier, when Kenneth returned from the Korean War. However, given the play's appropriation of its source text to centre White historical experience, *Clybourne Park* also does to *A Raisin* what Steve and Lindsey want to do to 406 Clybourne Street: it razes Hansberry's play and builds an oversized structure on top of it ('It just made more sense to start from scratch', says Lindsey).[56] At worst, it represents the 'gentrification' of Hansberry's play into a drama about how hard the 1950s was for White

---

[55] Ibid., 95.
[56] Ibid., 71.

people.[57] As Gregory S. Carr's article on the play proposes, *Clybourne Park* 'reinterprets *Raisin* from the white gaze'.[58] The play, like its White characters, is able to benefit from White privilege, achieving Broadway and Royal Court productions by 'broach[ing] sensitive racial issues by wrapping them in a veneer of satire'.[59] In this respect, Kwame Kwei-Armah's *Beneatha's Place* (2013), another sequel to *A Raisin in the Sun*, could be read as a re-appropriation of Hansberry's play that returns the focus to the Black characters, Beneatha and Asagai, as they begin their life together in Nigeria. After Asagai's assassination at the end of Act 1, the play imagines a subsequent academic and activist life and career for Dr (later Dean) Beneatha Asagai-Younger. Previously produced in the

---

[57] The above discussion may seem like an unnecessarily harsh evaluation of a play that was unanimously praised by London theatre critics at the time (as critics predicted, it went on to win the Olivier Award in 2011 for Best New Play). Lauded as 'sharp', 'spiky' and 'provocative' in reviews, several critics commented on the audience's laughter; they were reported as producing an exciting 'mixture of laughter and disbelief' (Charles Spencer, review of *Clybourne Park* by Bruce Norris, directed by Dominic Cooke, Royal Court Theatre, *Daily Telegraph*, 3 September 2010. Available online: https://www.telegraph. co.uk/culture/theatre/theatre-reviews/7980236/Clybourne-Park-Royal-Court-review. html (accessed 24 December 2022)), the play was 'cathartic' and 'left the audience howling with delight' (Aleks Sierz, review of *Clybourne Park* by Bruce Norris, directed by Dominic Cooke, Royal Court Theatre, *The Arts Desk*, 2 September 2010. Available online: https://theartsdesk.com/theatre/clybourne-park-royal-court-theatre (accessed 24 December 2022)); it 'had the audience gasping in shock and then rolling in cathartic laughter at the utter absence of political correctness' (John Nathan, review of *Clybourne Park* by Bruce Norris, directed by Dominic Cooke, Royal Court Theatre, London, *Jewish Chronicle*, 10 September 2010, reproduced in *Theatre Record* 30, no. 18 (2010): 924). Others agreed with Nathan in linking the play's generation of audience laughter with its willingness to say the (supposedly) unsayable, to 'indulge in the joys of politically incorrect transgression' (Sierz, *The Arts Desk*), to address 'the politically correct terrors of talking about race' (Paul Callan, review of *Clybourne Park* by Bruce Norris, directed by Dominic Cooke, Royal Court Theatre, *Daily Express*, 10 September 2010. Available online: https://www.express.co.uk/entertainment/theatre/198509/Review-Clybourne-Park-Royal-Court-London (accessed 24 December 2022)). With the benefit of a decade's hindsight, we might wonder whether 'confronting' racism by encouraging audiences to laugh at racist jokes was such a good idea, given how relentlessly public discourse has moved to the right since. Indeed, as Andrzej Lukowski observed in his review of a revival of the play in 2022, 'The discourse on race relations and white privilege has moved on a lot since it premiered to blockbuster effect at the Royal Court in 2010. And the liberal Obama-era America it satirises no longer exists' (Andrzej Lukowski, review of *Clybourne Park* by Bruce Norris, directed by Oliver Kaderbhai, Park Theatre, London, *Time Out*, 25 March 2022. Available online: https://www.timeout.com/london/theatre/clybourne-park-review (accessed 24 December 2022)).

[58] Gregory S. Carr, 'Interrogating Whiteness in Bruce Norris's *Clybourne Park*', *Theatre Symposium* 29 (2022): 64–72, 64.. doi:doi:10.1353/tsy.2022.0005

[59] Ibid., 69.

US at Baltimore Center Stage – where it played in rotating repertory with *A Raisin in the Sun* as The Raisin Cycle – *Beneatha's Place* was also revived in the UK when Kwei-Armah directed the play in 2023 at the Young Vic.[60] The idea of shared casting between *Raisin* and *Beneatha's Place* is an enticing example of two plays working together to create an extended timeline that an audience might experience in different sequences and combinations.

Love and Other Acts of Violence

Cordelia Lynn's play, *Love and Other Acts of Violence*, premiered at the reopened Donmar Warehouse in October 2021. The play serves as an example of a starker contrast between two diegetic timelines. Where *Clybourne Park* entwines its plots around an existing play, *Love and Other Acts* makes a point of creating a jarring dramaturgical contrast between the two timelines. As noted earlier in this chapter, this technique creates a conscious 'tear in the very canvas of the play; its breaks are not disguised, they are emphatically visible.'[61] The two historical periods are 'roughly now', where we witness a meeting and subsequent romance between 'Her' and 'Him' '*over roughly a decade*' (as the opening stage directions tell us), and Lemberg (now Lviv, in Ukraine) in 1918, which only appears in the Epilogue, about twenty minutes before the end of the play. The contrasting stories are complemented by contrasting styles, with the 'roughly now' scenes belonging to the contemporary 'meet-fast/talk-quickly genre of play', according to critic Matt Wolf.[62] Conversely, the Epilogue is presented according to a completely different set of design principles. Where the set for the present-day

---

[60] Carey Purcell, '*Beneatha's Place*, Part of Centerstage's *The Raisin Cycle*, Begins Performances May 8', *Playbill*, 8 May 2013. Available online: https://v.playbill.com/article/beneathas-place-part-of-centerstages-the-raisin-cycle-begins-performances-may-8-com-205018 (accessed 25 April 2023).

[61] Waters, *Secret Life*, 47.

[62] Matt Wolf, review of *Love and Other Acts of Violence* by Cordelia Lynn, directed by Elayce Ismail, Donmar Warehouse, London, londontheatre.co.uk, October 15, 2021. Available online: https://www.londontheatre.co.uk/reviews/love-and-other-acts-of-violence-review-donmar-warehouse (accessed 25 April 2023).

sequence 'consists of a bare wooden platform perched on a dirt bank', to herald the Epilogue 'Suddenly a fully furnished shtetl household drops from the ceiling'.[63] The performances in the Epilogue, like the new scenic design, are detailed and Naturalistic.

What's the relationship between the two timelines? Her and Him realize part way through their developing relationship that they share common family roots in Lviv: she as a Jew whose great-grandmother fled the pogrom at the end of the First World War, he as the descendant of the Polish troops who fought with the Austrians, Ukrainians and Russians over control of the city. Him has moved into Her's flat, and an important keepsake, a carved ram, goes missing. When, a long time later, Him reveals that he had stolen it, then panicked and denied it when confronted, and had thrown it into the river after they'd had a break-up, it precipitates a furious attack by Her that appears to leave Him dead. This violence does not come out of the blue, however; the country that the couple live in – which may be England – has been descending into fascism for some time. Both he, a history teacher and poet, and she, a physicist, lose their jobs, despite Her's initial assumption that the regime would not have an ideological problem with the laws of physics. They witness the state execution of protesters, and Him confesses to having joined a mob and killed a man, possibly the wrong person. Her and Him had traded blows and ethnic slurs prior to this point, with Him's declared feminism and passion for social justice proving wafer-thin compared to the depths of his entitlement, mansplaining and 'main character syndrome'. The most chilling moment of this part of the play is the very brief scene, seemingly early in the development of fascist rule, where they laugh at the ridiculousness of the sudden mania for 'FLAGS EVERYWHERE', a state that the Westminster government seemed to have reached already by 2021.[64]

---

[63] Nick Curtis, review of *Love and Other Acts of Violence* by Cordelia Lynn, directed by Elayce Ismail, Donmar Warehouse, London, *Evening Standard*, 21 October 2021. Available online: https://www.standard.co.uk/culture/theatre/love-and-other-acts-of-violence-donmar-warehouse-review-anti-semitism-b960718.html (accessed 17 March 2023).

[64] Cordelia Lynn, *Love and Other Acts of Violence* (London: Nick Hern, 2021), 40.

The Epilogue allows us to see Tatte, Her's great-great-grandfather, carving that treasured ram – a teething toy for a baby – in the drawing room where he chats with his daughter Baba and receives updates on the Polish advance. As feared, the soldiers force entry, find Baba's two young brothers under the floorboards and murder them and Tatte; Baba's hiding place is more secure, and she emerges to behold her dead family while a soldier watches her; he throws the ram away and says he will only let her go if she begs. Baba recites the Traveller's Prayer in Hebrew, which the man seems to think is her begging. It begins to snow, and Baba smiles (because she thinks that is what the Man expects, in order for her to escape? Because he is about to meet the same fate as Him in the present-day sequence? Because Baba knows that someday, somehow, he will?).

If we consider *Love and Other Acts of Violence* through the lens of the dual timeline history play, a number of features come into sharper focus. If the play had presented the events in chronological order, with the Epilogue first, it would have implied a straightforward cause-and-effect, still more so if both parts of the play were presented Naturalistically. By reversing the order and calling this scene an Epilogue, the relationship seems more tentative: is this a cyclical pattern rather than two simple nodal points? Her's apparent murder of Him over the ram, likewise, seems less an act of historical score-settling than it would have with a then-to-now timeline. Nevertheless, what would have been the 'big reveal' of a more conventional dual-timeline play – Her and Him's common historical provenance – is shared with a reader thirty pages into the script, so that it is the ram that becomes the concrete object of significance that unifies the two parts. As we have seen, the doubling of roles is a convention in dual timeline plays, and multi-rolling as subsequent generations of the same family is a frequently used pattern in the intergenerational history play (see Chapter 3). The script is clear that not only are the actors for Baba and the Man the same but that they are the great-grandparents of Her and Him; however, in performance, this instruction is not visible, creating a greater ambiguity. We might also note that the Naturalism of the Epilogue matches the dominant theatrical style of the beginning of the twentieth century – reflecting Grochala's 'solid modernity' – while the present-day scenes are more 'liquid': episodic, in indeterminate order, and beginning *in medias res*; it is 'a recognisably millennial couples play à la Nick Payne's *Constellations* or Duncan Macmillan's *Lungs*', as Rosemary Waugh observed in her review.[65] Thus, while *Love and Other Acts of Violence* is evidently a dual timeline play, it reverses the conventional chronology of this category of drama, yet remains an incomplete, multifaceted puzzle. It alludes to ideas of transgenerational trauma, but this may be an endless cycle rather than one historical incident explaining another; it brings in elements of the intergenerational history play, with the 'middle generations' left out; it challenges the social and political tendency to see current events sharply but the distant past more hazily. And, in its unexpected, sudden descent of a different world from the ceiling, the Donmar production recalled Tony Kushner's *Angels in America*.

In a pattern that will be very familiar by now, critics were divided on the quality of the play, accusing it of being 'at least three plays' and lamenting that it did not live up to the promise of the 'meet-fast/talk-quickly genre' that it began as. For Arifa Akbar it was 'an audaciously jagged creation' but it 'feels like one play latched onto another'.[66] Matt Wolf called it 'gerrymandered and contrived'.[67] Caroline McGinn thought the two parts of the play coexisted 'without much connection or correlation'; it is 'confusing' and, although the first part works well, it then 'goes and wanders off into at least three other plays'.[68] Nick Curtis

[65] Rosemary Waugh, review of *Love and Other Acts of Violence* by Cordelia Lynn, directed by Elayce Ismail, Donmar Warehouse, London, *iNews*, 20 October 2021. Available online: https://inews.co.uk/culture/arts/love-and-other-acts-of-violence-donmar-warehouse-review-1258815 (accessed 25 April 2023).

[66] Arifa Akbar, review of *Love and Other Acts of Violence* by Cordelia Lynn, directed by Elayce Ismail, Donmar Warehouse, London, *Guardian*, 18 October 2021. Available online: https://www.theguardian.com/stage/2021/oct/18/love-and-other-acts-of-violence-review-donmar-warehouse (accessed 25 April 2023).

[67] Wolf, review of *Love and Other Acts*.

[68] Caroline McGinn, review of *Love and Other Acts of Violence* by Cordelia Lynn, directed by Elayce Ismail, Donmar Warehouse, London, *Guardian*, 18 October 2021. Available online: https://www.timeout.com/london/theatre/love-and-other-acts-of-violence-review (accessed 25 April 2023).

agreed with McGinn's judgement that there are 'three different plays struggling to get out',[69] while Wolf praises the familiar pace, form and initial subject matter of the beginning and middle; it makes for 'two-thirds of a major play before going off the rails in a final sequence'.[70] The play is accused of being 'rushed and underdeveloped' by Dzifa Benson,[71] and yet 'much too schematic' by Clive Davis.[72] It is odd to note how, well over four decades after Churchill's *Cloud Nine*, similar leaps in historical time and switches of genre within a play are held to be lapses of taste or errors betraying inexperience.

A Museum in Baghdad

Hannah Khalil's play *A Museum in Baghdad*, first staged by the RSC in 2019, has a more complex dramaturgy than any of the plays discussed so far. Like *Seven Acts*, it mixes biodrama and fiction. It places the story of the early twentieth-century scholar, archaeologist, author, political agent and traveller Gertrude Bell – who helped found the Baghdad Archaeological Museum in 1926 – in juxtaposition with a fictional figure in 2006, Ghalia Hussein, an Iraqi recently returned from exile in London, and who is organizing the reopening of the museum after extensive looting during the chaos of the American-led invasion of Iraq in 2003. Hussein appears to be partly based on Lamia Al-Gailani Werr (1938–2019), one of Iraq's first female archaeologists and a key figure in

[69] Curtis, review of *Love and Other Acts*.

[70] Wolf, review of *Love and Other Acts*.

[71] Dzifa Benson, 'Intriguing Study of Whether Trauma is Passed Down in Our Genes', review of *Love and Other Acts of Violence* by Cordelia Lynn, directed by Elayce Ismail, Donmar Warehouse, London, *Daily Telegraph*, 18 October 2021. Available online: https://www.telegraph.co.uk/theatre/what-to-see/love-acts-violence-review-intriguing-study-whether-trauma-passed/ (accessed 25 April 2023).

[72] Clive Davis, 'A Callow Meditation on History', review of *Love and Other Acts of Violence* by Cordelia Lynn, directed by Elayce Ismail, Donmar Warehouse, London, *The Times*, 18 October 2021. Available online: https://www.thetimes.co.uk/article/love-and-other-acts-of-violence-review-a-callow-meditation-on-history-w8fvmp0w2 (accessed 17 March 2023).

the recovery of the museum and its artefacts after 2003.[73] In actuality, the museum was officially reopened in 2015, rather than 2006, as the Iraqi National Museum, and had to close again in the year of the play's premiere, 2019, during anti-government protests, reopening in 2022.[74] An audience will not necessarily know these components of fact-based and fictionalized history and how they are combined in performance; as noted in Chapter 1, one of the advantages that the playwright has over a history play's audience is that, on the whole, information has to be taken on face value as factual in real time, according to the world of the play – even if a mid-interval Google search may, for the curious, reveal spoilers or the playwright's use of creative license.

Additionally, while the audience may perceive *A Museum in Baghdad* to be operating on two timelines, the play script indicates that there are three: 'Then', meaning 1926, 'Now', referring to 2006, and 'Later', which 'could be in 50, 100, or 1,000 years in the future'.[75] As noted at the beginning of the chapter, we always already have more than two timelines in the dual timeline play, as the audience's 'now' makes up a third point of comparison – even if the play text labels 'Now' as 2006. As suggested above, an audience member's historical perspective may be influenced, in more or less specific ways, by the additional events of the period 2006–19, which may cast the looting of 2003 and its aftermath in a different light. Khalil's play also features two transhistorical characters, Abu Zaman, who '*straddles time and space, trying to affect the future*' and Nasiya, '*an Arab woman who is timeless*'.[76] At the play's climax – the opening ceremonies for the museum in 1926 and 2006, presented simultaneously – Nasiya climbs up and removes a 4,500-year old crown from its glass case and crushes it in protest: 'people are starving while

[73] Richard Sandomir, 'Lamia Al-Gailani Werr, 80, Dies; Archaeologist Rescued Iraqi Art', *New York Times*, 25 January 2019. Available online: https://www.nytimes.com/2019/01/25/obituaries/lamia-al-gailani-werr-80-dies-archaeologist-rescued-iraqi-art.html (accessed 25 April 2023).

[74] Hadani Ditmars, 'Iraq Museum Reopens after Three-Year Hiatus', *The Art Magazine*, 11 March 2022. Available online: https://www.theartnewspaper.com/2022/03/11/iraq-museum-baghdad-reopens (accessed 25 April 2023).

[75] Hannah Khalil, *A Museum in Baghdad* (London: Methuen Drama, 2019), 3.

[76] Ibid., 2.

you worry about dead things'.[77] Abu Zaman appears as a character in 1926 and 2006, a museum worker or caretaker, but also leader of the choral sections of the play, spoken in English and Arabic. He is said to 'haunt' the museum, to be a memory of all the missing artefacts, a 'stocktake of the missing', but also, 'something else', according to a US soldier stationed at the museum, something not necessarily disturbing, but nevertheless inexplicable. The play's dramaturgy has many other unusual features as it traces the parallel attempts of the two protagonists, Bell and Hussein, to open their respective museums in response to political imperatives. There is a large, empty glass exhibition case that dominates the set, which at times is used as a kind of crystal ball where characters attempt to see the future.[78] The performance space is gradually filled with sand,[79] culminating in Gertrude being covered in sand as she climbs inside the glass box.[80] Events are sometimes decided by a coin toss by Abu Zaman, which '*affects the timeline*', yet Abu Zaman is unable to prevent a recurring event that we see, the future head of the museum Mohammed – a curator in the 'Now' timeline – being kidnapped on his cigarette break.[81] Occasionally, what we have seen is called into question, as though the audience has witnessed an alternative version of events. For example, the soldier, Private York, confesses to Layla to having bought (what she thinks is) a stolen artefact, and only Layla realizes that the conversation has happened before, but now begins to think it was a dream, even though the audience witnessed it.[82] Conversely, we may now think that the present scene is a dream, and the earlier scene was real. This all leads us to question the repeated assertions from characters that the past is unchangeable.[83]

---

[77] Ibid., 79. The play script specifies that there are '*three ribbons, three pairs of scissors, three important people*', presumably for the three timelines, even though the 'Later' remains nebulous throughout (ibid., 71).

[78] Ibid., 38, 91.

[79] Ibid., 2.

[80] Ibid., 92.

[81] Ibid., 6.

[82] Ibid., 65.

[83] Ibid., 18, 38.

As the above analysis indicates, *A Museum in Baghdad* constitutes a refreshing change from the overdetermination of many previous dual timeline dramas. Its 'eccentricities', as Khalil calls them,[84] are a way of complicating western, industrialized notions of time and historical causality, even when the comparisons between periods are expressed with striking directness, for example when Nasiya begins a line with 'There was no food to eat, no water' each time Abu Zaman tosses a coin, applying the statement to 'the British', 'the Americans' and 'the state' in turn.[85] Nevertheless, such a fluid structure does have its drawbacks. Characters' motivations and fates can be unclear: the dedicated Ghalia abruptly leaves, Gertrude is buried in sand (a metaphor for physical or mental ill health, perhaps?) and we never get to see who is kidnapping Mohammed in the future and what happens to him. Because of the single setting of the museum, and the disparate characters assembled there, a considerable amount of offstage action and backstory has to be relayed to us (for example, Gertrude and Ghalia's contrasting mediations on 'home' just before the opening ceremonies).[86]

Reviewers disagreed over whether the play was 'over-wrangled and overwritten',[87] or whether its ten-year gestation period 'probably wasn't long enough'.[88] Predictably – given the critical patterns established in Chapter 2 – critics focused on the biographical subject of Gertrude Bell,

[84] Ibid., 'Author's Note', no pagination.

[85] Ibid., 77–8.

[86] Ibid., 68–70.

[87] Miriam Gillinson, review of *A Museum in Baghdad* by Hannah Khalil, directed by Erica Whyman, Swan Theatre, Stratford-upon-Avon, *Guardian*, 22 October 2019. Available online: https://www.theguardian.com/stage/2019/oct/22/a-museum-in-baghdad-review-hannah-khalil?CMP=gu_com (accessed 25 April 2023).

[88] Nick Curtis, review of *A Museum in Baghdad* by Hannah Khalil, directed by Erica Whyman, Swan Theatre, Stratford-upon-Avon, *Evening Standard*, 24 October 2019. Available online: https://www.standard.co.uk/culture/theatre/a-museum-in-baghdad-review-fascinating-history-of-a-nation-bogged-down-by-monotonous-mood-a4269701.html (accessed 25 April 2023).

lamenting that this was not a straightforward biodrama.[89] Dominic Cavendish noted that 'the theatre is crying out for strong female roles' and found himself 'yearning for more straightforward details of Bell's handling of herself in this far-off land';[90] similarly, Nick Curtis, while happy to have 'learned more about the history of the nation and of Middle Eastern geopolitics than I have from many Iraq War dramas', regretted that the play wasn't a 'drama that explored [Bell's] life in depth'.[91] Furthermore, it seems that critics remain unsettled by history plays that weave periods together rather than keeping them separate. For Miriam Gillinson, the play 'awkwardly straddles two worlds';[92] Cavendish advises: 'Were these chapters to sit largely separate, possibly either side of an interval, or even in two related plays, the result could not only be instructive but attain the accumulative force of a theatrical epic'.[93] This pattern of reviewing practice demonstrates the continuing critical resistance to history plays that experiment beyond the leaps in time that Caryl Churchill, Howard Brenton, David Hare and David Edgar, among others, first deployed in the 1970s and 1980s. The expectation to be educational and informative – in this case, to be either straightforward reportage or biodrama – seems to have become ever stronger in the intervening years.

Rockets and Blue Lights

The final play that I want to bring into dialogue with the other works in this chapter is Winsome Pinnock's *Rockets and Blue Lights*, first staged

---

[89] One reason for the play's avoidance of a conventional biographical structure, with Bell as the subject, may have been the release of the film *Queen of the Desert*, a biopic of Bell, starring Nicole Kidman in 2015; according to the reviews, Khalil first became interested in Bell in 2009 (Dominic Cavendish, review of *A Museum in Baghdad* by Hannah Khalil, directed by Erica Whyman, Swan Theatre, Stratford-upon-Avon, *Daily Telegraph*, 23 October 2019. Available online: https://www.telegraph.co.uk/theatre/what-to-see/museum-baghdad-review-rsc-swan-stratford-upon-avon-admirable/ (accessed 25 April 2023)).

[90] Cavendish, review of *A Museum in Baghdad*.

[91] Curtis, review of *A Museum in Baghdad*.

[92] Gillinson, review of *A Museum in Baghdad*.

[93] Cavendish, review of *A Museum in Baghdad*.

at Manchester Royal Exchange in 2020, transferring to the National Theatre, London in 2021. Like the plays of Khalil and Lustgarten considered earlier, Pinnock's play incorporates biographical elements. It contains a speculative account of J. M. W. Turner's sea voyage in 1840, when he posed as a ship's artist under an assumed name, a research trip that enabled him to paint two of his most famous works, *Slavers Throwing Overboard the Dead and Dying – Typhoon Coming On* (1840), sometimes referred to as *The Slave Ship*, and *Rockets and Blue Lights* (1840). As Clare Finburgh Delijani explains, Pinnock's play is named after the latter painting, 'to indicate that the legacies of the institution of slavery endure centuries after 1807, after official Emancipation' ('rockets and blue lights in the sky were a warning signal from the Royal Navy for those vessels engaging in human trafficking, which at this point was illegal under British law').[94] But Turner's is only one of the timelines and character groups featured in the play. Finburgh Delijani proposes that the play 'shifts between four time periods, providing a dramaturgical means for the past to haunt the present'.[95] In 2006, we see a script reading taking place involving the cast of a film, *The Ghost Ship*, supposedly based on the Zong massacre that Turner's *Slavers* depicts. Present at this read-through are the actors Lou, who plays the slave Olu, and Roy, who plays Turner, along with the Black director, Trevor, and Reuben, a marine archaeologist and consultant on the film. In the opening scene, set in 2007, we had already encountered Lou discussing the *Slavers* painting – which is on display in a museum on board a ship – with an art teacher, Essie. We see scenes from *The Ghost Ship*, set in 1781, where Olu is 'dragged from the hold of a ship and, after violently resisting, thrown overboard, joining adults and children thrashing for their lives'.[96] However, we are also shown arguments between Lou and Trevor, as the film's focus on the lost stories of the enslaved Africans gives way to a more bankable Turner biopic. Additionally, there are

---

[94] Clare Finburgh Delijani, 'The Afterlives of Enslavement: Histories of Racial Injustice in Contemporary Black British Theatre,' *Modern Drama* 65, no. 4 (2022): 473–98, 480.
[95] Ibid., 476.
[96] Ibid., 476.

scenes from *The Ghost Ship* that feature Turner in 1840 on board the merchant ship, the *Glory*. Finburgh Delijani sees Pinnock's *Rockets and Blue Lights* as belonging to a group of dramas that she calls 'postcolonial ghost plays'.[97] Hers is a convincing analysis, and would place the play in fruitful conversation with the nineteenth-century ghost plays I discussed in *Heritage, Nostalgia and Modern British Theatre*. However, in order to read it as a contemporary history play, in dialogue with the examples in the rest of this chapter, I want to offer a different interpretation focused on the play's doing/undoing/redoing of history – its action of 'repetition/reproduction', to recall the formulation used by Soyica Diggs Colbert, and cited in Chapter 2.

Despite the four timelines mentioned, *Rockets and Blue Lights* mostly follows the 1840 and the 2007 timelines, making it look and feel strongly like a dual-timeline play. If there is a single character whose through-line we follow, it is Lou's, from her arrival at the read-through, to the party that she holds instead of attending an awards ceremony for which she has received a nomination for *The Ghost Ship*. However, the key characters in the play's version of 1840 are a Black family – merchant seaman Thomas, the formerly enslaved Lucy and their daughter Jess – rather than Turner, who meets Thomas on board the *Glory* as it makes its journey to the Cape, where it is re-fitted with shackles in order to carry slaves to Brazil (enslaving Thomas, in turn, for trying to free those already shackled). This means that Turner exists in the play both as the film's clichéd 'tortured genius' artist, and also as a more deeply flawed historical character. To add a further dimension to this 'complex seeing', the actor playing Turner in *The Slave Ship* is Roy, a longstanding acquaintance of Lou's who has few qualms about centring himself professionally at Lou's expense.[98] In addition to playing skilfully with timelines, then, *Rockets and Blue Lights* is equally daring with

---

[97] Ibid., 473. The other plays that Finburgh Delijani considers are Janice Okoh's *The Gift* (2020), debbie tucker green's *ear for eye* (2018) and Selina Thompson's *Salt* (2018).

[98] In the 2021 NT production, Roy explains that he accepted his 'Best Actor' award but made a speech about how it really belonged to Lou, garnering applause for his performative generosity.

genre, mixing elements of the film-set romance (Lou and Reuben), the biopic, the ghost story and a satire on the heritage industry's treatment of the slave trade. There is even a sequence where Lou visits her dying grandfather, Clarke, a Windrush-era first generation immigrant, and he only appears to recognize her when she speaks in character as the role she plays in an American television series, Captain Sola Andrews. The conversation between Lou and Vonnie, her sister who stayed in their council flat to look after their mother and grandfather, calls to mind the final act of Churchill's *Top Girls*.

Certainly, the extended appearance of conversational ghosts is a recurring feature: Turner's mother appears to her son; a formerly enslaved woman, Meg, tells her story to Lou; in the scene with Vonnie and Clarke, Clarke seems to be simultaneously incapacitated in bed and speaking as a much younger version of himself, in a sharp 1950s suit. However, just as the play dramatizes history but also satirizes that process in the *Ghost Ship* plotline, so *Rockets* unpicks the 'ghost' motif. When Lou objects to the script changes that render her character Olu as a naked, abused body rather than a developed character – and, in the final sequence, a ghost – she says to Trevor: 'A ghost, for fuck's sake. We're always playing ghosts in one way or another. We're not seen as real functioning people. When is this shit going to stop?'[99] The intricate patterning of the play involves different timelines and generations of characters taking voyages, and being separated by the sea. The Atlantic slave trade is rendered as art, then rewritten and re-enacted in film, and reproduced as a heritage attraction; its steps are retraced by Reuben's research and also by Thomas, who unwittingly rejoins the slave trade in the supposedly post-abolition 1840s. Following him, Lucy and Jess sign articles for the same ship; Jess says, 'We make this journey for ourselves now.'[100] Injustices are repeated, compounded, echoed: the play's Turner, who invested in a sugar works and who insists as Thomas is chained and manacled, 'Leave me out of it. It's got nothing to do with me', doubles as

---

[99] Winsome Pinnock, *Rockets and Blue Lights* (London: Nick Hern, 2020), 39.
[100] Ibid., 77.

Roy, who colludes in expanding his role in the film, takes the glory, and yet insists to Lou, 'I have always had your back.'[101]

In these repetitions and reproductions, *Rockets* also functions as a historiographic metadrama,[102] ruminating on the means by which some individuals are commemorated, and others overlooked, forgotten or unrecorded, including in contemporary media that sets out to recuperate those lost voices. Moreover, as Finburgh Delijani comments, the throwing overboard of enslaved Africans 'has far-reaching consequences, since the unmemorialized cannot undertake the essential transmigration to the realm of the ancestors, where they are threaded to the unborn'.[103] In other words, while the play's dramaturgy threads these multiple timelines together, the historical rupture that it depicts concerns an *inability* to thread the living and the dead together, bringing about these restless ghosts. By the same token, the efforts to commemorate slavery's abolition and to educate current generations depict an inability to do so without repeating historical erasure and injustice. The answer, of course, is not to give up because of the difficulty and discomfort of it all, but as Lou says after the party, 'Do better. Educate yourself, Roy.'[104] At the play's end, Thomas becomes a transhistorical figure; as a Brazilian overseer cocks his rifle, he tells him, 'I'm not surprised by your fear of me, After all, I have survived much.'[105] Recalling the history of enslaved Africans and linking it to the New Cross and Grenfell fires, to the deaths of Black people in custody, and to contemporary racist murders, Thomas tells the overseer, 'I have lived and died ten million times. And I will live and live again.'[106] It is another powerful and moving instance of a play responding to Maurya

---

[101] Ibid., 56, 70.

[102] See Alexander Feldman, *Dramas of the Past on the Twentieth-Century Stage.*

[103] Finburgh Delijani, 'Afterlives', 476.

[104] Pinnock, *Rockets and Blue Lights*, 73. This line appears in the 2020 edition of the play but was not spoken in the National Theatre production.

[105] Ibid., 79.

[106] Ibid., 79–80.

Wickstrom's call, discussed in Chapter 2, to explore 'what happens when history is initiated, not finished'.[107]

Conclusion

In this chapter, I have sought to demonstrate how multiple temporalities can operate in even the most straightforward dual timeline plays, thanks to the difference between Elam's historical time ('the historical context of dramatic events') and *audience* historical time (the audience's historical distance from the events represented onstage). I have adopted the analogies of the hinge and the puzzle – in particular, the Rubik's Cube – to attempt to capture the contrary, intersecting and circular movements adopted by these plays: for them, time is always out of joint. The works examined have ranged from those whose timelines haunt each other more passively (*The Pride*) to those that merge or even reverse timelines, so that we struggle to locate our 'base temporality' (*Love and Other Acts of Violence, A Museum in Baghdad, Rockets and Blue Lights*). While the figure of the ghost is still alive and well as a means of rendering the past as present – and rendering the audience, in the present, as objects of a future memory – it is joined by a range of other techniques for achieving similar ends: the crystal-ball museum cabinet, the coin toss and the influx of sand; the film-within-a-play; the painter and their illuminating visions; the fully realized historical stage set, crashing onto the airy, unfixed present.

Khalil's, Pinnock's and Lustgarten's texts, in particular, illustrate the increasingly layered nature of contemporary history plays, a type of new writing that combines a sense of openness and possibility with a deft control of form and the demands of intersecting timelines. Nevertheless, theatre lends itself to feeling as much as argumentation, to metaphor and transposition rather than the didactic and the literal. These are 'embodied and emotional' investigations of the past, not

---

[107] Wickstrom, *Fiery Temporalities*, 61.

'academic and theoretical' ones.[108] This chapter has sought to highlight the benefits of being able to name the dramaturgical components with reference to established ways of representing the past. To be able to explain the 'aesthetic architecture' of new writing set in the past (or pasts) in the ways proposed by this book means that our critical tools are sharper: we are less likely to accept, without scrutiny, journalists' and scholars' complaints that such plays lack craft and sophistication. On the other hand, we are less likely, with these classifications of the history play to hand, to claim that a piece of new writing is unique when it is actually in dialogue with other staged histories, past and present.

Polychronic history plays offer a way for playwrights and productions to remake the past through the manipulation of historical material, conjuring correspondences and parallels into being. Yet they rely for their pathos and power on recognizing the limitations of what is historically possible for those characters. The interventionist strategies of polychronic playwrights also hold significant appeal for creators of fantastic and alternate history plays, which are not bound by such rules. It is a selection of these plays that form the substance of the Coda which follows.

---

[108] Finburgh Delijani, 'Afterlives', 479.

Coda: Alternate and Fantastic Histories

Introduction

A coda can mean a final event or section. In classical music, it refers to an elaborate passage following the end of the main part of a piece of music and is often the most technically demanding. In classical ballet, it describes a concerted dance; that is, with all the dancers in formation. The plays that will be discussed in this Coda, in different ways, are elaborate or concerted examples of the patterns identified in the previous sections of the book, multiplying timelines and periods, creating temporal puzzles and setting up complex metatheatrical and paratheatrical games. The last few chapters have each focused on a different dramaturgical approach to the history play, from biodrama to intergenerational family drama to polychronic timelines. This coda groups together four plays that are positioned at the far end of the 'posthistorical' play type that Mark Berninger identifies, and that I discussed in Chapter 1. As previously noted, Berninger calls this 'the most problematic type of history play since it transcends most extensively the limits of what is traditionally seen as a history play. It contains a high degree of fictionalized history. Whether an event is documented or not is irrelevant'.[1] In Chapter 1 I argued that, by this definition, all attempts to stage history are posthistorical to some degree, and that fictionalizing history is the norm in both the work of professional narrative historians and the work of playwrights, novelists and screenwriters, since the past does not speak for itself but has to be

[1] Berninger, 'Variations', 40.

selected and arranged using literary tropes and genres. It is also the case that the plays analysed in Chapters 2, 3 and 4 all use elements of the fantastic, especially the works that I highlight. Victorian Mary Seacole has her Bluetooth earpiece; the characters in *Wife* are catapulted into the future; and *Rockets and Blue Lights* includes extended conversations with ghosts. As Lucie Armitt concedes in her discussion of fantasy, in a sense 'all imaginative work is fantas-*tic*; creativity put through a filter of everyday experience'.[2] Moreover, Karen Hellekson's description of alternate histories in prose fiction also rings true for the polychronic plays covered in the previous chapter in particular:

> Alternate histories question the nature of history and of causality; they question accepted notions of time and space; they rupture linear movement; and they make readers rethink their world and how it has become what it has. They are a critique of the metaphors we use to discuss history. And they foreground the 'constructedness' of history and the role narrative plays in its construction.[3]

So, plays with disrupted timelines, or 'oppositional' narratives that highlight the experience of the marginalized and undocumented, or works that draw attention to their writerly or metatheatrical qualities, are already producing effects comparable to those of alternate histories.

The reason that these plays appear in a Coda of their own is that, rather than including *elements* of alternate histories or the fantastic as the plays just mentioned do, alternate history or fantastic history is their starting point: it is where they are based. Hence, in Martin McDonagh's *A Very Very Very Dark Matter* (2018) and Alistair McDowall's *The Glow* (2022), the 'real world' that we recognize is only very lightly sketched in, and the fantastical feats of time travel that are possible in these narratives are not explained, simply presented as how the world of the play operates. In the other two plays considered in this coda, *Rapture* by Lucy Kirkwood (2022) and *Mr Burns: A Post-Electric Play* by Anne

---

[2]   Lucie Armitt, *Fantasy* (Abingdon: Routledge, 2020), 24.
[3]   Karen Hellekson, 'Toward a Taxonomy of the Alternate History Genre', *Extrapolation* 41, no. 3 (2000): 254–5.

Washburn (2014), we are offered alternate histories of either the future or the very recent past.

Alternate and fantastic history plays, then, are linked in that they typically explore history that did not happen, could not happen or hasn't happened yet. The examples that are investigated here are not widely regarded as 'history plays' because their history is deliberately 'unreliable' – that is, they overtly reject the pretence that history plays are unmediated true stories, derived neutrally from the historical record. Alternate-history and fantastic dramaturgies can offer a new, freeing perspective on how historical events resonate through time. They are also able to emphasize the sense of live encounter over the narrative function of drama: none of these plays have linear plots, nor do they provide conventional narrative closure. The disadvantage of this type of production is how hard an audience may have to work to construct a cohesive world from the limited information given and from the epic sweep of the action. When the view is so elevated, the atmosphere can be very thin.

I have opted for the term 'alternate history' rather than 'counterfactual history' since – according to Catherine Gallagher in her landmark study, *Telling It Like It Wasn't: The Counterfactual Imagination in History and Fiction* – alternate-history narratives 'invent not only fictional historical events but also fictional characters. Thus they extend the reach of the counterfactual mode into the realm of imaginative literature.'[4] As noted previously, every play analysed in this book invents events and characters to some degree, but alternate histories in the case of *The Glow* and *Rapture* denote a kind of conspiracy-theory approach to what we think we know about how history operates, and *Mr Burns*, as I will show, pursues a chaos-theory idea of history where a *Simpsons*

---

[4] Catherine Gallagher, *Telling It Like It Wasn't: The Counterfactual Imagination in History and Fiction* (Chicago: University of Chicago Press, 2018), 48. Gallagher prefers the term 'alternative histories', but that seemed too close to the 'oppositional histories' discussed by Peacock in *Radical Stages* for my purposes here. Karen Hellekson's proposed taxonomy of 'alternate histories' uses this term primarily (Hellekson, 'Toward', 248).

episode – rather than the flapping of a butterfly's wings – has enormous consequences for future civilizations.[5]

I have chosen to use 'fantastic' as an additional descriptor in acknowledgement of the element of fantasy in McDonagh and McDowall's time-travel plays. Lucie Armitt proposes that a key component of fantasy is its use of competing worlds, 'wherein one world, purportedly representing "reality", is left behind in preference for another which is unknown and "foreign" in the sense of being strange, fabulous or grotesque'.[6] Counterfactual histories hinge on a 'what if?', a 'nexus' where a decisive event could have turned out differently.[7] For Armitt, the 'what if?' in fantasy means that 'the laws of physics, logic, time, physiognomy, life and death and/or geography are usually subverted'.[8] Josy Miller uses 'the fantastic' to explain non-realist theatrical responses to 9/11. The incursion of the fantastic 'is incongruous with the established universe of the piece; this is why, in most cases, the fantastic emerges after the "rules" of the universe in which the piece is operating have been clearly established'.[9] Miller highlights, as an 'iconic example' of the use of the fantastic, Tony Kushner's *Angels in America*, which (as discussed in the Introduction) deploys such techniques in order to make sense of the devastation of AIDS.[10] A further example might be Katori Hall's *The Mountaintop* (2009). Set in Memphis in 1968, the night before Martin Luther King Jr's assassination, the play imagines an encounter between King and a motel maid, Camae, who is revealed to be an angel of death who will guide him to the afterlife. It begins by imitating realist form but breaks with it decisively part-way through, introducing snowstorms outside, flowers growing though the carpet, and a telephone line to God. In this, Hall's play represents a compressed version of the approach of August Wilson, whose plays

---

[5] Gallagher writes of 'the centuries-old connection between secret-history and counterfactual-history narrative' (*Telling*, 283).
[6] Armitt, *Fantasy*, 3.
[7] Gallagher, *Telling*, 52.
[8] Armitt, *Fantasy*, 3.
[9] Miller, 'Performing Collective Trauma', 200.
[10] Ibid., 201.

appear to have realist historical settings but reveal themselves on closer inspection, and over the course of his 'century cycle', to have magical and fantastical elements.[11] By contrast, the plays by McDonagh and McDowall that I am including as 'fantastic histories' announce their intentions from the start, with situations so outlandish, and presented in such a mannered way, that they cannot be read as realism.

Time Travel and Theatre

Before examining the four plays named above in detail, it may be helpful to consider the ways that audiences are primed to understand alternate timelines. Predominantly, this prior understanding is likely to come from television, prose fiction and film, where time travel tropes are seemingly ubiquitous.[12] However, experiments with time were also a particular feature of inter-war theatre, most famously the 'time plays' of J. B. Priestley, including *Dangerous Corner* (1932), *I Have Been Here Before* (1937), *An Inspector Calls* (1945) and *Time and the Conways* (1937), the latter touched on in Chapter 3. Noël Coward, also discussed in that chapter, is seemingly preoccupied with time travel as a way of charting historical and social change, not only in *Cavalcade* (1931) and *This Happy Breed* (1942), but also in period pieces like *Family Album: A Victorian Comedy with Music* (1936), and *Quadrille* (1952), subtitled 'a romantic Victorian comedy'. Coward's early play *Post-Mortem* remained unperformed on stage in his lifetime, but experimented with a time frame in which a soldier dies on the Western Front in 1917 and, at the moment of death, is transported forward in time to 1930, to visit his mother, father, fiancée and his former comrades in the trenches, in civilian life. *Peace in Our Time*, which premiered in 1947, imagines a London pub in an alternate timeline where Britain was invaded by the

---

[11] For example, as Elam notes, in the Broadway revision of *King Hedley II*, Aunt Ester's death 'causes all the lights to go out in the Hill district of Pittsburgh', and her voice seems to have been transferred to the cat's meow at the play's conclusion (192, 196).

[12] See de Groot, *Remaking History*, 132–7.

Nazis in 1940 and liberated in 1945. Like the contemporary plays in this Coda, *Peace in Our Time* takes us straight into the alternate-history scenario; there is no induction or conceptual framework. Coward's working title for the play was *Might Have Been*, and presumably the public's long awareness of the possibility of invasion during the war years meant that the alternative timeline needed no introduction.

By contrast, *Post-Mortem* integrates a discussion of time into the dialogue. The protagonist, John Cavan, discusses theories of time in the trenches with his restless intellectual friend Perry:

> Time is very interesting. Nobody has found out much about it, perhaps there isn't any, perhaps it's just a circle and Past and Future are the same. Funny if the current got switched and we all started remembering twenty years hence and looking forward to last Tuesday.[13]

Similarly, Priestley's time plays usually include some discussion, or at least allusions to, the tricks that time plays on the mind and alternative theories of time, as in Kay and Alan's conversations in *Time and the Conways*. Priestley's plays in this mode are often structured as time loops, where we return to where we started at the end: revisiting the innocence of the Conway family in 1919 (*Time and the Conways*), or receiving notice that the real (?) Inspector Goole is on his way (*An Inspector Calls*), or replaying the play's opening dialogue, but this time with a song on the radio interrupting the conversation, which would otherwise have been headed for disaster (*Dangerous Corner*).

We might also consider how theatre thrives on other forms of looping time. Theatre is all about repetition, from a succession of play-drafts to the processes of rehearsal, previews, the press night, to the run and the revival, theatre relies on embedding change in repetition, on reproducing the same phenomena on a nightly (or twice-daily) basis, always the same but always changing. Margherita Laera writes of theatre as fundamentally an adaptive process, where both adaptation and performance 'are nostalgic in their "ache for return", their desire to

---

[13] Noël Coward, *Post-Mortem*, in *First World War Plays*, edited by Mark Rawlinson (London: Bloomsbury Methuen Drama, 2014), 147.

come "home" again and again, wherever "home" might be'.[14] She quotes Marvin Carlson's characterization of theatre as a 'memory machine': '[t]he retelling of stories already told, the re-enactment of events already enacted, the experience of emotions already experienced, these are and have always been central concerns in all times and places'.[15] Laera goes on to summarize the core principles of performance as 'restored behaviour, representation of the world and a relentless repetition lacking the exactness of machines'.[16] For Sarah Grochala, 'disrupted time' plays are one means by which theatre 'can reveal, negotiate and critique the increasingly liquid social structures of contemporary social reality'.[17] In other words, this pattern of 'relentless repetition' is not simply a playwriting whim or a fashion, but an attempt to express the way we live now: the 'space-time compression' that Grochala identifies as a core feature of liquid modernity. Grochala writes specifically about Caryl Churchill's 1997 work *Heart's Desire*, which begins 'as if it were the first scene of a normal play', with mother, father and aunt in the kitchen awaiting daughter Suzy's return from Australia, but where the action of the scene 'comes to a grinding halt, stops, is rewound and starts again', twenty-six times.[18] The scene is replayed with a variation which is either adopted or discarded and replaced.

This kind of playwriting – in which 'the story' is perpetually called into question, rehearsed but also seemingly randomly generated or improvised – has been used very successfully by several other writers. Martin Crimp's *Attempts on Her Life* (1997), is subtitled *Seventeen Scenarios for Theatre*. The play doesn't assign dialogue to characters, so it is subject to a wide range of directorial interpretation. Yet the play appears to be offering a variety of ways to describe or capture an elusive woman called Anne, the putative 'her' of the title. In a similar vein, Nick Payne's *Constellations* (2012) presents a love

---

[14] Margherita Laera, 'Introduction', in *Theatre and Adaptation: Return, Rewrite, Repeat*, edited by Margherita Laera (London: Bloomsbury Methuen Drama, 2014), 3.

[15] Carlson, *The Haunted Stage*, 3.

[16] Laera, *Theatre and Adaptation*, 3.

[17] Grochala, *The Contemporary Political Play*, 89.

[18] Ibid., 106.

story between Roland and Marianne that is inflected with theories of multiple universes and quantum mechanics; so, the love story develops differently – is replayed with variations, as in Churchill's *Heart's Desire* – from scene to scene.[19] Some narrative variations are given a longer timeline, while others are abandoned sooner, like a chose-your-own-adventure book that someone else is playing. Or, of course, like the processes of improvisation and devising that have been key developments in theatre-making of the past half-century. In these plays, the process of 'making', of performance construction, becomes the dramatic action and the object of scrutiny, rather than something that must be concealed in order to reach the goal of a smooth-running, undisrupted final product. Bearing all this in mind, then, we can say that theatre that depicts time travel is simultaneously importing a set of references from popular media, operating in a tradition of twentieth-century drama, mimicking in its content what theatre does as a form, *and* using disrupted time and repetition with variation to reflect the experience of contemporary life.

A Very Very Very Dark Matter

Martin McDonagh's *A Very Very Very Dark Matter* (hereafter referred to as *Dark Matter*) was first staged at the Bridge Theatre in 2018. It makes extensive use of time travel and time loops and proposes an alternate history of nineteenth-century European popular fiction. Mbute is, according to the play's Narrator, 'a Congolese pygmy, imprisoned for sixteen years in a three-foot by three-foot mahogany box'.[20] Her jailer is the Danish author Hans Christian Andersen, who has cut off Mbute's foot, and whose fairytales are really written by Mbute, whom he insists

---

[19] Payne acknowledged Churchill's influence, and that of *Blue Heart* in particular, when *Constellations* won the *Evening Standard* Award for Best Play in 2012 (R. Darren Gobert, *The Theatre of Caryl Churchill* (London: Bloomsbury, 2014), 180). *Blue Heart* was the portmanteau title for the two one-act plays, *Heart's Desire* and *Blue Kettle*, that were staged together in 1997 (Gobert, *Theatre of Caryl Churchill*, 177).

[20] Martin McDonagh, *A Very Very Very Dark Matter* (London: Faber, 2018), 4.

on calling Marjory (as does the play script, despite Mbute's insistence on her African name).[21] The play has two major twists, neither of which are concealed from the audience. The first is that Mbute is being pursued through time by two 'bloody Belgians', Dirk and Barry, because she herself is a time traveller seeking to prevent the Congolese genocide (1885–1908), in which ten million Africans were killed.[22] The second twist is that Mbute has a sister, Ogechi, who is being imprisoned and exploited in precisely the same way by English author Charles Dickens, who keeps Ogechi in his cellar in Kent. What we think of as Andersen's fairytales are Mbute's; Dickens's plots, characters and social critiques are likewise stolen from Ogechi's imagination. When Ogechi dies, according to the play, Dickens's purported talent evaporates; he is a 'spent force' and all he can produce is the subpar and incomplete *Mystery of Edwin Drood*.[23] However, Ogechi's ghost is able to tell Mbute about a haunted concertina that hangs in the attic room in Denmark; it conceals a machine gun, and Mbute is able to use this to kill Dirk and Barry and – she hopes – to travel forward in time again to prevent the genocide. We understand that this is one of many attempts to do so, and one of many times that Mbute has been pursued by Belgians trying to kill her. As she says, exiting with her weaponry and a cigar in her mouth, and winking to the audience, 'The story isn't over yet. Is it?'[24]

The play pursues a justified premise: that nineteenth-century European culture is understood as complicit in colonial exploitation and murder, the metaphor placed alongside the horrific reality, the part

---

[21] This decision in the published script implicitly sides with Andersen, suggesting that his imposed, European name for her somehow takes precedence over Mbute's choice and identity. It is hard not to read this as an undermining, or even a mocking, of Mbute's belief in her self-definition and self-determination. Even when the play delivers her pay-off line as she kills one of the genocidal Belgians, Barry – 'Me name's Mbute, bitch' – the script is still calling her Marjory (McDonagh, *Dark Matter*, 52).

[22] McDonagh, *Dark Matter*, 19. Dirk and Barry and represented as literally 'bloody' in their first appearance: 'naked to the waist. Heads and torsos totally covered in what looks like blood, strange stitches down their arms and sides' (McDonagh, *Dark Matter*, 6).

[23] McDonagh, *Dark Matter*, 36–7.

[24] McDonagh, *Dark Matter*, 59.

juxtaposed with the whole. Yet this premise, I suggest, is undermined by the play's treatment of it. Mark O'Connell has observed of McDonagh's body of work that it 'self-consciously [plays] with clichés of Irishness without ever trying to say anything about those signifiers or what it might mean to employ them'.[25] Something similar is happening in this play, when McDonagh applies the cinematic clichés of time travel and 'Pekinpah-like' violence to colonial genocide.[26] The play's ending, with Andersen turning to the audience and saying of Mbute's mission, 'Be good if she did it though, wouldn't it?' also follows O'Connell's identification of the genre he calls 'light tragedy' in the writer's *oeuvre*: '[F]or all its reputation for darkness and perversity, his work is expertly crafted light entertainment passing itself off, sometimes almost convincingly, as provocative, serious art ... so many of his films and plays [follow] an inexorable logic of tragedy, but [are] mostly too glib to be properly unsettling or emotionally cathartic'[27]

Dramaturgically, *Dark Matter* struggles to bring its constituent tropes and allusions into a coherent whole. The overlong visit of Hans Christian Andersen to Charles Dickens's house in 1857 – at the same time as Dickens was beginning his affair with Ellen Ternan and seeking to dissolve his marriage to Catherine – has been a popular subject for biographical history plays.[28] Yet McDonagh has difficulty making the timings work, something that one would think crucial in a time-travel play. We are told that the story opens in Copenhagen in the 'late 1800s', which would imply that the Congolese genocide was taking place at that time, but Andersen is able to travel to Dickens's house

[25] Mark O'Connell, 'Blarney: The Put-On Irishness of Martin McDonagh', *Slate*, 26 January 2023. Available online: https://slate.com/culture/2023/01/martin-mcdonagh-irish-banshees-inisherin-blarney.html?s=09 (accessed 26 January 2023).

[26] The stage directions instruct us that the Belgians should be torn to horrifying pieces '*Pekinpah-like in their awful death dance, arterial spray spattering the walls behind them*' (McDonagh, *Dark Matter*, 51).

[27] O'Connell, 'Blarney'.

[28] Sebastian Barry's *Andersen's English* was produced by Out of Joint in 2010 and toured England in a co-production with Hampstead Theatre. Simon Gray's *Little Nell* (2006) covered similar territory in the form of a memory play and Richard Pinner's *Penny Dreadful* (2011) was an at times farcical take on Dickens and Ternan.

at Gad's Hill, staying with him as he did in 1857. Dickens complains about the problems he is having with *Edwin Drood*, when he still had *A Tale of Two Cities*, *Great Expectations* and *Our Mutual Friend* ahead of him, with *Drood* incomplete at his death in 1870. Catherine and Charles's separation in May 1858 is also telescoped into Andersen's visit.[29] Even character motivation collapses in the second Act, since Dickens, we are told, loathes Andersen, but repeatedly confides in him. Hence, he says things like 'It's not that I don't like him. He's just doing my fucking head in!' while also dismissing everything he says as 'senseless fucking nonsense' and demanding, 'When are you going to fucking leave?!'[30] Dickens is presented as a philanderer and, implicitly, a rapist (how can Ogechi, his underground prisoner, have freely given consent?),[31] but his incredulous tone and unremitting use of expletives make it seem as though the play wants us to be entertained by his behaviour. The fact that Andersen has been an obnoxious, self-absorbed philistine without challenge up to this point, and is finally getting his theatrical comeuppance, led to a great deal of laughter at Dickens's Basil Fawlty-like exasperation when I saw the production. The casting of popular and well-regarded actors Phil Daniels (Dickens) and Jim Broadbent (Andersen), both cast somewhat against type – Broadbent a loathsome egotist, Daniels a Victorian patriarch with the speech patterns of a gangster – added to the incongruity and the sense that we were not meant to take any of the play's ideas too seriously.

Desirée Baptiste's article in *Exeunt* magazine explains the play's ethical failure: 'This is a play about race matters by a writer for whom race matters not.'[32] Baptiste argues that the play fails as satire

[29] McDonagh, *Dark Matter*, 49.
[30] McDonagh, *Dark Matter*, 34, 36, 34.
[31] McDonagh, *Dark Matter*, 48.
[32] Desirée Baptiste, 'A Very Very Very Dark Matter, and the Limits of Satire', *Exeunt Magazine*, 16 November 2018. Available online: https://exeuntmagazine.com/features/dark-matter-limits-satire/ (accessed 28 April 2023).

because of its stylistic inconsistencies, and because it fails to offer a better standard against which to judge the actions of the 'red men' who speak so lightly of their mutilation of Congolese people.[33] Furthermore, 'it fails as documentary' for the same reasons; the play cannot justify its treatment of the genocide by the claim that it somehow educating or raising awareness, 'because of the play's wild juxtaposition of atrocity, parody and fantasy which makes it hard for those in the dark to know real from made-up'.[34] Jackie Sibblies Drury's *We Are Proud to Present*, analysed in Chapter 1, is specifically about the limitations of theatre as a vehicle for remembering and recognizing genocide. Having initially had the impulse to use the play to tell the story, Drury ultimately chose to parody her own 'well-meaningness' by showing an under-equipped company trying, and failing, to make moving documentary theatre, and revealing unspeakable truths about themselves in the process. McDonagh, by contrast, seems to revel in the perception that he is ill-equipped to share the story of the Congolese genocide.

It is perhaps overkill to cite the play's critical reception to support the case against it, but it is worth noting that most of the reviews, after some complaints about *Dark Matter* being muddled and confusing, accurately identified the metaphorical thrust of the play's set-up. Matt Trueman, for instance, came to the conclusion that 'Essentially, McDonagh makes literal the debt that white, western culture owes to colonialism, insinuating that all its artistic achievements – not just its economic strength – sit on a crest of global suppression.'[35] What each critic makes of this metaphor, however, is usually down to their

---

[34] Baptiste, 'Limits of Satire'.

[35] Matt Trueman, review of *A Very Very Very Dark Matter* by Martin McDonagh, directed by Matthew Dunster, Bridge Theatre, London, *Variety*, 25 October 2018, reproduced in *Theatre Record* 38, no. 19–20 (2018): 966.

[33] 'Satire fails, as the scene is outdistanced by the reality ... The play's juxtaposition of satire with its other forms of comedy: parody, fantasy and nonsense, reduces the satire, already teetering at the brink of collapse for the above reasons, to the in-*signifi*-cant.' Baptiste, 'Limits of Satire'.

newspaper's political standpoint.[36] What is much less remarked upon is the affective contradiction between this reckoning, however clumsy, with European barbarism, and *Dark Matter*'s attempts to provoke and offend by voicing the same racist and other dehumanizing bigotries that the central metaphor condemns. Ann Treneman notes, in a generally approving review, that the play's '[t]argets include the Chinese, Belgians, colonialism, war and (why?) Spaniards'.[37] Like Richard Bean's *Harvest*, analysed in Chapter 3, *Dark Matter* is a history play that wants to have its cake and eat it – in this case, to be aggressively cartoonish, but to expect its central historical idea to remain somehow pure and untouched by the outrage that the play seeks to provoke and capitalize on. As Baptiste argues, *Dark Matter* is not interested in the Congo as history, or as an encounter with a possible past. Rather, it speaks to the present by inviting us to revel in its grotesque caricatures of Andersen and Dickens, inversions of the sentimentalized, heritage reputations that they have accrued. It relies on, and trades in, familiar 'Great Writers' history, even as it gestures towards an underacknowledged past that it cannot confront and that it must repeatedly attempt to narrativize out of existence using Mbute. McDonagh attempts to use his central character both as a *deus ex machina*, and as a human shield: his theatrical insurance against

---

36 For example, for Christopher Hart at the *Sunday Times* it was 'a clunkingly clumsy great metaphor' (Christopher Hart, review of *A Very Very Very Dark Matter* by Martin McDonagh, directed by Matthew Dunster, Bridge Theatre, London, *Sunday Times*, 28 October 2018, reproduced in *Theatre Record* 38, no. 19–20 (2018): 967). Similarly, for the *Spectator*'s Lloyd Evans it was an attempt to 'parrot the orthodoxy' (Lloyd Evans, review of *A Very Very Very Dark Matter* by Martin McDonagh, directed by Matthew Dunster, Bridge Theatre, London, *Spectator*, 3 November 2018, reproduced in *Theatre Record* 38, no. 19–20 (2018): 968). By contrast, Andrzej Lukowski calls it a 'savage but cryptic allegory for the means by which Western culture is built upon the back of colonial plunder' (Andrzej Lukowski, review of *A Very Very Very Dark Matter* by Martin McDonagh, directed by Matthew Dunster, Bridge Theatre, London, *Time Out*, 25 October 2018, reproduced in *Theatre Record* 38, no.19–20 (2018): 966). Michael Billington, meanwhile, opined sympathetically that the 'link between literary plagiarism and genocidal oppression is a risky one but you see what McDonagh is driving at' (Michael Billington, review of *A Very Very Very Dark Matter* by Martin McDonagh, directed by Matthew Dunster, Bridge Theatre, London, *Guardian*, 25 October 2018, reproduced in *Theatre Record* 38, no. 19–20 (2018): 965).

37 Ann Treneman, review of *A Very Very Very Dark Matter* by Martin McDonagh, directed by Matthew Dunster, Bridge Theatre, London, *The Times*, 25 October 2018, reproduced in *Theatre Record* 38, no. 19–20 (2018): 965.

the accusation that he is mocking the genocide in the Congo. In this way, *Dark Matter* squanders its subject matter, and the dramaturgical possibilities – and indeed the ethical responsibilities – that it raises.

The Glow

A productive point of comparison with *Dark Matter* is Alistair McDowall's play *The Glow*, which premiered at the Royal Court in January 2022. Though it, too, falls short of its initial promise, the play is a compelling experiment, fusing elements of myth, history and the fantastic. *The Glow* is an extreme example of a polychronic play, one that uses history to invite us to consider that rationality cannot offer a full account of existence, and to question whether history is ever really confined to the past. The first scenes take place in 1863, at one of the Victorian era's high points of interest in spiritualism. The forceful and ambitious Mrs Lyall removes a woman from an asylum and sets her to work as a spirit medium; her son, Mason, is extremely resentful at having to share space and lose his privileges to this confused woman with a '*cracked bark*' of a voice.[38] For her part, Mrs Lyall has no sentimental attachment to 'Sadie' (as the character originally designated 'The Woman' in the script is now known). Mrs Lyall wants the world to know her as 'the woman who tore the veil between worlds' and to hold absolute power, but she regards Sadie as 'waste/Thrown away like spoiled meat ... You are a tool for my using.'[39] The set-up is familiar from séance plays like Conor McPherson's *The Veil* (2011). We anticipate that there may be more to Sadie's power than Mrs Lyall understands, and that she will – perhaps at the play's climax – realize her mistake. But *The Glow* has already made preparations to abandon this timeline, and this historical drama subgenre. Sadie can produce a bright spark of hovering light in her palm;[40] momentarily, we see a knight in armour emerge from the darkness;[41] when Mason grabs her wrist, she transports them

---

[38] Alistair McDowall, *The Glow* (London: Methuen, 2022), 12.
[39] McDowall, *The Glow*, 38.
[40] McDowall, *The Glow*, 31.
[41] McDowall, *The Glow*, 13.

both to a 'scorched battlefield'[42] and moments later bites off his nose as Mason is simultaneously a Roman soldier, Aulus.[43] When Mrs Lyall tries to punish and control Sadie, breaking each of her fingers, Sadie snaps her fingers back into place and '*vomits a glowing lava into Mrs Lyall's mouth*'.[44] At that, we are in 343 AD, and the Victorian plot is only revisited in glimpses from this point on.

In the second Act, we move to 1348, where an ageing knight, Haster, is attempting to take The Woman to the king as a captive. When Haster and The Woman form an unlikely alliance, he names her Brooke. We see a flash of an ARP warden from the Second World War, and a 'figure in a fallout suit',[45] before changing eras again, to Wales in 1993, where The Woman appears without warning in the house of a retired nurse, Ellen. Brooke also meets with Evan, a countercultural historian in 1979 who tells her about the legend of The Woman in Time, a female figure who appears in all manner of paintings, historical accounts, tapestries and statues, 'kind of a game that's been running for centuries', as Evan says.[46] This theory, we are told, was elaborated in a book, *The Woman in Time*, by an eccentric scholar named Dorothy Waites. In one of the play's final scenes, Ellen reveals that Evan is her deceased son; for a moment, Brooke is able to make her see him as she does, alive in 1979. The play grows increasingly melancholy as The Woman outlives everyone she has come to care for, particularly Ellen and Haster. In Evan's final speech, we learn that the ARP warden was another believer in The Woman who had encountered her and the knight and had also written a book about it.

This offers a payoff of sorts, but *The Glow* adds further finishes. There is a monologue from The Woman, seeming to declare to the audience that she has existed since long before human life and will exist until the heat-death of the universe.[47] The published play text (which

---

[42] McDowall, *The Glow*, 29.
[43] McDowall, *The Glow*, 31.
[44] McDowall, *The Glow*, 40.
[45] McDowall, *The Glow*, 48.
[46] McDowall, *The Glow*, 69.
[47] McDowall, *The Glow*, 98–101.

doubled, as per Royal Court tradition, as the theatre programme during the production's run) featured an Appendix and then an Afterword, a lengthy mock-programme note by a historian, 'Professor Helen Cullwick' of the 'University of Irwell' in which Cullwick expresses scepticism about Dorothy Waites's theory of The Woman.

As a history play, *The Glow* extends many of the tropes identified in this book to absurd proportions. I counted eight named timelines, and The Woman is evidently a transhistorical figure to rival Khalil's Abu Zaman and to completely outstrip Woolf's Orlando and Drury's Mary Seacole in potency and longevity. A kind of Victorian-waif edition of the Terminator, she is indestructible and yet always vulnerable, always seeking safety, home and family. In its metafictional self-awareness, and dabbling in conspiratorial versions of history, *The Glow* anticipates Kirkwood's *Rapture*, discussed later in this Coda; in its catapulting backwards and forwards in time it recalls some of the paradoxes of MacDonagh's *Dark Matter*, Ella Hickson's *Oil* (2016) and Zinnie Harris's *The Wheel* (2011). For most of its playing time, it fulfils the promise of history plays to offer encounters with possible pasts, rather than superficially realistic educational nuggets.

However, while the refusal to develop and conclude the spirit-medium plot is an enjoyably radical departure, in a sense this is undone by the final monologue and its need to explain The Woman's cosmic dimensions, to narrate to the end of the universe in search of a big finish. Coupled with the published script's pastiche of a scholarly essay, it suggests a certain lack of faith in an audience's ability to comprehend the connections that Evan in the dialogue has already explicitly made. Perhaps this is deliberate, this heavy-handedness, to show that McDowall doesn't really 'mean it'; just possibly, the play and its supplementary notes are parodying conspiracy-seekers. Are we meant to recognize the trope of the sceptical academic (a staple of the stories of M. R. James, where such characters are punished for their overconfident rationality), and to reject it, but then are we also meant to reject the earnest 'I want to believe' attitude that such a rejection might imply? What does the play say about women, if *The* Woman is an otherworldly being, rather than a person: is she some manifestation of 'the eternal feminine'?[48]

The Glow deserves credit for its lightness and flexibility of staging; in the Royal Court production, rarely was historical period denoted by anything other than costume and hand props. The seemingly insurmountable challenge of creating an epic time-hopping adventure of the kind that television has done for decades, turns out to be disarmingly simple: make use of darkness and shadow, keep the playing space flexible, don't try to recreate full settings and landscapes, and let the costumes do the talking. There were some moments that were difficult to follow: it was hard to tell, for instance, that Sadie was meant to be vomiting lava into Mrs Lyall's mouth in the stage direction quoted earlier. In her book *Performing the Unstageable*, Karen Quigley explores McDowall's previous use of stage directions that 'defy categorization' in *X* (2016).[49] Vicky Featherstone directed both *X* and *The Glow* in their premieres at the Royal Court. As in the directorial choices discussed by Quigley, Featherstone made use of similar sharp blackouts and snapshots in *The Glow*.[50] In retrospect, as an audience member, regardless of whether I was able to perceive an action of vomiting or that the lighting was meant to convey the idea of lava, the key impressions were that, firstly, we were somehow crossing over timelines, and secondly, that Mrs Lyall had been overpowered in spectacular fashion, demonstrating the capabilities of The Woman's 'glow'. Costume, scenography, light and sound combined to convey the 'impossible' stage action, creating an unsettling and historically disorientating experience. This achievement made the play's final recourse to language – in the form of a monologue and the professorial postscript – feel unnecessary. Where McDonagh's *Dark Matter* is under-written in some key respects, *The Glow*'s ending felt over-written, losing the previous scenes' immediacy in order to

---

[48] The 'eternal feminine' is a concept first introduced at the end of Part Two of Johann Wolfgang von Goethe's *Faust* (1832). The idea has since been considered and developed by a range of thinkers.

[49] Karen Quigley, *Performing the Unstageable: Success, Imagination, Failure* (London: Bloomsbury Methuen, 2020), 70.

[50] Quigley, *Performing the Unstageable*, 72.

describe and allude to events at one remove, offering several consecutive endings.

Rapture

Lucy Kirkwood's play *Rapture* was also first staged at the Royal Court, in June 2022. It offers an alternate history dealing with very recent events, spanning from 2011 to the present. The play presents itself as '[t]he story of Noah and Celeste Quilter', a tale that the government wants to prevent being told, having blocked publication of a report into their deaths.[51] In a projected message at the start of the performance, it is explained further that Kirkwood 'was asked by a campaign group to produce a dramatization of their relationship' which has been produced covertly and illegally by the Royal Court.[52] Indeed, in the Royal Court's real-life programming announcements, the play was advertised under a completely different name, *That Is Not Who I Am* by Dave Davidson. As Sarah Hemming writes in her review for the *Financial Times*, 'the publicity surrounding the play has become a real-time extension of it. Announced by the Royal Court as a new play by an unknown writer – one Dave Davidson, said to have worked in the security services for 38 years – the play immediately sparked intrigue.'[53] Only when audiences arrived at the theatre, and once the false covers for their playscripts/programmes were removed, did it become clear that they were attending the premiere of a new Lucy Kirkwood drama. On one hand this ruse could have been intended to encourage new audiences – perhaps those inclined to the Quilters' suspicion of the state and its security agencies – into the theatre by foregrounding the subject-matter rather than by the theatrical cachet of 'a new Lucy Kirkwood play'. On

---

[51] Lucy Kirkwood, *Rapture* (London: Nick Hern Books, 2022), 5.

[52] Kirkwood, *Rapture*, 5.

[53] Sarah Hemming, review of *That Is Not Who I Am* (*Rapture*) by Lucy Kirkwood, directed by Lucy Morrison, Royal Court Theatre, London, *Financial Times*, 23 June 2022, reproduced in *Theatre Record* 42, no. 6 (2022). Available online: www-theatrerecord-com.libproxy.york.ac.uk/magazine/production/1075 (accessed 28 April 2023).

the other hand, the invented persona of Dave Davidson seemed so self-parodic ('Dave' as an abbreviation of David is often associated in UK culture with a forced blokey informality) that many surmised it could not possibly be real; their (ultimately correct) supposition made it feel more like a smug Royal Court in-joke than a break from the usual programming.[54]

In *Rapture*, Celeste, a nurse, and Noah, a former soldier, meet on a blind date, and over a period of years gradually withdraw from society. They become online activists, posting YouTube videos together about the working of power in the modern state, and developing a substantial following; then, they go offline and disappear, apparently murdered. We do not discover what it was that Noah and Celeste were planning that made them targets for state assassination. We are introduced to a character called Lucy Kirkwood, who explains, 'I'm playing Lucy Kirkwood as she thought she'd be brave enough to do this herself but decided, quite late in the day, that it wouldn't be a good idea, given her condition.'[55] Towards the end of the play, 'The Real Lucy Kirkwood', 'heavily pregnant', 'emerges onstage' to interrupt the action as 'Lucy Kirkwood' reads out a legal disclaimer by the Royal Court.[56] As an argument erupts between the apparently 'real' playwright and her fictional counterpart, 'The Real Lucy Kirkwood' is assassinated after telling the audience, 'A conspiracy theory is just the wrong answer to the right question! You are being lied to! You are being lied to!'[57] As the programme cast list indicates, in some performances 'The Real Lucy Kirkwood' really is played by Lucy Kirkwood; in others, she is played by the actors Ellie Kendrick, Sophie Melville or Letty Thomas. Thus, depending on the specific performance that an audience member saw – and on whether they

---

[54] The title of Michael Ashcroft and Isabel Oakeshott's 2015 'unauthorised biography' of Conservative Prime Minister David Cameron was *Call Me Dave*.

[55] Kirkwood, *Rapture*, 17–18.

[56] Ibid., 82.

[57] Ibid., 84.

were able to recognize Kirkwood, Kendrick, Melville or Thomas – they would be experiencing a slightly different level of fictionality when 'The Real Lucy Kirkwood' is assassinated in the world of the play (that insists, at this point, that it is *not* a play).

Rapture's metatheatrical, conspiratorial staging of a conspiracy plot about a conspiracy irritated some critics, who may have been expecting the play to be a political thriller with a clear thesis. Aleks Sierz perceived a 'cynical sensibility' and judged it to be 'intricate without being illuminating', adding that it 'feels like a middle-class slap in the face to anyone who really wants to change the world'.[58] Patrick Marmion in the *Daily Mail* called the Royal Court a 'haute-bourgeois theatrical salon', and announced that it had 'very nearly accomplished the difficult task of disappearing up its own fundament'.[59] At least two reviews commented on the production design: Stephen Bates remarked that 'Designer Naomi Dawson's ingenious revolving set frames the claustrophobic world of a couple glued together, with the narrator and stagehands roaming around outside it to suggest constant intrusions on their privacy',[60] while Frey Kwa Hawking observed,

> All the way to the back wall of the Royal Court's Downstairs is shown in Naomi Dawson's set, as the incredibly active and visible stage managers (Lizzie Chapman, Jen McTaggart, Elle Hutchinson, and Ophir Westman) manipulate the structure of the Quilters' home. It feels like it offers the increasingly vulnerable bodies of the couple brief

[58] Aleks Sierz, review of *That Is Not Who I Am* (*Rapture*) by Lucy Kirkwood, directed by Lucy Morrison, Royal Court Theatre, London, *The Arts Desk*, 20 June 2022, reproduced in *Theatre Record* 42, no.6. Available online: https://www-theatrerecord-com.libproxy.york.ac.uk/magazine/production/1075 (accessed 28 April 2023).

[59] Patrick Marmion, review of *That Is Not Who I Am* (*Rapture*) by Lucy Kirkwood, directed by Lucy Morrison, Royal Court Theatre, London, *Daily Mail*, 14 June 2022, reproduced in *Theatre Record* 42, no. 6 (2022). Available online: https://www-theatrerecord-com.libproxy.york.ac.uk/magazine/production/1075 (accessed 28 April 2023).

[60] Stephen Bates, review of *That Is Not Who I Am* (*Rapture*) by Lucy Kirkwood, directed by Lucy Morrison, Royal Court Theatre, London, *The Reviews Hub*, 19 June 2022, reproduced in *Theatre Record* 42, no. 6 (2022). Available online: https://www-theatrerecord-com.libproxy.york.ac.uk/magazine/production/1075 (accessed 28 April 2023).

moments of being shielded from the audience, and the government monitoring they imagine, as it's turned.[61]

Such design choices offer a materialization of the construction of narratives and counternarratives around the Quilters, at the same time constructing and reconstructing history. Rather than the production being cynical or self-indulgent, as reviewers suggested, I would counter that the production's dramaturgy combined content with form very effectively, offering an experience in which meaning could not be derived or settled from speech alone.

Lucy Kirkwood has previous form in playing with historical events to create factitious versions of the past that nod to their own unreliability. *Chimerica* (2013) premiered at the Almeida Theatre, transferred to the West End and was adapted for television by Kirkwood in 2019. It is a dual-timeline play that imagines the story of the 'Tank Man' who stood up to the Chinese military forces in their response to the Tiananmen Square protests of 1989, and a modern journalist who goes in search of him. Like *Rapture*, it has a political-thriller flavour to it; in reviewing *Rapture*, Matt Wolf was reminded of 'those great political-paranoia/ surveillance-themed films of the 1970s like *The Parallax View* and *The Conversation*. This is cut from the same sceptical, anxious cloth', and the same can certainly be said of *Chimerica*.[62] Both plays grow invented events around historical fact and enact the overcoming of many obstacles to get at a truth that has itself been invented. Even Kirkwood's relatively Naturalistic large-scale play at the National Theatre, *The Welkin* (2020) has moments of anachronism where the illusion of the late eighteenth-century setting is deliberately punctured. What feels new in *Rapture* is that Kirkwood is one of the first playwrights to attempt to historicize

---

[61] Freya Kwa Hawking, review of *That Is Not Who I Am* (*Rapture*) by Lucy Kirkwood, directed by Lucy Morrison, Royal Court Theatre, London, *WhatsOnStage*, 19 June 2022, reproduced in *Theatre Record* 42, no. 6 (2022). Available online: https://www-theatrerecord-com. libproxy.york.ac.uk/magazine/production/1075 (accessed 28 April 2023).

[62] Matt Wolf, review of *That Is Not Who I Am* (*Rapture)* by Lucy Kirkwood, directed by Lucy Morrison, Royal Court Theatre, London, *London Theatre*, 21 June 2022, reproduced in *Theatre Record* 42, no. 6 (2022). Available online: https://www-theatrerecord-com. libproxy.york.ac.uk/magazine/production/1075 (accessed 28 April 2023).

the Covid lockdowns of 2020 and 2021. Susannah Clapp comments in the *Observer*, 'The documentary claim is quickly punctured yet the play contains a marvellous record of lockdown life. It is already easy to forget how essential it seemed to wash tinfoil',[63] and Marlowe notes that Noah and Celeste's interactions 'span the Covid crisis and the nightmarish surrealism of lockdown'.[64] One of the things the play achieves is to bring to our attention the strangeness of the very recent past. The conspiracy theories that took hold during the lockdowns are both shown to have been rooted in a pre-existing conspiratorial mindset, and also to have exacerbated such tendencies, especially for those kept at home making, sharing and commenting on YouTube videos. Lloyd Evans in the *Spectator* even managed to construe the play as 'a funny, sweet-natured marital comedy with a powerful anti-lockdown message'.[65] As with several of the other plays discussed in this section, many readers might object to *Rapture* being classified as a history play, but these dramas are involved in a process of, or imagining a process of, historicization. In Kirkwood's case, it is a form of historicization through fabulation, self-consciously revelling in its own artifice.

In their article 'Lockdown Time, Time Loops, and the Crisis of the Future', cultural geographer Anna J. Secor and literary scholar Virginia Blum examine the proliferation of time-loop films and television series around the time of the Covid lockdowns, including *Palm Springs* (2020), *The Map of Tiny Perfect Things* (2021) and *Russian Doll* (2019–). They note how the experience of lockdown was frequently framed in terms of the 1993 movie *Groundhog Day* and point out that the TV

[63] Susannah Clapp, review of *That Is Not Who I Am* (*Rapture*) by Lucy Kirkwood, directed by Lucy Morrison, Royal Court Theatre, London, *Observer*, 19 June 2022, reproduced in *Theatre Record* 42, no. 6 (2022). Available online: https://www-theatrerecord-com.libproxy.york.ac.uk/magazine/production/1075 (accessed 28 April 2023).

[64] Sam Marlowe, review of *That Is Not Who I Am* (*Rapture*) by Lucy Kirkwood, directed by Lucy Morrison, Royal Court Theatre, London, *iNews*, 24 June 2022, reproduced in *Theatre Record* 42, no. 6 (2022). Available online: https://www-theatrerecord-com.libproxy.york.ac.uk/magazine/production/1075 (accessed 28 April 2023).

[65] Lloyd Evans, review of *That Is Not Who I Am* (*Rapture*) by Lucy Kirkwood, directed by Lucy Morrison, Royal Court Theatre, London, *Observer*, 19 June 2022, reproduced in *Theatre Record* 42, no. 6 (2022). Available online: https://www-theatrerecord-com.libproxy.york.ac.uk/magazine/production/1075 (accessed 28 April 2023).

and film that appeared to be reflecting the lockdowns of 2020–21 were actually conceived and commissioned well before the pandemic.[66] They maintain that something else is at work in the culture to precipitate these preoccupations, and identify the 'slow cancellation of the future', as discussed in the Introduction to the present volume, as the root of this 'problem of stuckness'.[67] Secor and Blum go on to state: 'The time loop offers to take Berardi's proposition literally, cancelling future disappointments … a promise for our anxious times in which both the everyday failure of the promises of liberal democracy and neoliberal governance and the horror of catastrophic futures hover over the impasse of the present.'[68] The same principle can, I propose, be applied to the time loops in *Dark Matter*, *The Glow* and *Rapture*. Though McDonagh's play predates Covid, all three plays seem stuck in unending loops, where the genocide keeps on happening, a place to call home is always beyond reach, and the online recordings of Noah and Celeste are replayed over and over, while competing truth-claims – and conspiracy claims – about what happened lead us into a spiral of epistemological doubt.[69]

Indeed, the time loops in these plays are more pessimistic than the screen media that Secor and Blum discuss, where 'the time-loop conceit offers *not one but two* fantasies of time: an infinite time for working out (without decaying towards death) and a time beyond this in which

---

[66] A. J. Secor and V. Blum, 'Lockdown Time, Time Loops, and the Crisis of the Future', *Psychoanalysis, Culture & Society* 28 (2023): 251, 260. doi:10.1057/s41282-023-00379-4

[67] Secor and Blum, 'Lockdown Time', 262.

[68] Ibid., 262.

[69] Kirkwood's *Rapture* premiered shortly after Prime Minister Boris Johnson was forced from office as a result of, among other factors, the 'Partygate' scandal of MPs and government employees breaching their own lockdown restrictions at the same time that, elsewhere in the country, the police were enforcing the rules with draconian zeal. The attempts to defend Johnson by his supporters by playing down the seriousness of Covid and the emergency measures of only two years earlier were a highly topical example of politicians attempting to rewrite recent history to suit their own purposes. See, for example, Adam Bienkov, 'Party by Gaslight: Boris Johnson Rewrites History at the Privileges Committee', *Byline Times*, 22 March 2023. Available online: https://bylinetimes.com/2023/03/22/boris-johnson-rewrites-history-at-the-privileges-committee/ (accessed 24 April 2023).

we are fully reconciled to our finitude'.[70] In *Dark Matter*, Andersen reduces the size of the wooden box in which he keeps Mbute each time she leaves it; her sister has already died, and Andersen has removed Mbute's foot, so that even though Andersen on the one hand wishes her well in her time-travelling mission, on the other he casually and sadistically reduces her chances of succeeding by increments. In *The Glow*, it was notable in the Royal Court production just how young and vulnerable The Woman/Sadie/Brooke seemed, as played by Ria Zmitrowicz with self-conscious adolescent body language. She could be read as a representative of young people in lockdown, watching time pass but cut off from real connection. In this metaphorical reading, the young during lockdown had all the power and potential that comes from their mastery of technology (their 'glow'), yet they had to watch impotently as those they care for age and die in accelerated time. All that is left to look forward to, apparently, is the end of the universe. In *Rapture*, Kirkwood chronicles how the apparent blessings of technology during lockdown (the ability to video call with isolating loved ones, for instance) were countered by the ability and propensity of contemporary media to produce and reproduce endless conspiracies: QAnon, Stop the Steal, 5G, Chemtrails, Bill Gates and vaccines, and so on.

The cover image of the play script of *Rapture* depicts a sequence of four photographs of a Victorian couple, a man and woman. In the two images on the left, they are still and rather sombre, in accordance with the familiar conventions of Victorian studio photography. The shots on the right are blurred as the couple seem to be laughing and cuddling, the woman hiding her face in the bottom right image as the man looks towards the lens, smiling. The cover (which is reproduced in the US edition) can be interpreted in several ways: perhaps Celeste and Noah have hoaxed their followers and the government; perhaps Lucy Kirkwood, presenting multiple versions of Lucy Kirkwood, is provoking us to think again about the rhetorics of 'truth' and 'authenticity' that circulate in political theatre and documentary drama. Perhaps the

---

[70] Secor and Blum, 'Lockdown Time', 262.

playscript is suggesting that we can never know what people were really like and what their intentions were from the traces of media that they leave behind; equally, the photographs in conjunction with the play title imply a link to Victorian evangelism and spiritualism; perhaps our ideas of the truth beyond 'the veil' will seem as strange in 150 years' time as theirs do to us now.[71]

Mr Burns

I want to end with a discussion of a play that is not a historical drama, but a drama of historicization. Anne Washburn's play *Mr Burns* was first performed in the UK at the Almeida in 2014, having been produced at Woolly Mammoth Theatre Company in Washington DC in 2012. I include it as this book's final play since it takes the tendencies of contemporary history plays to project their action into the future in their final act or part (as in *Oil*, *Wife*, *The Glow*) and instead begins the play at that point. *Mr Burns* invites us to imagine how societies (mis) remember their pasts and construct histories from the remnants of the past. It therefore also offers some insights into the way that theatre makers themselves historicize and invent that may serve as reflections on this book's project.

Subtitled 'a post-electric play', *Mr Burns* consists of three acts, one 'set in the very near future', a second seven years later and the third act seventy-five years after the second act. In the first act, we are aware that some catastrophe in North America has led to the breakdown of the electricity grid, and that five survivors of this event are in New England, trying to recall a *Simpsons* episode, with varying degrees of knowledge and engagement. They are joined by a new arrival, Gibson, who as well as bringing news and advice from the breakdown of civilization, helps to supply one of the *Simpsons* lines that the group had not got quite right (and indeed, is almost killed for it when one of the group

---

[71] In *The Glow*, Mrs Lyall, Mason and Sadie sing the spiritualist hymn, 'Only A Thin Veil Between Us', an assertion that seems apt here (McDowall, *The Glow*, 18–20).

misunderstands his quotation: 'O I'll stay away alright. I'll stay away …
forever').[72] In the second act, this recalling of culture from before
the apocalypse has become a makeshift entertainment industry, with
rival companies vying for the rights to stage *Simpsons* episodes, and
Shakespeare, and to recreate TV commercials, in what literary scholar
Camille Barrera calls a 'kind of post-apocalyptic intellectual property
battle'.[73] By the third act, *The Simpsons* has mutated to become, in the
words of drama scholar Ariel Watson, 'fully ritualized theatre in which
its previous purposes have attained a religious level of abstraction'.[74] In
this act, for Barrera, 'All comedy has seemingly been eradicated' and
Bart Simpson's 'characteristic irreverence has been superseded by a trite
earnestness'.[75] This is a play, then, about simulacra: representations of
an original that no longer exists.[76]

In some ways, the performance culture that emerges in the second
act is more akin to nineteenth-century theatre companies than the
present day. With no way of proving copyright, claims of theft of ideas
proliferate, and each company is chasing the latest fad as they seek to
evoke and emulate a different world – now lost – that it is beyond their
technology to bring into being. Watson notes that in the play 'chooses
theatricality – ever repeating, ever changing – as its post-apocalyptic
form',[77] and concludes that 'Washburn is tracing not simply the historical
process that produces high culture out of low (the Immortal Bard out of
the upstart groundling-baiting crow) but more richly the way in which

---

[72] Anne Washburn, *Mr Burns* (London: Oberon, 2014), 36.
[73] Camille Barrera, '"For We Are American": Postmodern Pastiche and National Identity in Anne Washburn's *Mr. Burns, a Post-Electric Play*', *Journal of Contemporary Drama in English* 6, no. 1 (2018): 132, doi:10.1515/jcde-2018-0016
[74] Ariel Watson, 'Apocalypse Masque: Post-Electric Theatricality in *Mr. Burns*', *Canadian Theatre Review* 175 (2018): 23. doi:10.3138/ctr.175.004
[75] Barrera, 'Postmodern Pastiche', 133.
[76] Moreover, the idea of an 'original' is especially complicated by *The Simpsons*' recurrent referencing of other artworks and media. As Barrera notes, 'Almost nothing in *The Simpsons* could strictly be called "original," and yet its indiscriminate copying and regurgitation of culture has somehow resulted in something unique' (Barrera, 'Postmodern Pastiche', 138).
[77] Watson, 'Apocalypse Masque', 22.

cultural texts can survive their own deaths, or rather the death of their form.[78] This is a significant analogy, I would suggest, for how history plays have developed. Certainly, Shakespeare's popular playwriting, including his histories, has become canonical high culture; but history plays are also made out of cultural texts that originally existed in older forms and have now been adapted for the 'historical-realist' dramas that I discuss in the Introduction and Chapter 1. These conventional forms of history play tend to flatten nuance and reproduce familiar generic plots, heroes and villains; like the third-act wrestling match between Bart and Mr Burns, they fictionalize history so that familiar dramaturgy is always fixed as the winner.

Washburn's play is notable for its process as much as its product, since it began as a week-long workshop with the theatre group the Civilians, where they tried collectively to remember *Simpsons* episodes.[79] As the playwright recalls, 'I knew I wanted to start with an act of recollection, with a group of survivors trying to piece together a TV episode. And to do that, I wanted to work with a group of actors; remembering is complicated; I could make remembering up, but it would never be as rich and complex as the real thing.'[80] Like the characters in the play, the actors were engaged in 'Fashioning ... the pastiche of a pastiche-dependent text into a new mythology'.[81] This, again, is one way to describe the process of creation that is writing and performing a history play, building from partial and incomplete textual fragments that assume familiarity with lost sources to which we have no access. In describing how the 'history' of these future Simpsonites might be negotiated and fashioned, Washburn could almost be talking about the present day:

I think that after an apocalypse, there'd be a lot of powerful but simplistic stories about what happened and why. For me, it would

---

[78] Ibid., 24.
[79] Washburn, *Mr Burns*, 8.
[80] Quoted in Watson, 'Apocalypse Masque', 21.
[81] Barrera, 'Postmodern Pastiche', 139.

be really important to be brave and bold about piecing together the exactitude of our history, while making sure people understand there are a lot of alternative ways of viewing it. There used to be only one 'history' that people knew about, but now, a big push in education has encouraged different ways of understanding our past. Many narratives are incommensurate, but exist side by side. There is a multiplicity in looking at the world that I think people find really stressful and would love to get away from. However, I'd want to find a way of maintaining this complexity of discussion at a time when people would be tempted to reach for simpler explanations.[82]

The point I seek to make is, I hope, a more developed one than the truism that future dystopias are as much about the here and now as history plays are. Rather, in Washburn's words we can see the appeal of the comforting, historical-realist history play that presents graspable facts, educational gobbets or instant hot takes. The alternative is a potentially 'stressful' type of play where '[m]any narratives are incommensurate, but exist side by side'; one that does not seek to ape the episodic and the spectacular representation of the past that television and film have long since been able to invent and to franchise more lucratively. Such history plays – with their bespoke dramaturgies, their plurality and their openness about the process of being made, being written, being 'put on' – would, unlike Washburn's post-apocalyptic players, have partial access to the historical record, but would not be ruled by it. They would not be seduced into thinking that using the record guaranteed 'authenticity', because to act as such would be just as absurd as to position a memory of a memory of *The Simpsons* as a foundational narrative or a revealed truth. Because of how the cracks and gaps – the made-ness and collective process – are always showing in theatre, it is able to resist 'powerful but simplistic stories'.

---

[82] Washburn in Nataraj, quoted in Barrera, 'Postmodern Pastiche', 142.

Conclusion

This book's Coda has examined theatrical works that bring together different history play dramaturgies 'in concert'. As I have argued, not all of these are successfully realized, and *Dark Matter*, I have proposed, illustrates what can happen when ideas are too casually thrown together and are unequal to the historical subject matter. The last two examples considered here, *Rapture* and *Mr Burns*, operate on very different timescales but are both highly topical, in that the 'now' that we are invited to view events from – the audience historical time, as I call it in Chapter 4 – is acutely subject to change. *Mr Burns* relies on the recognition of the cultural ubiquity of *The Simpsons* for Generation X and Millennials as they were growing up; it speaks of a period in cultural history when the family television set was always on, transmitting scheduled programming, so that the adults of Washburn's apocalypse quote the show almost like a reflex action. *Rapture* captures, and reproduces, a particular kind of 2020s lockdown paranoia with such specificity that a reader approaching the text in a few decades' time may need extensive footnotes to make sense of it. While *Mr Burns* is plainly not a history play according to the definitions proposed by this book, it is a polychronic drama that makes use of the techniques of the contemporary history play. The exchange goes both ways. As the Introduction and this Coda in particular have emphasized, twenty-first-century history plays do not cut themselves off from contemporary playwriting approaches in the doomed pursuit of historical realism. They *are* new writing, applied to historical subjects.

This book has set out to explore the revival of interest in history plays in the twenty-first century among contemporary playwrights. It has approached the subject from the positions of audience member, close reader and scholar, interpreting the dramaturgy of the plays from the evidence of published play scripts and performances. Necessarily, it has not devoted space to questions of how such work reaches the stages of flagship theatre institutions in the first place. In calling for more history plays that explore the interplay of content and form, I acknowledge that these can often be expensive works to produce. In particular, the kind of large-cast, main-stage production with a running time of around three hours tends to be the norm at the RSC and the Globe. This is tied to the repertory playing conditions of these two theatre institutions and also, perhaps, to the expectations of a theatrical experience in a 'Shakespearean' venue. Vera Cantoni, in her book on new writing at the Globe, collates the various techniques used to gain and hold the attention of audiences at performances on the main stage, demonstrating convincingly that there is a specific kind of 'Globe play' that caters to the venue and its demands.[83] But as I have shown in the present volume, history plays can successfully develop their ideas with small casts, as for example in *Wild Swimming*, *An Adventure* and *Curious*, and/or over shorter running times, like Ella Hickson's play on Queen Elizabeth I, *Swive [Elizabeth]*, which was staged at the Globe's Sam Wanamaker indoor venue with a cast of four.

In the wider theatre ecology, history plays, especially those that feel experimental in approach, or that deal with unfamiliar histories, can still be perceived as a risk. Indhu Rubasingham, as Artistic Director of the Kiln Theatre in Kilburn, north-west London, programmed, directed and revived a significant number of history plays, from Buffini's *Handbagged* and Chinonyerem Odimba's *The Seven Ages of Patience* (2019) to Lolita Chakrabarti's *Red Velvet* (2012) to the multi-writer, three-era piece *NW Trilogy*.[84] Rubasingham has talked about the complex considerations in balancing risk, when in-house productions are more costly: 'So the challenge is: "How do you find a clever way to curate a season, so it comes under the same umbrella of the mission statement?"'[85] She explains that a producing theatre needs to 'find plays that will attract and entertain

[83] Vera Cantoni, *New Writing at Shakespeare's Globe* (London: Bloomsbury Methuen Drama, 2017), 89–90.

[84] *NW Trilogy* consisted of an intersecting play each by Moira Buffini (*Dance Floor*, set in the 1950s), Roy Williams (*Life of Riley*, set in the 1970s) and Suhalyla El-Bushra (*Waking/Walking*, also set in the 1970s).

[85] Indhu Rubasingham, quoted in Christopher Haydon, *The Art of the Artistic Director* (London: Bloomsbury Methuen Drama, 2019), 135.

audiences', that will ideally 'land beautifully' for all of the theatre's diverse audiences; but at the same time artistic directors shouldn't 'start to second-guess [their] choices' on the basis of what they imagine will be successful, mustn't be afraid to court controversy, and 'have to be battle-ready'.[86] Moreover, as playwright and theatre academic Bridget Foreman argues, commissioned playwrights increasingly do not start with a 'blank page' and the invitation to write whatever interests them; instead, via the practice of 'directive commissioning', 'a playwright is directed towards certain constraints of subject matter and/or approach, or is directly instructed to work within such constraints'.[87] While this can lead to productive and innovative partnerships – as Foreman's community history plays such as *Everything Is Possible* attest – this may, in some cases, have the effect of commissioning bodies directing would-be historical dramatists towards what the historian Martin L. Davies calls 'affirmative culture', reinforcing well-known and popular events and figures from the past rather than challenging their dominance.[88]

In the above paragraphs I have written of individual playwrights and their agency over their writing, or otherwise, but the 'lone dramatist' model of interpretation is one that this book has mostly sought to avoid. That is, rather than seeking out the writers' intentions I have sought to analyse their effects and impacts on the page and in performance, and to view plays laterally to see what they hold in common with other dramaturgies of the history play. In de-emphasizing this particular understanding of the individual playwright's voice, I am going against the new-writing orthodoxies of the Royal Court, the 'writers' theatre' where productions should 'serve the text'.[89] (The Royal Court is also a venue where, as noted in the Introduction, historical drama has been specifically discouraged.) The history plays discussed in depth

---

[86] Rubasingham, quoted in Haydon, *The Art*, 134, 136, 153, 137.
[87] Bridget Foreman, 'A New Way of Working – Practice and Process in Directive Commissioning', PhD dissertation, University of York, 2019, 11.
[88] Martin L. Davies, *Historics: Why History Dominates Contemporary Society* (Abingdon: Routledge, 2006), 5.
[89] Ruth Little and Emily McLaughlin, *The Royal Court Theatre Inside Out*, (London: Oberon, 2007), 17.

in the present study are more likely to be the product of devised and collaborative work than the conception of a single creative artist. We might think of Jackie Sibblies Drury and Nadia Latif, who worked together as writer and director on the London premieres of *Fairview* and then *Marys Seacole*, which underwent a number of textual changes for the Donmar production. We might consider the creative relationship between Ella Hickson, director Carrie Cracknell and dramaturg Jenny Worton in the long development of *Oil*, and Director Natalie Abrahami, who is credited as 'Director/Creator' in the text of Hickson's *Swive [Elizabeth]*.[90] Hannah Khalil credits dramaturgs Hanna Slättne and Chris White in her note on *A Museum in Baghdad*, calling them the 'masterbuilders'.[91] Moira Buffini, whose collaborations with Indhu Rubasingham on *Handbagged* and other plays extend over more than a decade, speaks of the need to bring together 'what's seen as the written play (the playwright's play) and the made play (the devised play)', to combine the visual and the spectacle with 'the word' which 'in the theater is too powerful a weapon to ignore'.[92] However, I would suggest that this gap is already being closed in the practice of making performances about the past. In addition to the partnerships mentioned above, we might add Irish company Malaprop Theatre's *Everything Not Saved* (2018),[93] Jennifer Kidwell and Scott R. Sheppard's *Underground Railroad Game*[94] and the TEAM's *Mission Drift* as particularly strong examples of history 'plays' that come from collaborative devising and making processes.[95] It is probably not coincidental that they all contain alternate histories or elements of the fantastic, making for highly unpredictable, exciting and moving work in performance. Although there is not the space here to do them justice, it is to these productions

[90] Hickson, *Swive*, 3.

[91] Khalil, *A Museum*, no pagination.

[92] Moira Buffini, quoted in Jeffrey Sweet, *What Playwrights Talk About When They Talk About Writing* (New Haven: Yale University Press, 2017), 181–2.

[93] The production ran at the Edinburgh Fringe and Brighton Fringe in 2018.

[94] *Underground Railroad Game*, devised with the company Lightning Rod Special, ran off-Broadway in 2017 and was staged at Edinburgh Fringe in 2017 and Soho Theatre, London in 2018.

[95] *Mission Drift* has been produced, among other places, at Edinburgh Fringe in 2011 and the Shed at the National Theatre, London, in 2013.

that future work on contemporary history plays might turn, in order to further develop the dramaturgical accounts presented in this book.

This book's project has been to develop a critical vocabulary for history plays, so that their connections and correspondences can be analysed more accurately. It has also argued that to trust a play's announcement that it is set in the past – rather than to fret over whether a text 'qualifies' as a history play – shifts the emphasis from the *what* (the perceived fidelity of the play to the historical record) to the *how* (the processes through which we are invited to encounter the past). This is important if Theatre Studies is to avoid treating history plays as either discrete artefacts without immediate comparators, or else as historical misinformation that needs to be exposed and corrected through a misguided 'fidelity criticism'. Proposing a set of models for this *how* – however provisional they may be, and however much plays in practice might overspill these categories – is a significant first step to understanding how theatre uses history. In a field of scholarship where plays are still commonly taught and interpreted as either 'realistic' or 'non-realistic', this further nuance continues to be necessary, and the problem of the 'realness' of the past offers a way into more developed discussions of the 'nonreal' and its theatrical properties.[96]

These methods of dramatizing the past are not going to change England's relationship with its history on their own. But they can, I contend, help to popularize – to bring directly to the people – more creative ways of thinking about our pasts. At the same time, they can argue forcefully for a revisioning of what should constitute history, who is included in that history, and to whom and for whom that history might speak. Such reckonings should be destabilizing and discomfiting, but in doing so they would fulfil a key criterion for new writing in the twenty-first century: that it be an experience and an encounter, not a narration or a thesis. Our cultural and political climate will continue

---

[96] For example, the fourth edition of the popular textbook *Script Analysis for Actors, Directors, and Designers* by James Thomas (Oxford: Focal Press, 2009) features 'New Material on Non-Realistic Plays'. Similarly, Robin Shrift's *The Director's Toolkit* (New York: Routledge, 2018) contains one chapter on 'Directing Nonrealistic Styles' (chapter 19).

to deteriorate if overfamiliar plays, subjects and dramaturgies are revived time after time on English stages. The 'heritage' versions of history that promote 'affirmative culture' or 'processional history' need to be disrupted and dismantled, made live and contingent, in every performance. At its best, historical theatre offers a place to be together, to feel as a collective and to encounter unfinished thinking about who we are in relation to our past. The history play is an idea whose time, once again, has come.

Bibliography

'About'. *Value Engineering: Scenes from the Grenfell Inquiry* website. Available online: https://part1.grenfellsystemfailure.com/about.html (accessed 29 April 2023).

Adamson, Samuel. *Wife*. London: Faber and Faber, 2019.

Akbar, Arifa. Review of *Love and Other Acts of Violence* by Cordelia Lynn, directed by Elayce Ismail, Donmar Warehouse, London. *The Guardian*, 18 October 2021. Available online: https://www.theguardian.com/ stage/2021/oct/18/love-and-other-acts-of-violence-review-donmar-warehouse (accessed 25 April 2023).

Akbar, Arifa. '*Marys Seacole* review: Mystifying Drama about Caring Through the Ages', review of *Marys Seacole* by Jackie Sibblies Drury, directed by Nadia Latif, at Donmar Warehouse. *Guardian*, 2 April 2022. Available online: https://www.theguardian.com/stage/2022/apr/22/marys-seacole-review-donmar-warehouse-london (accessed 21 March 2023).

Akita, Lizzie. '*Marys Seacole* review: Muddled Drama Takes Too Long to Make Its Point', review of *Marys Seacole* by Jackie Sibblies Drury, directed by Nadia Latif, at Donmar Warehouse. *Time Out*, 22 April 2022. Available online: https://www.standard.co.uk/culture/theatre/marys-seacole-review-donmar-warehouse-jackie-sibblies-drury-b995683.html (accessed 21 March 2023).

Andress, David. *Cultural Dementia*. Kindle ebook. London: Head of Zeus, 2018.

Armitt, Lucie. *Fantasy*. Abingdon: Routledge, 2020.

Babbage, Frances. *Adaptation in Contemporary Theatre: Performing Literature*. London: Bloomsbury Methuen Drama, 2018.

Bachrach, Hailey. 'Quilted History: *Emilia* and *Swive*', *Hailey Bachrach* (blog), 22 January 2020. Available online: https://hbachrach.com/ (accessed 21 March 2023).

Bachrach, Hailey. 'Review: *The Normal Heart* at National Theatre'. *Exeunt Magazine*, 1 October 2021. Available online: https://exeuntmagazine.com/ reviews/review-normal-heart-national-theatre/ (accessed 1 November 2021).

Baldick, Chris. 'Chronicle Play'. In *The Oxford Dictionary of Literary Terms*. Oxford: Oxford University Press, 2015. Available online: https://www-oxfordreference-com.libproxy.york.ac.uk/view/10.1093/ acref/9780198715443.001.0001/acref-9780198715443 e-201

Baptiste, Desirée. 'A *Very Very Very Dark Matter*, and the Limits of Satire'. *Exeunt Magazine*, 16 November 2018. Available online: https://exeuntmagazine.com/features/dark-matter-limits-satire/ (accessed 28 April 2023).

Barfield, Steven. 'Dark Matter: The Controversy Surrounding Michael Frayn's *Copenhagen*'. *Archipelago: An International Journal of Literature, the Arts and Opinion* 8, no. 3 (2004): 80–103. Available online: http://www.archipelago.org/vol8-3/barfield.htm

Barnett, Anthony. *The Lure of Greatness: England's Brexit and America's Trump*. Harmondsworth: Penguin, 2017.

Barnett, David. '"I've been told … that the play is far too German": The Interplay of Institution and Dramaturgy in Shaping British Reactions to German Theatre'. In *Cultural Impact in the German Context: Studies in Transmission, Reception, and Influence*, edited by Rebecca Braun and Lyn Marvin, 150–66. Rochester, NY: Camden House, 2010.

Barrera, Camille. '"For We Are American": Postmodern Pastiche and National Identity in Anne Washburn's *Mr. Burns, a Post-Electric Play*'. *Journal of Contemporary Drama in English* 6, no. 1 (2018): 131–45. doi:10.1515/jcde-2018-0016

Bates, Stephen. Review of *That Is Not Who I Am* (*Rapture*) by Lucy Kirkwood, directed by Lucy Morrison, Royal Court Theatre, London. *The Reviews Hub*, 19 June 2022, reproduced in *Theatre Record* 42, no. 6 (2022). Available online: https://www-theatrerecord-com.libproxy.york.ac.uk/magazine/production/1075

Bean, Richard. *Harvest*. London: Oberon, 2005.

Bennett, Michael Y. *Narrating the Past Through Theatre: Four Crucial Texts*. New York: Palgrave, 2013.

Benson, Dzifa. 'Intriguing Study of Whether Trauma is Passed Down in Our Genes', review of *Love and Other Acts of Violence* by Cordelia Lynn, directed by Elayce Ismail, Donmar Warehouse, London. *Daily Telegraph*, 18 October 2021. Available online: https://www.telegraph.co.uk/theatre/what-to-see/love-acts-violence-review-intriguing-study-whether-trauma-passed/ (accessed 25 April 2023).

Benzie, Rebecca, and Benjamin Poore. 'History Plays in the Twenty-First Century: New Tools for Interpreting the Contemporary Performance of the Past'. *Studies in Theatre and Performance* (2023). doi:10.1080/14682761.2023.2266205

Berardi, Franco 'Bifo'. *After the Future*. New York: AK Press, 2011.

Berninger, Mark. 'Variations of a Genre: The British History Play in the Nineties'. In *British Drama of the 1990s*, edited by Annelie Knapp, Erwin Otto, Gerd Stratmann and Merle Tönnies, 37–64. Heidelberg: Universitätsverlag C. Winter, 2002.

Bienkov, Adam. 'Party by Gaslight: Boris Johnson Rewrites History at the Privileges Committee'. *Byline Times*, 22 March 2023. Available online: https://bylinetimes.com/2023/03/22/boris-johnson-rewrites-history-at-the-privileges-committee/ (accessed 24 April 2023).

Billington, Michael. Review of *A Very Very Very Dark Matter* by Martin McDonagh, directed by Matthew Dunster, Bridge Theatre, London. *Guardian*, 25 October 2018, reproduced in *Theatre Record* 38, no. 19–20 (2018): 965.

Bird, Caroline. *Red Ellen*. London: Nick Hern, 2021.

Botham, Paola. 'Howard Brenton and the Improbable Revival of the Brechtian History Play'. *Journal of Contemporary Drama in English* 2, no. 1 (2014): 170–84.

Botham Paola. 'The Twenty-First Century History Play'. In *Twenty-First Century Drama: What Happens Now*, edited by Siân Adiseshiah and Louise LePage, 81–103. Basingstoke: Palgrave, 2016.

Brecht, Bertolt. *Brecht on Theatre*, edited by Marc Silberman, Steve Giles and Tom Kuhn. London: Bloomsbury, 2015.

British Theatre Consortium, SOLT/UKTheatre, and BON Culture. *British Theatre Repertoire 2014* (report). Available online: https://static1.squarespace.com/static/513c543ce4b0abff73bc0a82/t/57347c792b8dde48ff9c18e1/1463057537574/British+Theatre+Repertoire+2014.pdf (accessed 3 February 2023).

Brown, Ian. *History as Theatrical Metaphor: History, Myth and National Identities in Modern Scottish Drama*. Cham, Switzerland: Palgrave, 2016.

Buffini, Moira. *Handbagged*. London: Faber and Faber, 2013.

Buffini, Moira. *Handbagged*. London: Faber and Faber, 2022.

Butler, Isaac, and Dan Kois. *The World Only Spins Forward: The Ascent of Angels in America*. New York: Bloomsbury, 2018.

Bush, Chris. *Faustus: That Damned Woman*. London: Nick Hern, 2020.

Bush, Chris, and Richard Hawley. *Standing at the Sky's Edge*. London: Nick Hern, 2022.

Callan, Paul. Review of *Clybourne Park* by Bruce Norris, directed by Dominic Cooke, Royal Court Theatre. *Daily Express*, 10 September 2010. Available online: https://www.express.co.uk/entertainment/theatre/198509/Review-Clybourne-Park-Royal-Court-London (accessed 17 March 2023).

Campanella, Edoardo, and Marta Dassù. *Anglo Nostalgia: The Politics of Emotion in a Fractured West*. Oxford: Oxford University Press, 2020.

Campbell, Alexi Kaye. *The Pride*. London: Nick Hern, 2013.

Canton, Ursula. *Biographical Theatre: Re-Presenting Real People?* Basingstoke: Palgrave Macmillan, 2011.

Cantoni, Vera. *New Writing at Shakespeare's Globe*. London: Bloomsbury Methuen Drama, 2017.

Carr, Gregory S. 'Interrogating Whiteness in Bruce Norris's *Clybourne Park*'. *Theatre Symposium* 29 (2022): 64–72. doi:10.1353/tsy.2022.0005

Carson, Marvin. *The Haunted Stage: Theatre as Memory Machine*. Ann Arbor: University of Michigan Press, 2001.

Cavendish, Dominic. Review of *A Museum in Baghdad* by Hannah Khalil, directed by Erica Whyman, Swan Theatre, Stratford-upon-Avon. *Daily Telegraph*, 23 October 2019. Available online: https://www.telegraph.co.uk/theatre/what-to-see/museum-baghdad-review-rsc-swan-stratford-upon-avon-admirable/ (accessed 25 April 2023).

Chadwick, Eleanor. 'History, Her Story, or Our Story? Navigating the Tensions of Historically-Responsive Storytelling in *Emilia*'. In Kressly et al., *Notelets*, 105–17.

Chambers, Colin. *Inside the Royal Shakespeare Company: Creativity and the Institution*. Abingdon: Routledge, 2004.

Chandrasekhar, Anupama. *The Father and the Assassin*. London: Nick Hern, 2022.

Chemers, Michael. *Ghost Light: An Introductory Handbook for Dramaturgy*. Carbondale, IL: Southern Illinois University Press, 2011.

Churchill, Caryl. *Vinegar Tom*, in *Plays: One*. London: Methuen, 1985.

Clapp, Susannah. Review of *Common* by D. C. Moore, directed by Jeremy Herrin, National Theatre, London. *Observer*, 11 June 2017. Available online: https://www.theguardian.com/stage/2017/jun/11/common-olivier-anne-marie-duff-theatre-national-review (accessed 3 February 2023).

Clapp, Susannah. Review of *I, Joan* by Charlie Josephine, directed by Ilinca Radulian, Shakespeare's Globe, London. *Observer*, 11 September 2022. Available online: https://www.theguardian.com/stage/2022/sep/11/i-joan-shakespeares-globe-review-charlie-josephine-isobel-thom-non-binary-joan-of-arc-the-glass-menagerie-royal-exchange-manchester-silence-review (accessed 3 October 2022).

Clapp, Susannah. Review of *That Is Not Who I Am* (*Rapture*) by Lucy Kirkwood, directed by Lucy Morrison, Royal Court Theatre, London. *Observer*, 19 June 2022. Available online: https://www.theguardian.com/stage/2022/jun/19/the-week-in-theatre-that-is-not-who-i-am-the-false-servant (accessed 28 April 2023).

Colbert, Soyica Diggs. 'Black Leadership at the Crossroads: Unfixing Martin Luther King Jr. in Katori Hall's *The Mountaintop*'. *The South Atlantic Quarterly* 112, no. 2 (2013): 261–83. doi:10.1215/00382876-2020199

Costa, Maddy. 'The Well-Made Play and the Play Made Well'. *Write A Play* (blog), *The Bruntwood Prize for Playwriting*, 5 March 2019. Available online: https://www.writeaplay.co.uk/the-well-made-play-and-the-play-made-well-by-maddy-costa/ (accessed 3 February 2023).

Coveney, Michael. Review of *Harvest* by Richard Bean, directed by Wilson Milam, Royal Court Theatre, London. *The Independent*, 12 September 2005, reproduced in *Theatre Record* 25 no. 9 (2005): 1125.

Coward, Noël. *Cavalcade*. In *Noël Coward: Collected Plays Three*, 97–158. London: Methuen Drama, 1994.

Coward, Noël. *Post-Mortem*. In *First World War Plays*, edited by Mark Rawlinson, 137–214. London: Bloomsbury Methuen Drama, 2014.

Coward, Noël. *This Happy Breed*. In *Noël Coward: Collected Plays Four*, 149–372. London: Methuen Drama, 1999.

Cullen, Jim. '"*Hamilton*: A Musical Inquiry" Course Syllabus'. In Romano and Potter, *Historians on Hamilton*, 351–60.

Currie, Mark. *About Time: Narrative, Fiction and the Philosophy of Time.* Edinburgh: Edinburgh University Press, 2010.

Curtis, Nick. Review of *A Museum in Baghdad* by Hannah Khalil, directed by Erica Whyman, Swan Theatre, Stratford-upon-Avon. *Evening Standard*, 24 October 2019. Available online: https://www.standard.co.uk/culture/theatre/a-museum-in-baghdad-review-fascinating-history-of-a-nation-bogged-down-by-monotonous-mood-a4269701.html (accessed 25 April 2023).

Curtis, Nick. Review of *I, Joan* by Charlie Josephine, directed by Ilinca Radulian, Shakespeare's Globe, London. *Evening Standard*, 2 September 2022. Available online: https://www.standard.co.uk/culture/theatre/i-joan-shakespeares-globe-review-non-binary-game-changer-women-b1022607.html (accessed 3 October 2022).

Curtis, Nick. Review of *Love and Other Acts of Violence* by Cordelia Lynn, directed by Elayce Ismail, Donmar Warehouse, London. *Evening Standard*, 21 October 2021. Available online: https://www.standard.co.uk/culture/

theatre/love-and-other-acts-of-violence-donmar-warehouse-review-anti-semitism-b960718.html (accessed 17 March 2023).

Dallison, Paul. 'A Brief History of Having Cake and Eating It'. *Politico*, 31 August 2017. Available online: https://www.politico.eu/article/a-brief-history-of-having-cake-and-eating-it/ (accessed 28 June 2022).

Davies, Martin L. *Historics*. London: Routledge, 2006.

Davies, William. *This Is Not Normal: The Collapse of Liberal Britain*. London: Verso, 2021.

Davis, Clive. 'A Callow Meditation on History', review of *Love and Other Acts of Violence* by Cordelia Lynn, directed by Elayce Ismail, Donmar Warehouse, London. *The Times*, 18 October 2021. Available online: https://www.thetimes.co.uk/article/love-and-other-acts-of-violence-review-a-callow-meditation-on-history-w8fvmp0w2 (accessed 17 March 2023).

De Groot, Jerome. *Remaking History: The Past in Contemporary Historical Fictions*. Abingdon: Routledge, 2016.

De Jongh, Nicholas. Review of *Harvest* by Richard Bean, directed by Wilson Milam, Royal Court Theatre, London. *Evening Standard*, 9 September 2005, reproduced in *Theatre Record* 25 no. 9 (2005): 1123.

Diggs Colbert, Soyica. *The African American Theatrical Body: Reception, Performance, and the Stage*. Cambridge: Cambridge University Press, 2011.

Ditmars, Hadani. 'Iraq Museum Reopens after Three-Year Hiatus'. *The Art Magazine*, 11 March 2022. https://www.theartnewspaper.com/2022/03/11/iraq-museum-baghdad-reopens (accessed 25 April 2023).

Donington, Katie. 'Relics of Empire? Colonialism and the Culture Wars'. In *Embers of Empire in Brexit Britain*, edited by Stuart Ward and Astrid Rasch, 121–32. London: Bloomsbury Academic, 2019.

Drury, Jackie Sibblies. *Marys Seacole*. New York: Dramatists Play Service. Ebook. 2022.

Drury, Jackie Sibblies. *We are Proud to Present a Presentation about the Herero of Namibia, Formerly Known as Southwest Africa, from the German Sudwestafrika, between the Years 1884–1915*. London: Methuen Drama, 2021.

Eaglestone, Robert. 'Cruel Nostalgia and the Memory of the Second World War'. In *Brexit and Literature: Critical and Cultural Responses*, 92–104. Abingdon: Routledge, 2018.

Edgar, David. *How Plays Work*. London: Nick Hern, 2009.

Elam, Jr, Harry. *The Past as Present in the Drama of August Wilson*. Ann Arbor: University of Michigan Press, 2006.

Evans, Lloyd. Review of *A Very Very Very Dark Matter* by Martin McDonagh, directed by Matthew Dunster, Bridge Theatre, London. *Spectator*, 3 November 2018, reproduced in *Theatre Record* 38, no. 19–20 (2018): 968.

Evans, Lloyd. Review of *That Is Not Who I Am* (*Rapture*) by Lucy Kirkwood, directed by Lucy Morrison, Royal Court Theatre, London. *Spectator*, 19 June 2022, reproduced in *Theatre Record* 42, no. 6 (2022). Available online: https://www-theatrerecord-com.libproxy.york.ac.uk/magazine/production/1075 (accessed 28 April 2023).

Fallow, Catriona. 'New Work in and Beyond Repertory at the Royal Shakespeare Company and Shakespeare's Globe'. *Early Theatre* 25 no. 2 (2022): 173–85. doi:10.12745/et.25.2.4739

Faye, Shon. *The Transgender Issue: An Argument for Justice*. London: Penguin, 2021.

Feldman, Alexander. *Dramas of the Past on the Twentieth-Century Stage: In History's Wings*. Abingdon: Routledge, 2013.

Finburgh Delijani, Clare. 'The Afterlives of Enslavement: Histories of Racial Injustice in Contemporary Black British Theatre'. *Modern Drama* 65, no. 4 (2022): 473–98.

Finburgh Delijani, Clare. *Watching War on the Twenty-First Century Stage: Spectacles of Conflict*. London: Bloomsbury Methuen Drama, 2017.

Fisher, Mark. 'Lost Futures'. In *Ghosts of My Life*, 2–29. London: Zero Books, 2014.

Foreman, Bridget. 'A New Way of Working – Practice and Process in Directive Commissioning'. PhD dissertation, University of York, 2019. oai:etheses.whiterose.ac.uk:25442

Gallagher, Catherine. *Telling It Like It Wasn't: The Counterfactual Imagination in History and Fiction*. Chicago: University of Chicago Press, 2018.

Geiss, Deborah R. *Suzan-Lori Parks*. Ann Arbor: University of Michigan Press, 2008.

Gems, Pam. *Queen Christina* in *Plays One*. London: Oberon, 2004.

Gilkes Romero, Juliet. *The Whip*. London: Oberon, 2020.

Gillinson, Miriam. Review of *A Museum in Baghdad* by Hannah Khalil, directed by Erica Whyman, Swan Theatre, Stratford-upon-Avon. *Guardian*, 22 October 2019. Available online: https://www.theguardian.com/stage/2019/oct/22/a-museum-in-baghdad-review-hannah-khalil?CMP=gu_com (accessed 25 April 2023).

Gilroy, Paul. *After Empire: Melancholia or Convivial Culture?* Abingdon: Routledge, 2004.

Gilroy, Paul. *Postcolonial Melancholia*. New York: Columbia University Press, 2005.

'A Glimpse into our 1970s Measure for Measure'. *Shakespeare's Globe* (blog). Available online: https://www.shakespearesglobe.com/discover/blogs-and-features/2021/11/10/a-glimpse-into-our-1970s-measure-for-measure/ (accessed 8 December 2021).

Gobert, R. Darren. *The Theatre of Caryl Churchill*. London: Bloomsbury, 2014.

Goodhart, David. *The Road to Somewhere: The New Tribes Shaping British Politics*. London: Penguin, 2017.

Graham, James. *Best of Enemies*. London: Methuen Drama, 2021.

Green, Jesse. 'Review: When the "Light Shining" on Revolution Falters'. Review of *Light Shining in Buckinghamshire* by Caryl Churchill, directed by Rachel Chavkin, New York Theatre Workshop, New York. *New York Times*, 7 May 2018. Available online: https://www.nytimes.com/2018/05/07/theater/review-light-shining-on-buckinghamshire-caryl-churchill.html (accessed 3 February 2023).

Grochala, Sarah. *The Contemporary Political Play: Rethinking Dramaturgical Structure*. London: Bloomsbury Methuen, 2017.

Hall, Katori. *The Mountaintop*. In *Plays: 1*, 187–248. London: Methuen Drama, 2011.

Halliburton, Rachel. Review of *I, Joan* by Charlie Josephine, directed by Ilinca Radulian, Shakespeare's Globe, London. *The Arts Desk*, 2 September 2022. Available online: https://theartsdesk.com/theatre/i-joan-shakespeares-globe-review-non-binary-retelling-thats-ebullient-its-irreverent (accessed 3 October 2022).

Hammond, Brean S. '"Is everything history?": Churchill, Barker, and the Modern History Play'. *Comparative Drama* 41, no. 1 (2007): 1–23. doi:10.1353/cdr.2007.0004

Harben, Nilhoufer. *Twentieth-Century English History Plays*. New York: Barnes and Noble, 1988.

Hart, Christopher. Review of *A Very Very Very Dark Matter* by Martin McDonagh, directed by Matthew Dunster, Bridge Theatre, London. *Sunday Times*, 28 October 2018, reproduced in *Theatre Record* 38, no. 19–20 (2018): 967.

Hatherley, Owen. *The Ministry of Nostalgia*. London: Verso, 2017.

Hawkins, Ella. *Shakespeare in Elizabethan Costume: 'Period Dress' in Twenty-First-Century Performance*. London: Arden, 2022.

Haydon, Christopher. *The Art of the Artistic Director*. London: Bloomsbury Methuen Drama, 2019.

Head, Julia. 'Director's Note.' In *Wild Swimming* by Marek Horn, no pagination. London: Nick Hern, 2019.

Hellekson, Karen. 'Toward a Taxonomy of the Alternate History Genre.' *Extrapolation* 41, no. 3 (2000): 254–5.

Hemming, Sarah. Review of *I, Joan* by Charlie Josephine, directed by Ilinca Radulian, Shakespeare's Globe, London. *Financial Times*, 8 September 2022, reproduced in *Theatre Record* 42, no. 9 (2022). Available online: https://www-theatrerecord.com.libproxy.york.ac.uk/magazine/production/2579 (accessed 3 October 2022).

Hemming, Sarah. Review of *That Is Not Who I Am (Rapture)* by Lucy Kirkwood, directed by Lucy Morrison, Royal Court Theatre, London. *Financial Times*, 23 June 2022, reproduced in *Theatre Record* 42, no. 6. Available online: https://www-theatrerecord-com.libproxy.york.ac.uk/magazine/production/1075 (accessed 25 April 2023).

Here's What She Said to Me. Utopia Theatre (marketing pack). Available online: https://www.utopiatheatre.co.uk/wp-content/uploads/2022/08/HWSSTM-Marketing-Pack.pdf (accessed 22 December 2022).

Hewitson, Mark. *History and Causality*. Basingstoke: Palgrave Macmillan, 2014.

Hingorani, Dominic. 'Binglishing Britain: Tara Arts: *Journey to the West Trilogy*'. *Contemporary Theatre Review* 14, no. 4 (2004): 12–22.

Hinsliff, Gaby. 'Why Inheritance Is the Dirty Secret of the Middle Classes'. *Guardian*, 3 December 2022. Available online: https://www.theguardian.com/money/2022/dec/03/why-inheritance-is-the-dirty-secret-of-the-middle-classes-harder-to-talk-about-than-sex?CMP=Share_AndroidApp_Other (accessed 17 March 2023).

Holder, Heidi J. 'Strange Legacy: The History Plays of Suzan-Lori Parks'. In *Suzan-Lori Parks: A Casebook*, edited by Kevin J. Wetmore Jr and Alycia Smith-Howard, 18–28. Abingdon: Routledge, 2007.

Horn, Marek. *Wild Swimming*. London: Nick Hern, 2019.

Hughes-Warrington, Marnie. 'Introduction: Theory, Production, Reception'. In *The History on Film Reader*, edited by Marnie Hughes Warrington, 1–12. Abingdon: Routledge, 2009.

'I, Joan', Shakespeare's Globe (theatre programme), 2022, no pagination.

Inchley, Maggie. *Voice and New Writing, 1997–2007: Articulating the Demos*. Basingstoke: Palgrave Macmillan, 2015.

'Interview with Jackie Sibblies Drury'. InterAct Theatre Company, YouTube. Available online: https://www.youtube.com/watch?v=D6pkEYpoL3M (accessed 28 June 2022).

Jakobson, Roman. 'On Realism in Art'. In *Readings in Russian Poetics: Formalist and Structuralist Views*, edited by Ladislav Matejka and Krystyna Pomorska, 38–46. Chicago: Dalkey Archive, 2002.

Jenkins, Keith. *Re-thinking History*. London: Routledge, 1991.

Jenkins, Keith, and Alun Munslow, eds. *The Nature of History Reader*. London: Routledge, 2004.

Kaufmann, Eric. 'It's NOT the Economy, Stupid: Brexit as a Story of Personal Values'. *The London School of Economics and Political Science* (blog), 7 July 2016. Available online: https://blogs.lse.ac.uk/politicsandpolicy/personal-values-brexit-vote/ (accessed 22 May 2022).

Khalil, Hannah. *A Museum in Baghdad*. London: Methuen Drama, 2019.

Khalil, Hannah. 'Collaborating with Shakespeare and Fletcher on Henry VIII'. *Shakespeare's Globe* (blog), 17 May 2022. Available online: https://www.shakespearesglobe.com/discover/blogs-and-features/2022/05/17/collaborating-with-shakespeare-and-fletcher-on-henry-viii/ (accessed 3 February 2023).

Kirkwood, Lucy. *Rapture*. London: Nick Hern, 2022.

Kressly, Laura, Aida Patient and Kimberly A. Williams, eds. *Notelets of Filth: A Companion Reader to Morgan Lloyd Malcolm's Emilia*. Abingdon: Routledge, 2023.

Kressly, Laura. '"There's Only So Much Work Our Imaginations Can Do": *Emilia* and London's Privileged Theatre Critics'. In Kressly et al., *Notelets of Filth*, 151–62.

Kushner, Tony. *Angels in America*. London: Nick Hern, 2017.

Kwa Hawking, Frey. Review of *That Is Not Who I Am* (*Rapture*) by Lucy Kirkwood, directed by Lucy Morrison, Royal Court Theatre, London. *WhatsOnStage*, 19 June 2022. Available online: https://www.whatsonstage.com/news/this-is-not-who-i-am-at-the-royal-court-review_56742/ (accessed 28 April 2023).

Laera, Margherita. 'Introduction'. In *Theatre and Adaptation: Return, Rewrite, Repeat*, edited by Margherita Laera, 1–17. London: Bloomsbury Methuen Drama, 2014.

Lang, Theresa. *Essential Dramaturgy: The Mindset and Skillset*. New York: Routledge, 2017.

Lee-Jones, Jasmine. *Curious*. London: Methuen Drama, 2021.

Leonor Faber-Jonker, 'Introduction'. In *We Are Proud to Present ...*, by Jackie Sibblies Drury, vii–xxi.

Lester, Alan. 'History Reclaimed – But from What?', *Snapshots of Empire* (blog), University of Sussex, 15 September 2021. Available online: https://blogs.sussex.ac.uk/snapshotsofempire/2021/09/15/history-reclaimed-but-from-what/ (accessed 3 February 2023).

Letts, Quentin. Review of *Wife* by Samuel Adamson, directed by Indhu Rubasingham, Kiln Theatre, London. *Sunday Times*, 9 June 2019, reproduced in *Theatre Record* 39, no. 11 (2019). Available online: https://www-theatrerecord-com.libproxy.york.ac.uk/magazine/issue/1866 (accessed 25 April 2023).

Lewis, Isobel. Review of *I, Joan* by Charlie Josephine, directed by Ilinca Radulian, Shakespeare's Globe, London. *The Independent*, 3 September 2022, reproduced in *Theatre Record* 42, no. 9 (2022). Available online: https://www-theatrerecord-com.libproxy.york.ac.uk/magazine/production/2579

Lindenberger, Herbert. *Historical Drama: The Relation of Literature and Reality*. Chicago: University of Chicago Press, 1975.

'Literary Office', *Royal Court Theatre* website. Available online: https://royalcourttheatre.com/literary-office (accessed 29 April 2017).

Little, Ruth, and Emily McLaughlin. *The Royal Court Theatre Inside Out*. London: Oberon, 2007.

Lloyd Malcolm, Morgan. *Emilia*. London: Oberon, 2019.

Lukowski, Andrzej. Review of *Clybourne Park* by Bruce Norris, directed by Oliver Kaderbhai. Park Theatre, London. *Time Out*, 25 March 2022. Available online: https://www.timeout.com/london/theatre/clybourne-park-review (accessed 25 April 2023).

Lukowski, Andrzej. Review of *Common* by D. C. Moore, directed by Jeremy Herrin, National Theatre, London. *Time Out*, 7 June 2017. Available online: https://www.timeout.com/london/theatre/common (accessed 3 February 2023).

Lukowski, Andrzej. Review of *I, Joan* by Charlie Josephine, directed by Ilinca Radulian, Shakespeare's Globe, London. *Time Out*, 1 September 2022. Available online: https://www.timeout.com/london/theatre/i-joan-review (accessed 3 October 2022).

Lukowski, Andrzej. Review of *Marys Seacole* by Jackie Sibblies Drury, directed by Nadia Latif, at Donmar Warehouse, London. *Time Out*, 22 April 2022.

Available online: https://www.timeout.com/london/theatre/marys-seacole-review (accessed 21 March 2023).

Lukowski, Andrzej. Review of *A Very Very Very Dark Matter* by Martin McDonagh, directed by Matthew Dunster, Bridge Theatre, London. *Time Out*, 25 October 2018. Available online: https://www.timeout.com/london/theatre/a-very-very-very-dark-matter-review (accessed 28 April 2023).

Lustgarten, Anders. The *Seven Acts of Mercy*. London: Methuen Drama, 2016.

Lynn, Cordelia. *Love and Other Acts of Violence*. London: Nick Hern, 2021.

Maddocks, Archie. *A Place for We*. London: Samuel French, 2021.

Maguire, Tom. *Making Theatre in Northern Ireland: Through and Beyond the Troubles*. Exeter: Exeter University Press, 2006.

Maitland, Hayley. '*The Crown* Isn't the Problem'. *Vogue*, 22 October 2022. Available online: https://www.vogue.co.uk/arts-and-lifestyle/article/the-crown-disclaimer (accessed 22 December 2022).

Malik, Nesrine. *We Need New Stories*. London: Weidenfeld and Nicolson, 2019.

Marlowe, Sam. Review of *I, Joan* by Charlie Josephine, directed by Ilinca Radulian, Shakespeare's Globe, London. *The Stage*, 2 September 2022. Available online: https://www.thestage.co.uk/reviews/i-joan-review-shakespeares-globe-by-charlie-josephine-and-directed-by-ilinca-radulian (accessed 3 October 2022).

Marlowe, Sam. Review of *That Is Not Who I Am* (*Rapture*) by Lucy Kirkwood, directed by Lucy Morrison, Royal Court Theatre, London. *iNews*, 24 June 2022, reproduced in *Theatre Record* 42, no. 6. Available online: https://www-theatrerecord-com.libproxy.york.ac.uk/magazine/production/1075 (accessed 28 April 2023).

Marmion, Patrick. Review of *That Is Not Who I Am* (*Rapture*) by Lucy Kirkwood, directed by Lucy Morrison, Royal Court Theatre, London. *Daily Mail*, 14 June 2022. Available online: https://www.dailymail.co.uk/tvshowbiz/article-10947945/PATRICK-MARMION-reviews-Southbury-Child.html (accessed 28 April 2023).

'Marys Seacole'. Donmar Theatre website. Available online: https://booking.donmarwarehouse.com/events/1801APGQPRKNVLCHG SKJBCTJKDRMGPLNL?_ga=2.138071159.694363853.1654353699–105755424.1654353699 (accessed 28 April 2023).

Matthewman, Scott. Review of *I, Joan* by Charlie Josephine, directed by Ilinca Radulian, Shakespeare's Globe, London. *The Reviews Hub*, 2 September 2022. Available online: https://www.thereviewshub.com/i-joan-shakespeares-globe-london/ (accessed 3 October 2022).

McDonagh, Martin. *A Very Very Very Dark Matter*. London: Faber, 2018.

McDowall, Alistair. *The Glow*. London: Methuen, 2022.

McGinn, Caroline. Review of *Love and Other Acts of Violence* by Cordelia Lynn, directed by Elayce Ismail, Donmar Warehouse, London. *Guardian*, 18 October 2021. Available online: https://www.timeout.com/london/theatre/love-and-other-acts-of-violence-review (accessed 25 April 2023).

McHenry, Jackson, and Kathryn Van Arendonk. 'Does *The Crown* Like the Royals or Not?' *Vulture*, 10 November 2022. Available online: https://www.vulture.com/article/the-crown-season-5-charles-diana-royal-sympathy.html (accessed 22 December 2022).

McKinnie, Michael. *Theatre in Market Economies*. Cambridge: Cambridge University Press, 2021.

McLuskie, Kate, and Kate Rumbold. *Cultural Value in Twenty-First Century England: The Case of Shakespeare*. Manchester: Manchester University Press, 2014.

Miller, Josy. 'Performing Collective Trauma: 9/11 and the Reconstruction of American Identity'. In *History, Memory, Performance*, edited by David Dean, Yana Meerzon, and Kathryn Prince, 187–202. Basingstoke: Palgrave Macmillan, 2015.

Mitchell, Peter. *Imperial Nostalgia*. Manchester: Manchester University Press, 2021.

Monteiro, Lyra D. 'Race-Conscious Casting and the Erasure of the Black Past in *Hamilton*'. In Romano and Potter, *Historians on Hamilton*, 58–70.

Moore, D. C. *Common*. London: Methuen Drama, 2017.

Morgan, Peter. *Frost/Nixon*. New York: Faber and Faber, 2014.

Morley, Sheridan. 'Introduction'. In *Noël Coward: Collected Plays Three*, vii–xvii.

Morley, Sheridan. Review of *Harvest* by Richard Bean, directed by Wilson Milam, Royal Court Theatre, London. *Daily Express*, 9 September 2005, reproduced in *Theatre Record* 25 no. 9, 1126.

Natasha Tripney, 'Why Does Radical European Work Get Such a Bum Deal in the UK?', *The Stage*, 30 November 2022. Available online: https://www.thestage.co.uk/opinion/why-does-radical-european-work-get-such-a-bum-deal-in-the-uk (accessed 21 March 2023).

Nathan, John. Review of *Clybourne Park* by Bruce Norris, directed by Dominic Cooke, Royal Court Theatre, London. *Jewish Chronicle*, 10 September 2010, reproduced in *Theatre Record* 30, no. 18, 924.

Nathan, John. Review of *Harvest* by Richard Bean, directed by Wilson Milam, Royal Court Theatre, London. *Jewish Chronicle*, 16 September 2005, reproduced in *Theatre Record* 25 no. 9, 1127.

Nichols, Tom. *Our Own Worst Enemy: The Assault on Democracy from Within.* New York: Oxford University Press, 2021.

Nightingale, Benedict. Review of *Harvest* by Richard Bean, directed by Wilson Milam, Royal Court Theatre, London. *The Times,* 10 September 2005, reproduced in *Theatre Record* 25 no. 9, 1123.

Norris, Bruce. *Clybourne Park.* London: Nick Hern, 2010.

O'Connell, Mark. 'Blarney: The Put-On Irishness of Martin McDonagh'. *Slate,* 26 January 2023. Available online: https://slate.com/culture/2023/01/martin-mcdonagh-irish-banshees-inisherin-blarney.html?s=09 (accessed 26 January 2023).

O'Hara, Robert. *Insurrection: Holding History* in *The Fire This Time: African American Plays for the 21st Century.* Edited by Harry J. Elam Jr. and Robert Alexander. New York: Theatre Communications Group, 2004, 253–336.

Orwell, George. 'The Lion and the Unicorn'. In *The Penguin Essays of George Orwell,* 144–94. Harmondsworth: Penguin, 1984.

O'Toole, Fintan. *Heroic Failure.* London: Head of Zeus, 2018.

Palmer, Beth. 'Nineteenth-Century Women's Lives on the Contemporary Stage'. Keynote address, University of Valencia, 2022. Available online: https://www.youtube.com/watch?v=AxcnmkkBn6A (accessed 9 October 2023).

Palmer, Richard H. *The Contemporary British History Play.* Westport, CN: Greenwood Press, 1998.

Parks, Suzan-Lori. *The America Play and Other Works.* London: Nick Hern, 1995.

Parks, Suzan-Lori, and Kevin Wetmore Jr. 'It's an Oberammergau Thing: An Interview with Suzan-Lori Parks'. In *Suzan-Lori Parks: A Casebook,* edited by Kevin J. Wetmore Jr and Alycia Smith-Howard, 124–40. New York: Routledge, 2007.

Patel, Vinay. *An Adventure.* London: Methuen Drama, 2018.

Peacock, D. Keith. *Radical Stages: Alternative History in Modern British Drama.* Westport, CN: Greenwood, 1991.

Pellegrini, David. 'Metatheatre'. In *The Companion to Theatre and Performance.* Oxford: Oxford University Press, 2010. Available online: https://www-oxfordreference-com.libproxy.york.ac.uk/view/10.1093/acref/9780199574193.001.0001/acref-9780199574193-e-2606 (accessed 3 February 2023).

Pennino, Anthony P. *Staging the Past in the Age of Thatcher: The History We Haven't Had.* Cham, Switzerland: Palgrave, 2018.

Pinnock, Winsome. *Rockets and Blue Lights*. London: Nick Hern, 2020.

Poore, Benjamin. 'Before the Fall: Looking Back on the Royal Shakespeare Company's "This Other Eden" Season (2001)'. *Journal of Contemporary Drama in English* 6, no. 1 (2018): 176–90. doi:10.1515/jcde-2018-0019

Poore, Benjamin. *Heritage, Nostalgia and Modern British Theatre: Staging the Victorians*. Basingstoke: Palgrave, 2012.

Poore, Benjamin. '"You Can't Be Here": The Playwriting Dialectic in Ella Hickson's *Oil*'. *Modern Drama* 63, no. 1 (2020): 21–38. doi:10.3138/md.1054r

Potts, John. *The New Time and Space*. Basingstoke: Palgrave, 2015.

Priestley, J. B. *Time and the Conways, and Other Plays*. London: Penguin, 1969.

Purcell, Carey. '*Beneatha's Place*, Part of Centerstage's *The Raisin Cycle*, Begins Performances May 8'. *Playbill*, 8 May 2013. Available online: https://v.playbill.com/article/beneathas-place-part-of-centerstages-the-raisin-cycle-begins-performances-may-8-com–205018 (accessed 25 April 2023).

Quigley, Karen. *Performing the Unstageable: Success, Imagination, Failure*. London: Bloomsbury Methuen, 2020.

Quirk, Catherine. 'We are Emilia: Emilia as Witness, Witnessing Emilia'. 130–138. In Kressly et al., *Notelets*, 130–138.

Rabey, David Ian. *Theatre, Time and Temporality: Melting Clocks and Snapped Elastics*. Bristol: Intellect, 2016.

Rebellato, Dan. *1956 and All That: The Making of Modern British Drama*. London: Routledge, 1999.

Rebellato, Dan. 'Exit the Author'. In *Contemporary British Theatre: Breaking New Ground*, edited by Vicky Angelaki, 9–31. Basingstoke: Palgrave Macmillan, 2013.

Rokem, Freddie. *Performing History: Theatrical Representations of the Past in Contemporary Theatre*. Iowa City: University of Iowa Press, 2000.

Romano, Renee C., and Claire Bond Potter, eds. *Historians on Hamilton: How A Blockbuster Musical Is Restaging America's Past*. New Brunswick, NJ: Rutgers University Press, 2018.

Romano, Renee C., and Claire Bond Potter. 'Introduction'. In Romano and Potter, *Historians on Hamilton*, 1–14.

Romanska, Magda. 'Introduction'. In *The Routledge Companion to Dramaturgy*, edited by Magda Romanska, 1–15. Abingdon: Routledge, 2014.

Rubenhold, Hallie. *The Problem with Great Men*. Edinburgh: Edinburgh International Book Festival, 2020.

Sanders, Julie. *Adaptation and Appropriation*. Abingdon: Routledge, 2006.

Sandomir, Richard. 'Lamia Al-Gailani Werr, 80, Dies; Archaeologist Rescued Iraqi Art'. *New York Times*, 25 January 2019. Available online: https://www.nytimes.com/2019/01/25/obituaries/lamia-al-gailani-werr-80-dies-archaeologist-rescued-iraqi-art.html (accessed 25 April 2023).

Schneider, Rebecca. *Performing Remains: Art and War in Times of Theatrical Reenactment*. Abingdon: Routledge, 2011.

'Script Submissions'. Royal Court Theatre website. Available online: https://royalcourttheatre.com/script-submissions/ (accessed 8 December 2021).

Secor, A. J., and Blum, V. 'Lockdown Time, Time Loops, and the Crisis of the Future'. *Psychoanalysis, Culture & Society* 28 (2023): 250–67. doi:10.1057/s41282-023-00379-4

Sedgman, Kirsty. *Locating the Audience: How People Found Value in National Theatre Wales*. Bristol: Intellect, 2016.

Shaw, Bernard. *Saint Joan*. New Mermaids edition, edited by Jean Chothia. London: Methuen Drama, 2008.

Shields, Mark. 'Tony Martin: Man Who Shot Burglars Knows He Still Divides Opinion'. BBC News website. Available online: https://www.bbc.co.uk/news/uk-england-norfolk–49355814 (accessed 28 June 2022).

Shipman, Tim. 'How the Tories Weaponised Woke: Ministers Are Wading into Debates Over Trans Rights, Taking the Knee and Cricketers' Tweets. It's All Part of a Vote-Winning Plot Masterminded by Dougie Smith, the Most Powerful Man in Politics You've Never Heard Of. Tim Shipman Reports'. *The Sunday Times*, 13 June 2021. Available online: https://advance.lexis.com/api/document?collection=news&id=urn:contentItem:62X2-G5H1-DYTY-C05R-00000-00&context=1519360 (accessed 21 March 2023).

Shrift, Robin. *The Director's Toolkit*. New York: Routledge, 2018.

Sierz, Aleks. Review of *Clybourne Park* by Bruce Norris, directed by Dominic Cooke, Royal Court Theatre, London. *The Arts Desk*, 2 September 2010. Available online: https://theartsdesk.com/theatre/clybourne-park-royal-court-theatre (accessed 25 April 2023).

Sierz, Aleks. *Rewriting the Nation*. London: Bloomsbury Methuen, 2011.

Sierz, Aleks. Review of *Common* by D. C. Moore, directed by Jeremy Herrin, National Theatre, London. *Tribune*, 16 June 2017, reproduced in *Theatre Record* 37, no. 11–12, 611.

Sierz, Aleks. Review of *That Is Not Who I Am* (*Rapture*) by Lucy Kirkwood, directed by Lucy Morrison, Royal Court Theatre, London. *The Arts Desk*, 20 June 2022. Available online: https://theartsdesk.com/theatre/not-who-i-am-royal-court-review-%E2%80%93-gimmicky-post-truth-spoof (accessed 28 April 2023).

Slater, Niall W. '*Nostoi* and Nostalgia in *Heartbreak House*'. *SHAW: The Journal of Bernard Shaw Studies* 37, no. 1 (2017): 12–14. muse.jhu.edu/article/661062

Soden, Oliver. *Masquerade: The Lives of Noël Coward*. London: Weidenfeld and Nicolson, 2023.

Sorlin, Pierre. *The Film in History: Restaging the Past*. Oxford: Blackwell, 1980.

Spencer, Charles. Review of *Clybourne Park* by Bruce Norris, directed by Dominic Cooke, Royal Court Theatre. *Daily Telegraph*, 3 September 2010. Available online: https://www.telegraph.co.uk/culture/theatre/theatre-reviews/7980236/Clybourne-Park-Royal-Court-review.html (accessed 25 April 2023).

Steel, Beth. *The House of Shades*. London: Faber, 2022.

Stoppard, Tom. *Leopoldstadt*. London: Faber, 2020.

Stuart, Isabel. 'Feeling Collectives: Emotions, Feminist Solidarity, and Difference in *Emilia*'. In Kressly et al., *Notelets*, 185–193.

'*The Sugar House* by Alana Valentine'. *Finborough Theatre*. Available online: https://finboroughtheatre.co.uk/production/the-sugar-house/ (accessed 30 October 2021).

Sweet, Jeffrey. *What Playwrights Talk About When They Talk About Writing*. New Haven: Yale University Press, 2017.

Taylor, Diana. *The Archive and the Repertoire: Performing Cultural Memory in the Americas*. London: Duke University Press, 2003.

Thomas, James. *Script Analysis for Actors, Directors, and Designers*. Oxford: Focal Press, 2009.

Treneman, Ann. Review of *A Very Very Very Dark Matter* by Martin McDonagh, directed by Matthew Dunster, Bridge Theatre, London. *The Times*, 25 October 2018, reproduced in *Theatre Record* 38, no. 19–20 (2018): 965.

Tripney, Natasha. Review of *Common* by D. C. Moore, directed by Jeremy Herrin, National Theatre, London. *The Stage*, 7 June 2017. Available online: https://www.thestage.co.uk/reviews/common-review-at-national-theatre-london-ambitious-but-impenetrable (accessed 3 February 2023).

Trueman, Matt. Review of *A Very Very Very Dark Matter* by Martin McDonagh, directed by Matthew Dunster, Bridge Theatre, London. *Variety*, 25 October 2018, reproduced in *Theatre Record* 38, no. 19–20 (2018): 966.

Turner, Cathy, and Synne K. Behrndt. *Dramaturgy and Performance*. Basingstoke: Palgrave Macmillan, 2008.

Ue, Tom. 'Going on *An Adventure* with Vinay Patel'. *New Writing*, 17, no. 2 (2020): 192–8. doi:10.1080/14790726.2019.1586956

Verma, Jatinder. 'The Challenges of Binglish: Analysing Multi-Cultural Productions'. In *Analysing Performance: A Critical Reader*, edited by Patrick Campbell, 193–202. Manchester: Manchester University Press, 1996.

Von Tunzelmann, Alex. *Fallen Idols: History Is Not Erased When Statues Are Pulled Down. It Is Made*. London: Headline, 2021.

Waldstreicher, David, and Jeffrey L. Pasley. 'Hamilton as Founders Chic: A Neo-Federalist, Antislavery, Usable Past?' In Romano and Potter, *Historians on Hamilton*, 137–66.

Washburn, Anne. *Mr Burns: A Post-Electric Play*. London: Oberon, 2014.

Waters, Steve. *The Secret Life of Plays*. London: Nick Hern, 2010.

Watson, Ariel. 'Apocalypse Masque: Post-Electric Theatricality in *Mr. Burns*'. *Canadian Theatre Review* 175 (2018): 19–24. doi:10.3138/ctr.175.004

Waugh, Rosemary. Review of *Emilia* by Morgan Lloyd Malcolm, directed by Nicole Charles, Shakespeare's Globe, London. *Exeunt Magazine*, 16 August 2018. Available online: https://exeuntmagazine.com/reviews/review-emilia-shakespeares-globe/ (accessed 21 March 2023).

Waugh, Rosemary. Review of *Love and Other Acts of Violence* by Cordelia Lynn, directed by Elayce Ismail, Donmar Warehouse, London. *iNews*, 20 October 2021. Available online: https://inews.co.uk/culture/arts/love-and-other-acts-of-violence-donmar-warehouse-review–1258815 (accessed 25 April 2023).

Wesker, Arnold. *Plays: 1: The Wesker Trilogy*. London: Methuen, 2001.

Wesker, Arnold. 'Introduction'. In *Plays: 1: The Wesker Trilogy*, ix–xxvii. London: Methuen, 2001.

White, Hayden. *Metahistory: The Historical Imagination in 19th-Century Europe*. Baltimore, ML: Johns Hopkins University Press, 2014.

'Why Vote Leave'. Vote Leave website. Available online: http://www.voteleavetakecontrol.org/why_vote_leave.html (accessed 28 June 2022).

Wickstrom, Maurya. *Fiery Temporalities in Theatre and Performance: The Initiation of History*. London: Bloomsbury Methuen Drama, 2018.

Williams, Raymond. *Marxism and Literature*. Oxford: Oxford University Press, 1977.

Willis, Emma. 'Metatheatre and Dramaturgies of Reception in Jackie Sibblies Drury's *We Are Proud to Present*'. *Journal of Contemporary Drama in English* 4, no. 1 (2016): 196–211. doi:10.1515/jcde-2016-0015

Wolf, Matt. Review of *Love and Other Acts of Violence* by Cordelia Lynn, directed by Elayce Ismail, Donmar Warehouse, London. *London Theatre*, 15 October 2021. Available online: https://www.londontheatre.co.uk/reviews/love-and-other-acts-of-violence-review-donmar-warehouse (accessed 25 April 2023).

Wolf, Matt. Review of *That Is Not Who I Am* (*Rapture*) by Lucy Kirkwood, directed by Lucy Morrison, Royal Court Theatre, London. *London Theatre*, 21 June 2022. Available online: https://www.londontheatre.co.uk/reviews/that-is-not-who-i-am-review-royal-court (accessed 28 April 2023).

Woods, Hannah Rose. *Rule, Nostalgia: A Backwards History of Britain*. London: Penguin, 2022.

Woolf, Virginia. *Orlando*. London: Penguin, 1993.

Worth, Katharine. *Revolutions in Modern English Drama*. London: Bell, 1973.

Wright, Patrick. *On Living in an Old Country*. 1985. Oxford: Oxford University Press, 2009.

Index

Printed in the USA
CPSIA information can be obtained
at www.ICGtesting.com
LVHW020220240624
783850LV00003B/21